Tom Hutchinson
Jane Sunderland

hotline

elementary

teacher's book

D1247348

OXFORD UNIVERSITY PRESS

1991

Oxford University Press
Walton Street, Oxford OX2 6DP

Oxford New York Toronto
Delhi Bombay Calcutta Madras Karachi
Petaling Jaya Singapore Hong Kong Tokyo
Nairobi Dar es Salaam Cape Town
Melbourne Auckland

and associated companies in
Berlin Ibadan

Oxford and Oxford English are trade marks of Oxford
University Press

ISBN 0 19 435487 3

Designed by Holdsworth Associates
Printed by Mateu Cromo Artes Gráficas, S.A., Pinto, Madrid,
Spain

Acknowledgements

The author would especially like to record his gratitude to his wife Pamela and his children, without whose support and patience *Hotline* would not have been possible.

The publishers would like to thank all of the ELT teachers and advisors around the world who have given generously of their time to talk about their needs and to comment on the manuscript and sample units of *Hotline*. Our thanks are especially due to:

Silvia Ronchetti (Instituto Superior del Profesorado en Lenguas Vivas Buenos Aires) in Argentina. Freddy Désir (Inspection de l'Enseignement Secondaire de l'Etat, Brussels), Norbert Jacquinet (Institut Notre-Dame, Brussels) in Belgium. Edit Nagy (National Institute of Education, Budapest), Lyane Szentirmay (Madách Imre Gimnázium, Budapest), Judit Sióréti (Városmajori Gimnázium, Budapest), Ilona Jobbágy (Könyves Kálmán Gimnázium, Budapest) in Hungary. Orazio Marchi (Progetto Speciale Lingue Straniere, Forlì) in Italy. Diana England and Monica Green (International House, Lisbon) in Portugal. Patsy Fuller (Freeland Teacher), Luis Fernandez (I.B. Alexandre Satorras, Mataro), Vincenc Haro and Merce Fosch (I.B. Ferran Casablanca, Sabadell), Eleanor Tompkins (La Salle Congres, Barcelona), Ana Coll (I.B. Narcis Monturiol, Barcelona), Victoria Alcalde (I.B. San Isidro, Madrid), Joaquin Rojo (I.B. Francisco de Goya, Madrid), Pedro Horillo and Margarita Hernandez (I.B. Verdaguer Parc de la Ciutadella, Barcelona), Pilar Gomez (Instituto Cid Campeador, Valencia) in Spain. Carroll Klein (Koç Özel Lisesi, Istanbul) in Turkey.

Special thanks are due to a panel of British teenagers, Juliet Kinsman, Zuleika Melluish, Pema Radha, Alex Huskinson and Mark Killingley, who advised on the Victoria Road storyline and on the Reading and Listening topics and to whom we are indebted for the natural, colloquial teenage language of the Victoria Road characters,

'Blue Suede Shoes', words and music by Carl Lee Perkins, used by kind permission of Carlin Music Corporation, Iron Bridge House, 3 Bridge Approach, Chalk Farm, London NW1 8BD.

Illustrations by:
Stefan Chabluk, Robin Edmonds, Roger Fereday, Clive Goodyear, Robina Green, Ian Heard, Tony Kerins, Gordon Lawson, Kevin Lyles, Neil Pinkett, Nicki Palin, Sharon Pallent, John Ridgway, Mark Rowney, Martin Salisbury, Penny Sobr

Victoria Road photography by: John Walmsley
Victoria Road design by: Keith Shaw

The characters in Victoria Road were played by:
Denise Coppard, Dick Daley, Joseph Derrett, Richard Flavell, Karen Heath, Margaret Heath, Natalie Kowlessur, Jeremy Mason, Tito Menezes, Robert Page, Graham and Sue Page, Claire Ridler, Sarah Rose, Paul and Pat Rose, Patrick Short, Angela Torpey, Paula Whitefoot.

The publishers would like to thank the following for their help with the Victoria Road photo story:
St Andrews School (Leatherhead), Peter Anthony Signs, Epsom and Ewell High School (Ewell), Leatherhead Cricket Club, London Coaches, London Country Buses, Mrs Moretta, Frances Myers, NESCOT drama department, One Stop Shop (Burgh Heath), Pickfords, Richard Shops (Leatherhead), Texacana Restaurant (Epsom), Therfield School (Leatherhead), Thorndike Young Players (Leatherhead), Rose and Brian Walsh, Whitgift Centre (Croydon).

Studio photography by: Pat Downing

The publishers would also like to thank the following for their permission to reproduce photographs:
Age Concern 42; Andes Press Agency 13, 18, 38 (Carlos Reyes and Marcel Reyes); Barnaby's Picture Library 50 (Michael C Cole, Colin Underhill); Greg Evans Photo Library 50; Sally and Richard Greenhill 16, 18, 106; Robert Harding Picture Library 18, 44, 76/77; Katz Pictures 40 (Les Wilson), 72, 106 (Robin Kennedy); Pictorial Press Ltd 24, 25, 28, 40, 41 (T McGough); Radio Times Picture Library 26; Redferns 40, 104; Rex Features 28, 40 (Curley); Frank Spooner 72 (O Abolafia-Liason, Gamma); Tony Stone Worldwide 13 (Jean-Francois Causse), 82/83 (Doug Armand), 106; Animal Photography/ Sally Anne Thompson 42; Topham Picture Library 102, 103; Daily Telegraph Colour Library 72 (Sunstar, John Swannel, S Zarember); Tropix 42 (P Frances); John Walmsey 16, 104; Zefa Picture Library 13, 16, 18, 39, 42, 48, 50, 52, 82/83 (G Mabbs, R Kord), 106 (D Cattani)

Who is *Hotline* for?

Hotline is a four-year course for teenagers. The whole course takes learners from beginner to intermediate level. Each year provides approximately ninety hours of teaching. *Hotline Elementary* is the second year of the *Hotline* course. It can be used with learners who have completed one year of English, or with false beginners.

What are the special features of *Hotline*?

Hotline brings together the best of modern and traditional aspects of language teaching. It incorporates modern ideas, such as skills development, learner training and project work. At the same time, *Hotline* has a sound grammar-based syllabus and a clear, practical methodology. *Hotline* is, therefore, both learner-centred and teacher-friendly. Each of the features is explained in greater detail below.

What kind of language syllabus does *Hotline* use?

The syllabus in *Hotline* is structurally graded and develops on a loopback principle. This means that constant revision is built into the syllabus progression. This loopback principle operates in a number of ways:

- Each year (except the first) begins with a substantial revision cycle, which recycles the structures taught in the previous year(s). In *Hotline Elementary*, the first three units thoroughly revise the present tenses and the past simple tense taught in Year 1, before introducing new grammatical forms.

- At the end of each main unit there is a Learning diary. The learners are asked to look back through the unit and consider how well they have learnt the new items in the unit. A simple self-check is provided in the Workbook (see below).

- Units 4, 8 and 12 are revision units. Here learners revise the work of the previous units.

In these ways, learners are given every opportunity to refresh and reinforce their knowledge of basic grammar, so that they have a firm foundation on which to build.

What does *Hotline Elementary* consist of?

Student's Book. This contains:

- nine main units plus an introduction and three revision units;
- pronunciation practice activities;
- a vocabulary list.

Cassette. This contains:

- Victoria Road dialogues;
- texts for listening activities;
- pronunciation practice activities;
- songs.

Workbook. This provides further practice and reinforcement of the items in the Student's Book. It contains:

- grammar consolidation;
- write-in grammar activities;
- vocabulary activities;
- self-checks for students to assess how well they have learnt the work of the unit;
- culture spots. These describe aspects of life in Britain and invite the learners to compare them with those in their own country. Teacher's notes for these are included in the Teacher's Book.

The Workbook is tied closely to the Student's Book. Each section in the Student's Book has further practice activities in the Workbook.

Teacher's Book. This contains:

- a description of the course;
- an introduction to project work;
- lesson notes, which provide explanations of language and cultural points that arise in each unit, and detailed guidance for handling each activity;
- tapescripts;
- suggestions for further activities;
- answer keys for the Student's Book activities;
- answer keys for the Workbook activities;
- three tests (in the revision units).

What does a Student's Book unit contain?

Each of the nine main units (1, 2, 3, 5, 6, 7, 9, 10, 11) provides approximately eight hours of teaching. Each unit contains the following elements:

- Introduction page
- Victoria Road
- Language work
- Reading
- Listening
- Interaction
- Project
- Learning diary

A unit works like this:

The **Introduction page** tells the students what they are going to learn in the unit.

Victoria Road presents the main language items for the unit.

In **Language work** the students analyse and practise the new grammar points.

The **Reading** section develops the students' reading skills and provides further language practice.

The **Listening** section develops the students' listening skills and provides further language practice.

The **Interaction** section develops the students' speaking skills and provides further language practice.

The **Project** provides the opportunity for students to relate the language of the unit to their own lives. It also provides practice in writing.

Finally, in the **Learning diary**, the students review the unit. They look back to the Introduction page and consider how well they know the new language.

Each section ends with a **Follow-up** activity. These activities reinforce the work of the section. They are optional activities. They can be used either for additional classwork or for homework.

Let's look at the sections in more detail.

1 INTRODUCTION PAGE

The first page of each unit provides a list of what is in the unit. The list shows:

- the contents;
- the language syllabus;
- the learning objectives.

This Introduction page is part of the process of learner involvement. You can use the page in a number of ways:

a for discussion
Discuss the contents of the unit. Ask students to look through the unit and find the items in the lists. Ask how they feel about these items. Ask which parts of the unit look the most interesting.

b for revision
Ask students what they know about the content and/or the language items.

c for negotiation
Ask students if there are any other learning objectives they have connected with the theme of the unit.

d for pre-teaching
Pre-teach important elements of grammar.

2 VICTORIA ROAD

Each unit has an episode in a continuing story about the young people who live in Victoria Road.

The characters in *Victoria Road* are:
Terry Moore
Sue and Vince Scott. They are twins and they live next door to Terry.
Kamala Wijeratne, Sue's best friend. Kamala's parents own the local newsagent's shop.
Casey Royston, Terry and Vince's friend
Jackie Wright, who comes to live in Victoria Road
Greg, Jackie's cousin from America
Carmen Ramirez, Sue's Spanish penfriend

The characters are first introduced in *Hotline Starter*. In case you or your students have not used *Hotline Starter*, there is a brief summary of the story in *Starter* on the next page.

Terry has just moved in next door to Sue and Vince. Sue overhears Terry saying that she is bossy. She decides to get her revenge and she arranges a date for Terry with Jane Fox. Sue knows that Jane has got a boyfriend – a big boy called Darren. When Terry asks Jane to dance, Darren tells him to go away. Terry is annoyed with Sue. They have an argument in a cafe and Terry accidentally spills his drink over Darren. Darren and his friends come looking for Terry. They wait for him after school.

On the day that they are waiting for him, Terry meets Kamala. She is carrying Sue's coat and bag, because Sue has gone to the cinema. Terry puts on Sue's coat to try and get past Darren and his friends, but they recognize him. They take him to the park, intending to throw him in the lake.

Later that evening, Vince and Casey are in the park. They find Sue's books all over the grass and her coat in the lake. They think Sue has had an accident and they call the police. Eventually, Sue and Terry both appear safely. Sue is very sorry for getting Terry into trouble. Terry tells his friends how he fought Darren and his friends and beat them.

Later, they all meet Darren and his friends. They are very friendly to Terry and Terry's friends wonder why. Sue later finds out from Jane Fox. Terry hadn't fought Darren and his friends. He had told them about the trick Sue played on him. They agreed that it was all Sue's fault, not Terry's. So they had thrown Sue's books on the grass and her coat in the lake. When they learn the truth, Terry's friends are very annoyed and they chase Terry. The story ends there.

If your students have not studied *Hotline Starter*, you may like to read them this summary. You could use part of it as a dictation. If they have studied *Hotline Starter*, it may be useful to refresh their memories. Ask them to tell you the story before you read the summary.

In *Hotline Elementary*, we meet the Victoria Road characters again one year later.

The Victoria Road story plays a number of roles:

a It continues the story. *Victoria Road* is an amusing, but realistic 'soap opera'.

b It introduces the main language item for the unit. These are then analysed in detail in the Language work section.

c It provides 'Useful expressions'. The language in *Hotline* is natural, modern English. In the 'Useful expressions' component, students work out the meaning of idiomatic expressions that occur in the story. They give the equivalent in their own language. This activity has a number of aims:

• It encourages students to work out meaning from context.
• It provides useful everyday expressions.
• It develops a sense of linguistic comparison, so that students learn that they cannot translate word for word.

d It provides comprehension practice and oral practice.

e It illustrates aspects of daily life in Britain. Some of these are followed up in the Workbook.

3 LANGUAGE WORK

The focus in *Hotline* is on enabling learners to *use* language. But an important element in this is helping learners to understand and feel comfortable with the basic structures of English. They will then feel more confident in language use.

In the Language work section, students study the language structures introduced in *Victoria Road*. The most important aspect of this section is the cognitive approach to grammar. This works in a number of ways:

Firstly, the students find and complete examples of the structure in the Victoria Road story.

Secondly, in the 'Build up' activities, the students work out the grammar rules for themselves. They complete substitution tables and grammar rules.

Thirdly, the students are encouraged to compare the English structure to that in their own language.

Finally, when the students have thoroughly analysed the structure, they do controlled practice activities.

Smaller Language work sections also appear in other parts of a unit. These work in a similar way to the main section.

4 READING

A principal feature in *Hotline* is the development of skills as well as language knowledge.

The Reading section provides interesting texts on a variety of themes. Activities encourage students to develop good reading strategies, such as skimming, scanning, looking for information, matching texts to pictures, etc. Students do not have to understand everything in the texts.

The activities provide a step-by-step approach to each text, as well as pre-reading and post-reading tasks. It is important to follow the instructions for dealing with the texts carefully.

The Reading sections also include 'Word work'. These activities help the learners to consolidate and develop their vocabulary.

5 LISTENING

The Listening section provides a range of spoken texts, which develop the students' ability to listen effectively. The texts include conversations, set-piece dialogues (e.g. ordering a meal in a cafe), stories, factual texts, interviews, etc. The activities are intended to make the students think about what they are going to hear, so that they listen in a context. As with the Reading section, there are pre-listening, while-listening and post-listening tasks. It is important to follow the instructions for the activities carefully.

6 INTERACTION

The Interaction section provides opportunities for developing speaking skills. Four types of activity are used:

- role play in structured situations, e.g. at the shops;
- drama role play, where students make their own plays;
- free discussion, where students talk about their own experiences and feelings;
- interviews, e.g. with pop stars.

7 PROJECT

The Project section provides opportunities for students to use the language of the unit to write about their own lives. Project tasks are related to the theme of each unit. Detailed guidance for doing project work is provided below on pages viii–xi.

8 THE LEARNING DIARY

This completes the loop. The students look back to the Introduction page and say how they feel about the language items and the learning objectives. A self-check is provided in the Workbook for students to check their knowledge.

The Learning diary is part of the process of learner involvement. It encourages the students to become more active as learners and to take on more responsibility for their own learning. It also provides evidence for you, as teacher, of things that have not been learnt very well and which may need further practice.

The Learning diary also asks the students to say which parts of the unit they liked most/least. This will help you and your students to learn more about how they learn best.

PRONUNCIATION PRACTICE

This section is at the end of the book on pages T110–T113a. It contains:

- a review of the phonemic alphabet, showing the basic sounds of English;
- activities focusing on specific points of pronunciation. There is one activity for each unit.

The Pronunciation practice activities can be done at any time in the unit, as time allows.

Lesson notes

The lesson notes provide:

- detailed guidance for teaching each activity;
- notes on language use;
- notes on content and cultural points;
- further activities.

The remainder of this Introduction is concerned with general guidance for handling project work.

An introduction to project work

Project work is a major feature of *Hotline*. Project work is not a new methodology. Its benefits have been widely recognized for many years in the teaching of subjects like Science, Geography and History. In language teaching, however, it is a relative newcomer.

The aim of this section is to provide a simple introduction to project work, to enable you to introduce it smoothly into your classroom.

1 Why do project work?

What benefits does project work bring to the language class? This teacher from Spain expresses it very well:

'Pupils don't feel that English is a chore, but is a means of communication and enjoyment. They can experiment with the language as something real not as something that only appears in books.'
(*Marisa Cuesta, Spain*)

As this teacher indicates, project work captures better than any other activity the two principal elements of a communicative approach. These are:

a a concern for motivation, that is, how the learners relate to the task;

b a concern for relevance, that is, how the learners relate to the language.

We could add to these a third element:

c a concern for educational values, that is, how the language curriculum relates to the general educational development of the learner.

Let's look at these elements in a bit more detail.

a Motivation

Positive motivation is the key to successful language learning, and project work is particularly useful as a means of generating this positive motivation. If you talk to teachers who do project work in their classes, you will find that this is the feature that is always mentioned – the students really enjoy it. But why is project work so motivating? There are three reasons.

Firstly, project work is very personal. The students are writing about their own lives – their house, their family, their town, their dreams and fantasies, their own research into topics that interest them. Students, in other words, are being given the opportunity to tell the world about themselves.

Secondly, project work is a very active medium. Students aren't just receiving and producing words. They are:

- collecting information;
- drawing pictures, maps, diagrams and charts;
- cutting out pictures;
- arranging texts and visuals;
- colouring;
- carrying out interviews and surveys;
- possibly making recordings, too.

Project work is learning through doing.

Lastly, project work gives a clear sense of achievement. It enables all students to produce a worthwhile product. As another teacher comments:

'There is feedback from the students as they realize what they can do with the English they have learned.'
(*Jesus-Angel Vallejo Carrasco, Spain*)

This feature of project work makes it particularly well suited to the mixed-ability class, because students can work at their own pace and level. The brighter students can show what they know, unconstrained by the syllabus, while at the same time the slower learners can achieve something that they can take pride in, perhaps compensating for their lower language level by using more visuals.

b Relevance

A foreign language can often seem a remote and unreal thing. This inevitably has a negative effect on motivation, because the students don't see the language as relevant to their own lives. If learners are going to become real language users, they must learn that English can be used to talk about their own world.

Project work helps to bridge this relevance gap in three ways.

Firstly, project work helps to integrate the foreign language into the network of the learners' own communicative competence. It encourages the use of a wide range of communicative skills, enables learners to exploit other spheres of knowledge and provides opportunities for them to write about the things that are important in their own lives.

Secondly, project work helps to make the language more relevant to learners' actual needs, because they are learning how to communicate about their own world – about their house, their family, their town, etc. Project work thus enables students to rehearse the language and factual knowledge that will be of most value to them as language users.

Thirdly, project work establishes a sounder relationship between language and culture. The purpose of learning a foreign language is to make communication between *two* cultures possible. English is not just for talking about the ways of the English-speaking world. It should also be a means for learners to tell the world about their own culture. Project work helps to create this approach. With project work the language thus acts as a bridge, enabling two cultures to communicate with each other.

c Education

There is a growing awareness among language teachers that the process and content of the language class should contribute towards the general educational development of the learner. Project work is very much in tune with modern views about the purpose and nature of education.

Firstly, there is the question of educational values. Most modern school curricula require all subjects to encourage initiative, independence, imagination, self-discipline, co-operation and the development of useful research skills. Project work is a way of turning such general aims into practical classroom activity.

Secondly, cross-curricular approaches are encouraged. For language teaching, this means that students should have the opportunity to use the knowledge they gain in other subjects in the English class. Project work clearly encourages this.

2 Yes, but . . .

Project work brings considerable benefits to the language classroom, but it's important to be aware of the implications of the way of working.

a Noise

Teachers are often afraid that the project classroom will be noisier than the traditional classroom and that this will disturb other classes in the school.

But project work does not *have* to be noisier than any other activity. Students will often need to discuss things and they may be moving around to get a pair of scissors or to consult a reference book. And some activities do require a lot of talking. If the students are doing a survey in their class, for example, there will be a lot of moving around and talking. However, this kind of noise is a natural part of productive activity. We must remember that the traditional classroom has quite a lot of noise in it, too. There is usually at least one person talking (and teachers usually talk rather loudly!) and there may be a tape recorder playing, possibly with the whole class doing a drill. There is no reason why project work should be any noisier than thirty or forty students giving a choral response – quite the opposite, in fact.

Project work is a different way of working and one that requires a different form of control. In project work, students are working independently. They must, therefore, take on some of the responsibility for managing their learning environment. Part of this responsibility is learning what kind of, and what level of, noise is acceptable. When you introduce project work, you also need to encourage and guide the learners towards working quietly and sensibly. Remember that they will enjoy project work and will not want to stop doing it because it is causing too much noise, so it should not be too difficult to get your students to behave sensibly.

b Time

It takes longer to prepare, make and present a project than it does to do more traditional activities. But bear in mind two points.

Firstly, not all project work needs to be done in class time. Obviously, if the project is a group task, most of it must be done in class, but a lot of projects are individual tasks. Projects about 'Your daily life', 'Your dream holiday', etc., can be done at home. You will be surprised how much of their own time students will gladly devote to doing projects.

Secondly, when choosing to do project work, you need to recognize that you are making a philosophical choice in favour of the quality of the learning experience over the quantity. Project work provides rich learning experiences – rich in colour, movement, interaction and, most of all, involvement. In this respect, projects are doubly valuable. They are not just rich learning experiences in themselves. The positive motivation that they generate colours the students' attitude to all the other aspects of the language programme. Learning grammar and vocabulary will appear more relevant, because the students know they will need these things for their project work.

c Use of L1

It is likely that most students will speak in their mother tongue while they are working on their projects. However, rather than seeing this as a problem, we should consider its merits.

Firstly, it is a natural way of working. It is a mistake to think of L1 and L2 as two completely separate domains. Learners in fact operate in both domains, constantly switching from one to the other. So it is perfectly natural for learners to use L1 while working on an L2 product. As long as the final product is in English, it doesn't matter if the work is done in L1.

Secondly, project work can provide some good opportunities for realistic translation work. A lot of the source material for projects – leaflets, maps, interviews, texts from reference books, etc. – will be in the mother tongue. Using this material in a project provides useful translation activities.

Thirdly, there will be plenty of opportunities in other parts of the language course for learners to practise oral skills. Project work should be seen as a chance to practise that most difficult of skills – writing. There is no need to worry if the students use L1 to do it.

d Different levels

Some teachers are concerned that, without the teacher's firm control, the weaker students will be lost and will not be able to cope. Again, the answer to this worry is to see the positive side of it. Not all students want or need the teacher's constant supervision. By encouraging the more able students to work independently, you are free to devote your time to those students who need it most.

Paradoxically, it is often in the traditional classroom that the weaker students can be neglected, because the brighter students take more than their share of the teacher's attention.

It would be wrong to pretend that project work does not have its drawbacks. It certainly demands a lot of the teacher in terms of preparation and classroom management skills. It also requires a change of attitude about what is really valuable in language teaching and you need to work with your students to develop a responsible working environment. But, in practice, most teachers find that their worst fears about project work do not materialize. The work is so motivating for the students that it produces its own momentum. The noise of the well-managed project classroom is the sound of creativity. And that's what we want to encourage, not suppress.

3 Getting started

The key to successful project work is good preparation.

a You'll need some basic materials and equipment:
- scissors;
- rulers;
- glue;
- large sheets of paper or card.

b It's a good idea to have some reference books available:
- a dictionary;
- a grammar book;
- an atlas.

Students will want to know new words or constructions for expressing their ideas. And if you haven't got reference books available, the students will ask you! This will not only become tiresome for you, but it also destroys an opportunity for learners to become more independent and to develop some useful research skills.

c Try to keep a stock of magazines, maps and leaflets in the class. You need to develop squirrel habits. Collect any material you can find. It's amazing how much printed material is available free from shops, travel agents, banks, etc. Remember two important points.

Firstly, the material does not have to be in English. Indeed, as already noted, material in L1 can provide opportunities for some creative translation work.

Secondly, you do not have to provide all the material yourself. Encourage the students to provide material as well. They will often have a stock of old comics and magazines at home.

d Teach your learners how to do project work. Before starting any project, discuss with the students how they will tackle it. What materials will they need? Where will they get them? etc. If the project requires a particular kind of activity, such as an interview, a graph or a chart, make sure the students know how to do it.

Use each project not only to learn and practise language but also to help your students to learn a bit more about project work.

e In *Hotline*, project work comes at the end of a unit, so it practises the language students have learnt in the unit. But do bear in mind that you can't anticipate all the language the learners will need. A lot of language learning goes on during the actual project work itself, as students look for new words or expressions. In project work, learners not only learn new vocabulary, they also develop the skills of looking for words they do not know or alternative ways of expressing what they want to say.

Preparation, then, is the key to making project work a success. Prepare your classroom by providing some basic materials. Prepare your students by practising the skills and techniques they will need. Most important of all, prepare yourself for a new way of working that is challenging but very satisfying.

4 Evaluation

Assessment of project work is a difficult issue to tackle. This is not because project work is difficult to assess, but because the best way to assess project work may conflict with official procedures for assessing a student's work. There are some guidelines for assessing projects, but, of course, you know best what is necessary and possible in your own system.

There are two basic principles for assessing project work:

a The most obvious point to note about project work is that language is only a part of the total project. Consequently, it is not very appropriate to assess a project only on the basis of linguistic accuracy. Credit must be given for the overall impact of the project, the level of creativity it displays, the neatness and clarity of presentation and, most of all, the effort that has gone into its production. There is nothing particularly unusual in this. It is normal practice in assessing creative writing to give marks for style and content. Many education systems also require similar factors to be taken into account in the assessment of students' oral performance in class.

So a wide-ranging 'profile' kind of assessment that evaluates the whole project is needed.

b The second principle is that, if at all possible, don't correct mistakes on the final project itself – or at least not in ink. It goes against the whole spirit of project work. A project usually represents a lot of effort and is something that the students will probably want to keep. It is thus a shame to put red marks all over it. This draws attention to things that are wrong about the project over the things that are good. On the other hand, students are more likely to take note of errors pointed out to them in project work, because the project means much more to them than just any piece of class work.

So what do you do about errors? There are two useful techniques:

a Encourage the students to do a rough draft of their project first. Correct this in your normal way. The students can then incorporate corrections in the final product.

b If errors occur in the final product, correct it in pencil or on a separate sheet of paper. It is then up to the students whether they wish to correct the finished piece of work.

But fundamentally, the most important thing to do about errors is to stop worrying about them. Projects are real communication. When we communicate, all we can do is the best we can with what we know. And because we usually concentrate on getting the meaning right, errors in form will naturally occur. It's a normal part of using and learning a language.

Students invest a lot of themselves in a project and so they will usually make every effort to do their best work. And remember that any project will only form part of the total amount of work that the students produce in the language course. There will be plenty of opportunities to evaluate accuracy in other parts of the language programme. Project work provides an opportunity to develop creativity, imagination, enquiry and self-expression and the assessment of the project should reflect this.

5 Conclusion

Project work is one of the most exciting developments in language teaching. It combines in practical form both the fundamental principles of a communicative approach and the values of good education. It has the added virtue of being a long-established and well-tried method of teaching in other subject areas.

	LANGUAGE WORK	READING	LISTENING	WORD WORK
Introductory unit p.3 VICTORIA ROAD Sue's penfriend	Tense revision			
1 Daily life p.9 VICTORIA ROAD Terry's problem	Telling the time The present simple – positive – negative	Sleep	Views of Britain	Verbs in expressions
2 The past p.19 VICTORIA ROAD Sue teases Terry	The past simple – *to be* regular verbs – positive – negative – irregular verbs – questions with *did* – negatives	The King of Rock and Roll	Fans	Pop music
3 Places p.29 VICTORIA ROAD Jackie arrives	The present continuous – positive – negative – questions The present simple and the present continuous	Hartfield	How observant are you?	Places
4 Revision p.39		Charity in Covent Garden	An interview with Rick Astley	Stars and stardom Shops
5 Travel p.43 VICTORIA ROAD Sue goes to Spain	The future simple *will* – positive – negative – questions *must, mustn't, needn't*	A long way to travel for your dinner	A day at the seaside	Geographical names Seasons
6 Problems p.53 VICTORIA ROAD Kamala's story	The past continuous – positive – negative – questions The past continuous and the past simple	The brave village	The cat	Disease Indefinite pronouns *(someone, etc)*

INTERACTION	PROJECT	PRONUNCIATION	LEARNING OBJECTIVES
	A letter to a penfriend	Phonetic alphabet revision	Asking for and giving personal information
What do you know about your classmates?	Your daily life	/z/, /ɪz/	Talk about your daily life Tell the time Describe regular events Talk about likes and dislikes Ask people about their lives
An interview with a pop star Ask people about their life story	A biography of a pop star	-ed endings	Talk about recent events Tell someone's life story Talk about pop music Talk about your favourite pop star
Giving directions	Your neighbourhood	/ɪ/, /iː/	Talk about what people are doing Contrast regular and current activities Describe a town Talk about what you can do in a town Ask for and give directions
A quiz	A charity event	Phonetic alphabet revision	
At the station	Your dream holiday	/r/	Talk about future plans Make suggestions Express conditions Describe a route Make arrangements for a journey Buy a train ticket Ask about train times Describe a holiday
My scar	A newspaper story	/h/	Tell a story Ask about a story Describe a historical event Talk about an event in your life

	LANGUAGE WORK	READING	LISTENING	WORD WORK
7 Comparisons p.63 VICTORIA ROAD Sue fights back	The comparative and superlative – regular – irregular Singular and plural with clothes *a pair of*	20th century fashion	A sound journey	Clothes
8 Revision p.73		Jailbreak	A news broadcast	
9 Visitors p.77 VICTORIA ROAD Jackie's cousin arrives	The present perfect – positive – negative – questions The present perfect and the past simple	A visit to London	Strange visitors	Places in a city
10 Food p.87 VICTORIA ROAD Jackie's surprise	*some/any* Quantity Countable/uncountable	Pizza Palace	Boston burgers	Food *a bottle of*, etc
11 Communication p.97 VICTORIA ROAD Terry in trouble	The passive voice – present – past – future – present perfect	Why weren't we warned?	The Top 40	Destruction The weather Pop music Computers
12 Revision p.107		The Florida Galleons		Treasure

Wordlist p.114

Irregular verbs p.119

INTERACTION	PROJECT	PRONUNCIATION	LEARNING OBJECTIVES
Shopping Sizes	Modern fashions	/tʃ/, /ʃ/	Compare people and things Describe clothes Buy a bus ticket Buy things in shops Ask about and give sizes of clothes
Quiz	Game: Escape from the evil Professor X	A secret message	
Contact with English	Important events in your life	Intonation	Introduce people Talk about past events that affect the present Ask about and say what you have done Talk about your contacts with the English- speaking world Talk about recent events in your life
In a cafe	Your own menu	/ɪz/ plural endings	Express quantities Describe what a meal consists of Read a menu Order a meal in a cafe Understand and give a recipe
Buying a record	Forms of communication	/n/ or /m/ + consonant	Describe a process Produce a flow chart Talk about the weather Talk about natural disasters Buy a record in a shop
Translation	Your final episode	A secret message	

Points to watch out for in this unit

- The verb *to have got* is very common in British English but not in American English. American people say *I have, I don't have,* and *He/She has* ... and so on in declarative sentences, and *Do you have* ...? / *Don't you have* ...? / *Does he/she have* ...? in interrogative ones.

VICTORIA ROAD

 a
- Students look at the picture of the people.
- Ask students to think of all the characters' names they remember from Book 1. Say *Now remind yourself of the others.*
- Or (if students have *not* used Book 1) say *'Victoria Road' is a story about some young people in Britain. Victoria Road is the name of the road they live in. Let's learn their names.*
- They look quickly through the story on pages 4–5 for their names.
- They write the full name of each person above the picture.
- Check answers, including spelling.

Answer key	
(from left to right)	
Casey Royston	*(unknown)*
Terry Moore	*Kamala Wijeratne*
Sue Scott	*Vince Scott*

b
- Students read instructions.
- They look for another girl's full name in the book.
- The student who finds the name calls it out.

Answer key
Jackie Wright (She first appears in Unit 3.)

INTRODUCTORY UNIT

1 a Look at these people. Do you know them?
Look quickly through the story on page 4
and find their names.

b You won't find one of the girls' names in
this unit. Look through the book. Can you
find her name?

Sue's penfriend

 • Read the questions aloud.
• Students look at the picture story to find the answers.
• Students give their answers.

Answer key
a At Sue and Vince's house
b Carmen, Sue's new penfriend
c She is writing to Carmen.
d Terry says he doesn't like girls with short hair. Sue has got short hair.

 • Play the tape.
• Students listen to the tape and follow in their books.

Notes
Tell This is a nickname often used for men and boys whose name is Terry.

Hang on a minute This means 'Wait a minute'. It is very informal.

Shh This means 'be quiet'.

big mouth Someone with a 'big mouth' is someone who often says tactless or rude things.

Come on here means 'Come with me, quickly'. It is not the same as 'Come in', which people say when someone knocks at the door.

Hurry up is an informal way of saying 'Hurry'.

Oh, he's all right here means 'He's not a bad person really'.

Don't worry about it here means 'It's not important'. Here Kamala means 'Don't spend too much time thinking about the things Terry says'.

See you is an informal way of saying 'I'll see you later'. It is very common between friends. If someone says *See you*, the reply is often *See you* (or *Yes, see you*) as well.

• English words often have two of the same letters next to each other. When we spell these, we say 'double' and then say the letter. Terry's surname is Moore, so he spells it 'M double-O R E'.

• In English, a person's family name (or 'surname') follows his or her given name.

• In Britain now, many young people have small 'personal computers' with word processing facilities which they use for playing computer games or writing letters.

 • Students read the questions.
• Elicit answers.

Answer key
(possible answers)
a He is at the Scotts' house.
b He is upstairs.
c He is outside.
d Sue is writing a letter to her penfriend on her word processor and Kamala is helping her.
e Sue's grandparents bought the word processor.
f She is Sue's new Spanish penfriend.
g Carmen, her mother, her father and her brother are in the photograph.
h He likes her long hair.
i Terry was rude to her. He said, 'I don't like girls with short hair' – and **her** hair is short! (Perhaps she also secretly likes Terry, and wants him to like her.)

 • Play the tape again. Students listen carefully.

Sue's penfriend

Look at the story.

 a Where are the people?

 b Who is the girl in the photograph?

 c What is Sue doing?

 d Why is Sue angry at the end?

Hello, Mrs Scott. Is Vince in?

Hello, Terry. Come in.

What are you doing?

I'm writing a letter to my new penfriend.

3 🔈 **Now listen and follow in your books.**

Terry Hello, Mr Scott. Hello, Mrs Scott. Is Vince in?

Mrs Scott Hello, Terry. Come in. Vince was upstairs just now. Vince!

Vince Hi, Tell. Is Casey with you?

Terry He's outside. Have you got your money?

Vince Oh no, I haven't. Hang on a minute.

Sue How do you spell your surname, Terry? Has it got an 'e' at the end?

Terry It's M – double O – R – E. Why? What are you doing?

Sue I'm writing a letter to my new penfriend.

Terry When did you get your computer?

Sue It's a word processor. My grandma and grandpa bought it for my birthday last week. Now ssh. I'm trying to concentrate.

Terry What's the penfriend's name, Kamala?

Kamala Carmen. She's from Spain. I've got a photo here.

Kamala Look. That's Carmen with her mum and dad and her brother. They're outside their flat.

Terry Mmm. She's very pretty. I like long hair.

Sue She hasn't got long hair now. It's short like mine.

Terry Oh, that's a pity. I don't like girls with short hair.

Sue Thank you very much, Terry Moore. Well, I don't like boys with small brains and big mouths. So don't be rude.

Terry What? Oh, er, I'm sorry, Sue. I didn't mean . . .

Casey Come on, Terry, Vince. The bus is coming. Hurry up.

Vince Bye.

Terry Bye.

Kamala See you.

Sue 'I don't like girls with short hair.' He's such a fool, that Terry Moore, and so rude.

Kamala Oh, he's all right, Sue. Don't worry about it.

4 **Answer these questions.**

a Where is Terry?

b Where is Vince when Terry arrives?

c Where is Casey?

d What are Sue and Kamala doing?

e Who bought the word processor?

f Who is Carmen?

g Who is in the photograph?

h What does Terry like about Carmen?

i Why is Sue annoyed?

5 Close your book. Listen again.

Useful expressions

- Students read 'Useful expressions'.
- Say *Complete the chart with the expressions that mean the same in (your language).*
- Add *If you've got no idea of the meaning, look back at the story. Work out the meaning from the situation. What would you say in that situation?*
- Students complete the chart.
- In pairs, students compare charts.
- Check answers. Discuss and explain as necessary.

 a
- Divide the class into groups of three.
- Students decide who will read each part.

> **Note**
> If students are not used to making decisions in groups, give everyone in each group a letter: A, B or C. Say *A reads Terry, B reads Sue and C reads all the other parts.*

b
- Students read the dialogue. All groups read at the same time. Go round the class listening for serious pronunciation problems. Answer questions as necessary.
- Ask one group to read the dialogue to the class. Other students listen and follow in their books.

FOLLOW UP

- Students number the sentences 1–10 to show the correct order. Say *Do this without looking back.*
- In pairs, students compare answers.
- Get one pair to read their dialogue.

> **Answer key**
> The sentences should be numbered from top to bottom as follows:
> 4 9 2 6 1 5 10 8 3 7

LANGUAGE WORK

Tense revision

 a
- Say *We will now look at the different tenses in the story.*
- Students read the headings in the chart.
- Remind students about the *uses* of the three different tenses. Do this in the mother tongue if necessary.
- Students turn back to *Victoria Road* to find examples.

- Write the headings on the blackboard.
- Elicit one example of each tense from the story. Write these on the blackboard. Students check their own lists.

> **Note**
> They should only give the relevant part of a sentence, e.g. *Vince was upstairs . . .*

- Elicit new examples. Add these to the list on the board.

> **Answer key**
> **Present simple**
> *Is Vince in?*
> *Is Casey with you?*
> *He's outside.*
> *Have you got your money?*
> *Oh no, I haven't.*
> *How do you spell your surname . . . ?*
> *Has it got an 'e' . . . ?*
> *It's M- double-O-R-E.*
> *It's a word processor.*
> *What's the penfriend's name . . . ?*
> *She's from Spain.*
> *I've got a photo . . .*
> *That's Carmen . . .*
> *They're outside their house.*
> *She's very pretty.*
> *I like long hair.*
> *She hasn't got long hair . . .*
> *It's short . . .*
> *Oh, that's a pity.*
> *I don't like girls . . .*
> *I don't like boys . . .*
>
> **Present continuous**
> *What are you doing?*
> *I'm writing a letter . . .*
> *I'm trying to concentrate.*
> *The bus is coming.*
>
> **Past simple**
> *Vince was upstairs.*
> *When did you get your computer?*
> *My grandma and grandpa bought it . . .*
> *I didn't mean . . .*

b
- Get students to come out and identify examples of each form in the list on the blackboard.
- Elicit further examples from students' own lists.

BUILD UP

2 • Using their lists from **1**, students copy and complete the tables.

• While they are doing this, copy the tables on the blackboard.

• One student completes Table **a** (*to be*) on the blackboard.

• Another student completes Table **b** (*have got*).

• Students amend their own tables.

Answer key

Table a		Table b	
He		*I*	
She	*is*	*You*	*have*
It	*is not*	*We*	*have not*
		They	
We			
You	*are*	*He*	
They	*are not*	*She*	*has*
		It	*has not*

• Read aloud the examples of full form and short form.

• Students add *'s got* to Table **b**.

• Students find the other short forms of *to have got* and *to be*. They add them to their tables.

• Elicit answers. Write them in the table on the blackboard.

Answer key

Add to Table a		Add to Table b	
I	*'m not*	*I*	
		You	
He		*We*	*haven't*
She	*isn't*	*They*	
It			
		He	
We		*She*	*hasn't*
You	*aren't*	*It*	
They			

Giving personal information

3 • Read instructions aloud (*Sue is on . . . the questions*).

• Check understanding.

• Ask *Look at Sue's answers. Can you guess what the questions are?*

• Students suggest questions.

a • Play the cassette. Students listen. Students write down the *questions*.

b • Play the cassette again. Students check their answers.

• Check answers.

• Play the cassette again as necessary.

Man Right, well, can I have some details? What's your name?
Sue Susan Scott.
Man How do you spell your surname?
Sue S-C-O double-T.
Man Where do you live?
Sue In Hartfield.
Man What's your address?
Sue 18 Victoria Road.
Man Victoria Road. What's your postcode?
Sue HA6 4BJ.
Man What's your telephone number?
Sue (0386) 754921.
Man And how old are you, Susan?
Sue 16.
Man When is your birthday?
Sue The twelfth of September.
Man Thank you very much. Now we'll send this information to . . .

Answer key
(See tapescript.)

• Give students practice in *dates*, e.g. today's date, different students' birthdays.

c • In pairs, one student interviews the other. They use the questions they have written down in Exercise 3 and write down answers.

• Students change roles and repeat.

d • Three or four students introduce their partners to the class.

Answer key

This is . . .	*He's/She's (age).*
His/Her name is . . .	*His/Her birthday is on . . .*
He/She lives in . . .	
His/Her address is . . .	
His/Her postcode is . . .	
His/Her telephone number is . . .	

FOLLOW UP

4 • Students complete the sentences using the words provided.

• Elicit answers.

Answer key

a	*Are*	*am*	**e**	*has got*	*is*	*has*
b	*is*	*has got*	**f**	*is*	*her*	*penfriend's*
c	*are*		**g**	*have got*	*from*	
d	*don't*	*He*	**h**	*a*	*my*	*are*	*our*

Useful expressions

 6 How do you say these expressions in your language?

Come in.

just now.

Hang on a minute.

Don't be rude.

Come on.

Hurry up.

See you.

He's all right.

Don't worry about it.

7 a Work in groups of three. One person is Terry, one is Sue and one is all the other parts.

b Read the dialogue.

FOLLOW UP

 8 Number this conversation in the correct order.

She's my penfriend.
Who are the other people in the photograph?
I'm writing a letter to Carmen.
She's from Spain.
What are you doing, Sue?
Oh. Where's she from?
They're Carmen's mum and dad. The boy is her brother.
Yes, here you are.
Who's Carmen?
Have you got a photograph of her?

LANGUAGE WORK

Tense revision

1 Look at the Victoria Road story again.

a Find more examples of these tenses. Make a list for each one.

present simple	present continuous	past simple
do you?	I'm writing	bought

b Look at your list and find two questions, two negative verbs and three short forms.

Examples
- question · · · · · Is Vince in?
- negative verb · · · · · I don't like
- short form · · · · · haven't

BUILD UP

2 Complete these tables.

to be

I	am	
	am not	
		from Greece.
He She It	....	15 years old.
	... .	Spanish.
We You They	....	here.
	... .	

have got

....	have	long hair.
....	have not	
....		a big house.
....		got green eyes.
....	has	
....	has not	two brothers.

Look. We can say:

She **has** got short hair. **Full form**
or She**'s** got short hair. **Short form**

Find other short forms in the story. Add them to the tables.

6

Giving personal information

3 📼 **Sue is on the telephone. She is talking to someone at the penfriend agency. Listen to their conversation.**

a Here are Sue's answers. Write the questions.

....
Susan Scott.

....
S–C–O– double T.

....
In Hartfield.

....
18 Victoria Road.

....
HA6 4BJ

....
(0386) 754921

....
Sixteen.

....
12th September.
(**Note:** We say 'the twelfth of September')

b Listen again and check your answers.

c Work in pairs. Use the questions from Sue's interview. Interview your partner.

d Introduce your partner to the class.

This is . . .
His/Her name is . . .

FOLLOW UP

4 **Complete the sentences with these words. Some of them are used more than once.**

are	he	my	her	is	am
penfriend's		have got		from	our
has got	don't	has	a		

a .... you Spanish? No, I .... from Argentina.

b She .... tall and she .... short hair.

c Casey and Vince .... sixteen years old.

d I .... like Terry. .... is such a fool.

e Vince .... a sister. Her name .... Susan. Terry .... not got any brothers or sisters.

f Carmen .... writing a letter to .... penfriend in England. Her .... name is Sue.

g I .... a penfriend. He is .... Brazil.

h Here is .... photograph of .... family. We .... in .... garden.

PROJECT

- Students complete the letter. They look back if necessary.

Answer key

A6 4BJ	our
Susan Scott	mum and dad (or parents)
telephone number	Casey
sixteen	Terry Moore
12th September	red
birthday	Kamala Wijeratne
brother	favourite
Vince	speak
brothers	
photograph	

Your life

- Students' project files can *either* be a scrap book *or* a ring binder containing several sheets of paper which can be added to.

- Give students plenty of time to design and produce their project file. It should include their name, school and class. Students can illustrate it with drawings, magazine pictures and/or photographs.

- In class or for homework, students write a letter about themselves to one of the characters in *Victoria Road*. They use Sue's letter as a model.

- Correct the letters. Consider paragraphing, grammar and spelling.

- Students rewrite letters.

- Display the letters. Create a time for students to read each other's letters.

- Students stick their letters into their project files.

EXTRA ACTIVITY

Game: Who is it?
This game practises the verb *to be* as well as asking questions.

- Say *I'm going to teach you a new game. I'll show you how to play it. Now, I'm thinking of a particular person. You have to find out who it is. You have to ask me questions. I will answer 'Yes' or 'No' – nothing else.*

- Give examples of questions, e.g.
  Is it a man or a woman?
  Is he/she a sportsman/sportswoman/sportsperson?
  Is he/she alive/dead?
  Has he/she got long hair?
  Is he/she from … ?
  Is he/she on television?

- Think of a person – someone famous, or someone in the class.

- Students ask questions.

- When someone discovers who the person is, repeat.

- Repeat – but this time choose a student to choose a person.

- Students play the game in pairs.

▶ **Pronunciation: page T110**

PROJECT

Here is Sue's first letter to Carmen. Use the information in this unit to complete it.

18 Victoria Road,
H_____,
Bucks,
England

21 September

Dear Carmen

Hello. I'm your new penfriend. My name is _____ and I live near London. My _____ is 754921. I'm _____ years old and my birthday is _____ September. When is your _____? I have got one _____. His name is _____ and he's sixteen, too. We're twins. We both go to Hartfield Secondary School. I'm in class 5A and Vince is in 5B. Have you got any _____ or sisters?

You can see me and Vince in this _____. We're having a barbecue in _____ garden with our _____ and some friends. The two boys are Vince's friends, _____ Royston and _____. Terry is wearing a _____ shirt and Casey is holding a green ball. The girl is _____. She's my best friend.

I love cycling, badminton and pop music. My favourite groups are Aha and the Famous Five. Who is your favourite pop group? My _____ TV programme is Neighbours. It's an Australian programme.

I'm sorry my letter is in English. I can't _____ Spanish. We learn French and German at school. I hope you can understand my letter. Bye for now.

Love Sue

Your life

Make a project file about your life.

At the end of each unit there is a project task. Here is your first task.

Use Sue's letter as a model. Write a letter about yourself to one of the characters in Victoria Road. Stick your letter in your project file.

Illustrate your project with some labelled photographs of people and things in your life.

▶ Pronunciation: page 110   8

1 daily life

the present simple

Contents

Victoria Road: Terry's problem 10
Language work: Telling the time 12
The present simple tense 13
Reading: Sleep 14
Listening: Views of Britain 16
Interaction: What do you know about your classmate? 17
Project: Your daily life 18

Language work 😊 😐 ☹

Grammar

telling the time
It's five past nine.

the present simple tense - statements
I get up at ten to eight.
He gets up early.

- negatives
I don't like sport.
She doesn't stay in bed late.

- questions
Do you snore?
When does she get up?

Word work

verbs in expressions

😊 😐 ☹ Learning objectives

In this unit you will learn how to:

talk about your daily life

tell the time

describe regular events

talk about likes and dislikes

ask people about their lives

VICTORIA ROAD

Terry's problem

- Ask students what happened in *Victoria Road* in the Introduction.
- Elicit ideas.

- Read out the questions.
- Students look quickly at the picture story and find the answers.
- Elicit answers.

> **Answer key**
> **a** *The people are Terry and Mrs Moore, his mother.*
> **b** *It's Saturday.*
> **c** *He's bored.* or
> *He secretly really likes Sue, but she seems not to like him.*

> **Note**
> Accept both answers – but if the students only suggest one, do not mention the other.

- Students look at the picture story again.
- Get students to say what happens in the story.

> **Answer key**
> (possible answer)
> *It's Saturday. Terry is bored because he's got nothing to do. His mother suggests that he should go and see his friends. Terry says that they all do things on Saturday. His mother suggests that he should go and see Sue. Terry is embarrassed and says she's busy, too. His mother is surprised, because Sue telephoned him this morning. Then Mrs Moore moves Terry's hand and sees that he is drawing a heart with Sue's name on. Is Terry secretly in love with Sue?*

 • 🔊 Play the cassette. Students listen and follow in their books.

> **Notes**
> **make your bed** 'To make a bed' means 'to straighten the sheets and blankets (or duvet) so the bed is neat, tidy and ready to get into again at night'.
>
> **Dinner** sometimes means 'midday meal' and sometimes 'evening meal'. Here 'dinner' means 'evening meal.' It is the main meal of the day.
>
> **There's nothing to do** *around here.* Terry means nothing interesting happens in the area where he lives.
>
> **in my way** This means 'you're where I want to be.' Mrs Moore wants to get on with the housework. She can't do this when Terry is around.
>
> **that's funny** can mean 'that's amusing' or 'that's strange'. Here it means 'that's strange'.
>
> • **community work** In Britain, some young people do voluntary community work in their spare time. Sue's work at the hospital is not unusual.
>
> • In Britain, children do not go to school on Saturday or Sunday. Schools and clubs often organize sports matches on Saturday morning.

- Students read the questions underneath the story.
- Elicit suggestions.

> **Answer key**
> **Problems:**
> *he feels bored*
> *he secretly likes Sue, but she seems not to like him*
>
> **To stop feeling bored, Terry can:**
> *play football with Casey*
> *do community work at the hospital with Sue*
> *have guitar lessons, like Vince*
> *do some housework*
> *go shopping or help with the housework*
> *go swimming*
>
> **Because he secretly likes Sue, Terry can:**
> *offer to do community work with her at the hospital*
> *ask her to teach him how to use her word processor*
> *tell her he really likes her*
> *ask her if she likes him*
> *apologize for being rude to her when she was writing to her penfriend*

3 • Students read the questions.

   • Students give their answers.

> **Answer key**
> **a** *It's twenty-five past eleven.*
> **b** *It's Saturday.*
> **c** *He's at home.*
> **d** *He's bored.*
> **e** *He goes to bed at quarter past ten.*
> **f** (possible answer) *She wants him to get up, to find something to do on Saturdays, and to help her in the house or go out.*
> **g** *He plays football on Saturday mornings.*
> **h** *He washes the car and goes swimming.*
> **i** *He doesn't like playing sport./He only likes sports on TV.*
> **j** *Casey plays football, Vince has guitar lessons, Sue does community work at the hospital and Kamala helps in her parents' shop.*

4 • Students close their books.

   • ▣ Play the cassette again. Students listen carefully.

Terry's problem

1 Look at the story and find the answers to these questions.

   a Who are the people?

   b What day is it?

   c What's wrong with Terry?

> Come on. Terry. It's time you were up.

> What's the matter with you today?

> I'm bored. Every day's the same. I feel like a robot.

> I've got nothing to do.

2 🔊 **Listen and follow in your books.**

Terry I'm bored. Every day's the same. I feel like a robot. I get up at ten to eight, I get dressed, I have my breakfast, I go to school at twenty to nine, I come home at half past three, I do my homework, I watch TV, I get undressed and I go to bed at quarter past ten . And then the next day, I get up again at ten to eight, I get dressed, I . . .

Mrs Moore Come on, Terry. It's time you were up.

Terry What's the time?

Mrs Moore It's twenty-five past eleven. You can't stay in bed all day. Now get up. And make your bed, too.

Later

Terry What time is dinner, Mum?

Mrs Moore Dinner is at six o'clock. It's only five to two. What's the matter with you today?

Terry I've got nothing to do.

Mrs Moore Why don't you help me. You can tidy your room or wash up or iron some clothes or go to the shops for me?

Terry Oh, Mum. I don't want to do housework.

Mrs Moore Go out, then.

Terry There's nothing to do around here.

Mrs Moore Other people do things. Look at Casey. He doesn't stay in bed till half past eleven at the weekend. He gets up early and plays football on Saturday mornings. And in the afternoon he washes the car or goes swimming.

Terry Yes, well, I don't like sport – except on TV.

Mrs Moore You're lazy. That's your problem, Terry. Now, I don't want you in my way. Go and see one of your friends.

Terry I can't. They all do things on Saturdays. Casey plays football, Vince has guitar lessons, Kamala helps in her parents' shop.

Mrs Moore What about Sue?

Terry (blushing) Er, no. Er ... she does her community work at the hospital on Saturdays.

Mrs Moore Well, that's funny because she phoned you this morning.

What do you think?

- What is Terry's problem?
- What can he do?

 Answer these questions.

a What's the time at the beginning of the story?

b What day is it?

c Where is Terry?

d What's wrong with him?

e What time does Terry go to bed?

f What does his mother want him to do?

g When does Casey play football?

h What other things does Casey do?

i Why doesn't Terry play football?

j What do Terry's friends do on Saturdays?

Close your book. Listen again.

Useful expressions

- Say *Look at 'Useful expressions'. Write down what each one means in our (your) language. If you're not sure, go back to the story and work out the meaning from the situation.*

- Students complete the chart. While they are doing this, write the chart on the blackboard.

- In pairs, students compare answers.

- Elicit answers. Write them in the chart on the blackboard.

- Discuss and explain as necessary.

- Students correct and amend their expressions as necessary.

> **Note**
> Make sure students understand the difference between *I'm bored* and *It's boring*; also *I'm interested (in) ...* and *It's interesting*.

 a
- Put students into pairs. Students choose their roles.

- Remind them not to speak too loudly.

b
- Students read the dialogue.

- Walk round the class and listen for serious pronunciation problems. Answer any questions students ask.

- If time, ask one pair to read the dialogue to the class. The other students listen and read carefully.

- If time, in pairs, change roles and repeat.

- Read the questions aloud.
- Elicit ideas and suggestions

> **Note**
> Answers should be in the *present simple* tense.

FOLLOW UP

- Students write the heading 'Terry's day' in their exercise books.

- Students look at the example *Terry gets up at ten to eight*. Say *When we are talking about someone else, remember that the verb always has an 's' at the end – so, here, 'gets' with an 's'.*

- Students write a paragraph about Terry's day in their exercise books.

> **Answer key**
> (possible answer)
> **Terry's day**
> *Terry gets up at ten to eight. He gets dressed. He has his breakfast. He goes to school at twenty to nine. He comes home at half past three. He does his homework. He watches TV. He gets undressed and goes to bed at quarter past ten.*

LANGUAGE WORK

Telling the time

- Students look at the pictures of clocks and watches.

- Students look at the first picture.

- Ask *What's the time?*

- Elicit answer.

- Repeat with the other pictures. A different student should answer each time.

> **Answer key**
> | | |
> |---|---|
> | *twenty-five to three* | *five past eight* |
> | *ten to one* | *twenty past seven* |
> | *half past twelve* | *quarter past eleven* |

- Divide class into pairs. One student is A; the other is B.

- Students read **2** carefully.

- Demonstrate the activity:
  One student comes to the front and acts student A and you act student B.
  When you give a time, student A points to the clock or watch.
  The other students check if it's the correct clock/watch.

- All pairs carry out the activity. Walk round the class.

- Students look at the pictures of buildings and opening times.

- They read the clues and label each building.

- Check that students understand *bank, shop, post office* and *museum*.

- Students explain how they got the answer.

> **Answer key**
> | | |
> |---|---|
> | *museum* | *post office* |
> | *shop* | *bank* |

T12

The present simple tense

- Students read the gapped sentences. Point out that in each case it is the *verb* which is missing.

- Say *Look back at 'Victoria Road' on page 10 if you need help.*

- Students complete the sentences.

- In pairs, students compare answers.

- Check answers.

Answer key

a *get*	*do*	*go*	*don't like*
b *gets*	*does*	*goes*	*doesn't stay*

- Say *Look at your sentences in **a** and **b**. What's the difference?*

- Elicit answer.

Answer key

*The 3rd person singular verbs, in **b**, have an 's' at the end. The 1st person singular verbs, in **a**, do not.*

BUILD UP

- Students complete the tables using the words provided. While they are doing this, copy the table on to the blackboard.

- Elicit answers. One student writes them on the blackboard.

- Students amend their own tables as necessary.

Answer key

(top to bottom)

like	*play*	*likes*	*plays*	*don't*

- Point out that, in the negative sentences, the 3rd person verbs after *don't* do *not* end in 's'.

- Remind them that this is the 'present simple' tense.

- Students read the rule.

a
- Students rule four columns in their exercise books.

- They head these *Things Everyone in the Family Does*, *Things Only I Do*, *Things Only My Mother Does* and *Things Only My Father Does*.

- Students list five activities in each column.

Note

These need not be expressed in full sentences but the verb form should be correct, i.e. the verbs in the first, third and fourth columns should end in 's', e.g. . . . *washes the dishes*; those in the second column should not end in 's', e.g. . . . *feed the cat*.

b
- In pairs, students read and compare each other's lists.

- One or two students tell the class about how their own lists are different from their partners' lists, e.g. *In my family only my mother cleans the bathroom but in X's family everyone cleans the bathroom.*

FOLLOW UP

- Remind students that negative sentences in the 3rd person singular do *not* have an 's' at the end of the verb.

- Get students to read the example aloud.

- Students write three sentences for each of the different cues.

- Check answers.

Answer key

Terry doesn't like sport.
Casey likes sport.
I like/don't like sport.

Terry doesn't wash the car.
Casey washes the car.
I wash/don't wash the car.

Terry doesn't play football.
Casey plays football.
I play/don't play football.

Terry doesn't go swimming.
Casey goes swimming.
I go/don't go swimming.

Terry watches TV on Saturday afternoons.
Casey doesn't watch TV on Saturday afternoons.
I watch/don't watch TV on Saturday afternoons.

Useful expressions

5 a How do you say these expressions in your language?

I'm bored.

I feel like a robot.

It's time you were up.

What's the matter with you?

I've got nothing to do.

Why don't you . . .?

Tidy your room.

There's nothing to do round here.

in my way

That's funny.

6 a Work in pairs. One person is Terry and the other is Mrs Moore.

b Read the dialogue.

7 What do you think about Terry's problem? Are you ever bored? What do you do?

FOLLOW UP

8 Describe Terry's day.

Example
Terry gets up at ten to eight. He . . .

LANGUAGE WORK

Telling the time

1 Look at these clocks and watches. What's the time?

2 Work in pairs.

A Ask 'What's the time?'

B Choose one of the times above and say it.

Example
It's five past eight.

A Point to the correct clock or watch.

3 Opening times. Look at these opening times. Read the clues below. Match the opening times to the buildings.

Opening hours
Monday–Friday
9.00–12.30 and
2.00–5.30
Saturday ·
9.00–12.30
Sunday Closed

Opening Times
Tuesday–Sunday
from 10.00–6.00
closed every Monday

Opening Hours
Monday–Saturday
8.00–8.00
Sunday
9.00–6.00

HOURS OF BUSINESS
Monday–Friday
9.30–3.30

The bank doesn't open every day.
The shop opens before the museum.
The post office doesn't open on Sundays.
The museum and the bank don't close at lunchtime.
The bank opens for five days a week.

The present simple tense

4 Complete these sentences. Use the Victoria Road story on page 10 to help you.

a I .... up at ten to eight.

I .... my homework.

I .... to school at twenty to nine.

I .... sport.

b Casey .... up early on Saturday mornings.

Sue .... her community work.

Casey .... swimming.

Casey .... in bed till half past eleven.

BUILD UP

Look at the sentences in 4a and b. Can you see the differences?

5 Use these words to complete the tables.

don't   plays   like   likes   play

positive		
I We You They	l............ p............	football. tennis.
He She It	l............ p............	the piano. the guitar.

negative		
I We You They	.... like .	football. tennis.
He She It	doesn't play	the piano. the guitar.

> This is the 'present simple' tense. We use it to talk about regular activities.

6 a Think about your family. Write down five things which:

- everyone in the family does.
- only you do.
- only your mother does.
- only your father does.

b Compare your list with your partner's.

FOLLOW UP

7 Use these cues. Write three sentences for each: one about Terry, one about Casey and one about yourself.

stay in bed till half past eleven on Saturdays
like sport
wash the car
play football
go swimming
watch TV on Saturday afternoons

Example
Terry stays in bed till half past eleven on Saturdays.
Casey doesn't stay in bed till half past eleven on Saturdays.
I don't stay in bed till half past eleven on Saturdays.

READING

 This is a scanning activity. The students first scan the text to find out where information is located, before they read in detail. The aim is to encourage students to get a general picture of what the text is about, before they read. This will give them a context that will help them to read and understand the text more easily.

- Students look at page 14.
- Ask *What are you going to read about?*

> **Answer key**
> *sleep/sleepwalking*

- Say *Before you look at the text, read questions a–e.*
- Students read **a–e**. Do not let them read the text yet!
- Ask *What do you think a sleepwalker is?*
- Elicit suggestions.
- Tell students not to read the text carefully. Say *Find out which paragraph contains the answer to each question. Write the number of that paragraph next to the question.*
- Check understanding of this instruction. Say *Do not answer the questions themselves.*
- Students read text quickly and write down the number of the correct paragraph next to each question.

> **Answer key**
> a 5   b 4   c 1   d 2   e 3

- Say *Now read again and find the answers.*
- Elicit answers.

> **Answer key**
> a *Yes*
> b *She got up and went to the launderette with a shopping bag and the dog.*
> c *Eight and a half hours*
> d *Rapid eye movement sleep*
> e *Open doors and windows, ride bicycles, drive cars, take a bath or shower, shave, clean their teeth, get dressed, dig the garden and get into bed with other people*

 • Students read the statements **a–j**.
- Students look through the text again. They write 'Right', 'Wrong' or 'Don't Know' next to each.
- Students explain their answers.

> **Answer key**
> a *W*   b *W*   c *D*   d *R*   e *W*
> f *W*   g *D*   h *D*   i *W*   j *W*

 • Students read 'Sleep' again. This time they read in detail.
- They put each fact into the correct column. (While they are doing this, copy the column headings on the board.)
- Elicit answers. One student writes these under the headings on the board.
- Students amend their work as necessary.

> **Answer key**
> **Deep sleep**
> *Your temperature falls.*
> *Your body relaxes.*
> *You breathe more slowly.*
> *You dream in words.*
> *You can't remember your dreams.*
> *You can't wake up easily.*
> *People sleepwalk.*
> *You talk.*
>
> **REM sleep**
> *You dream in pictures.*
> *You breathe more quickly.*
> *Your temperature rises.*
> *You can remember your dreams.*
> *You can wake up easily.*

 • Students look at the pictures.
- Ask *What are the people doing?*
- Students find the incorrect ones.

> **Answer key**
> *paint*   *eat*
> *wash the car*   *write*

WORD WORK

5 • Students complete each expression with the correct verb. (The verbs have all been used in the story or the exercises.)

• In pairs, students compare answers.

• Check answers.

Note

Students may give an answer which is not from the text but which is correct. If this happens, accept the answer, then elicit the 'correct' verb.

Answer key

take (have)   ride   clean   dig   drive
open   open   wake/get   go   get   get

---

6 a • Divide the class into pairs.

• One student asks the other the questions from the questionnaire and writes down the answers.

• Change roles and repeat.

b • Choose one student to tell the class how his or her partner answered the questions.

• Student reports his/her partner's answers.

• Repeat with two or three more students.

EXTRA ACTIVITY

Summarize the results in a chart on the blackboard or OHP.

a Average the time spent sleeping every day (Question 1).

b Find the total number of students who answered 'Yes' to each of Questions 2–7.

c List the different sleepwalking activities (Question 7 – second part) – if any!

FOLLOW UP

7 • Read instructions aloud.

• Students read example.

• Students write two sentences about themselves and their partner for each question on the questionnaire.

Note

Alternatively, students can write *one* sentence for each question, e.g. *I sleep for nine hours every night, but my partner (only) sleeps for seven and a half hours.*

READING

1 **Read these questions.**

a Can sleepwalkers see?

b What did the girl from Wales do?

c How much sleep do teenagers need?

d What is REM sleep?

e What kinds of things do sleepwalkers do?

Look quickly at the text. In which paragraph will you find the answer to each question?

Sleep

In a normal life a person sleeps for about twenty-five years. But why do we sleep? The simple answer is: we don't know. We need more sleep when we are young. A baby sleeps for about ten hours. A teenager sleeps for eight and a half hours and an adult for seven or eight hours. Old people need only five or six hours.

There are two kinds of sleep. When you go to sleep you go into **deep sleep**. Your temperature falls, your body relaxes and you breathe slowly. After about half an hour you go into **active sleep**. This is also called **rapid eye movement sleep** (or **REM sleep**), because your eyes move. You dream in both deep sleep and REM sleep, but in REM sleep you dream in pictures. If you wake up in REM sleep you can usually remember your dream. Your body spends about twenty minutes in REM sleep and then goes back into deep sleep for an hour.

Do you ever talk or walk in your sleep? People sleepwalk in deep sleep and sleepwalkers do amazing things. They open doors and windows, they ride bicycles and drive cars. They cook, they take a bath or a shower (often in their pyjamas), they shave, they clean their teeth, they get dressed, they dig the garden and they get into bed with other people.

A man in Scotland woke up in his car two miles from his house. He had no clothes on. A girl from Wales woke up at five o'clock in the morning in a launderette. She had a shopping bag and the family's dog with her.

Sleepwalkers are asleep, but they have their eyes open and they can see. They can't wake up easily. If they do, they can't remember anything. Do you ever sleepwalk? Are you sure? Perhaps you do, but nobody sees you.

2 **Right, Wrong or Don't know?**

	✓	✗	?
a Everyone sleeps for eight hours a night.	☐	☐	☐
b Teenagers need less sleep than adults.	☐	☐	☐
c Some people sleep for only one or two hours.	☐	☐	☐
d REM sleep is the same as active sleep.	☐	☐	☐
e You only dream in deep sleep.	☐	☐	☐
f People sleepwalk in REM sleep.	☐	☐	☐
g The man from Scotland woke up at five o'clock in the morning.	☐	☐	☐
h The girl from Wales was in her pyjamas.	☐	☐	☐
i Sleepwalkers can't see.	☐	☐	☐
j Sleepwalkers remember everything they do.	☐	☐	☐

3 Put these facts in the correct column. They are all true.

You dream in pictures.
You breathe slowly.
Your temperature rises.
You dream in words.
Your temperature falls.
You can't wake up easily.
Your body relaxes.
You can't remember your dreams.
You breathe quickly.
You talk.
You can remember your dreams.
People sleepwalk.
You can wake up easily.

deep sleep	REM sleep

4 Which of these is not in the text?

5 Find the verbs to complete these expressions.

.... a shower   .... the door

.... a bicycle   .... up

.... your teeth   .... to sleep

.... the garden   .... into bed

.... a car   .... dressed

.... the window

6

QUESTIONNAIRE How do you sleep?

1 How long do you sleep every day? [   ] hrs

2 Can you remember your dreams? Yes ❑ No ❑

3 Do you dream in colour? Yes ❑ No ❑

4 Do you often dream about the same thing?
    Yes ❑ No ❑
    What do you dream about? [   ]

5 Do you snore? Yes ❑ No ❑

6 Do you talk in your sleep? Yes ❑ No ❑

7 Do you sleepwalk?
    Yes ❑ No ❑
    What do you do? [   ]

a Answer the questionnaire.

b Share your answers with others in the class.

FOLLOW UP

7 Work in pairs. Write your answers and your partner's answers to the questionnaire.

Example
I sleep for nine hours every night. My partner sleeps for seven and a half hours.

LISTENING

Views of Britain

 • Students read the introduction. Add that this may be particularly true if the other people are from overseas.

- Ask if students agree with this.
- Ask what *sort* of things people might learn about themselves from someone from overseas.
- Elicit suggestions.
- Tell students they are going to listen to a cassette of someone from overseas talking about Britain.
- Say *First, listen for the name, **where** the speaker is from and **why** he/she is in Britain.*
- Play the cassette.
- Students listen.
- Elicit answers.

> **Answer key**
> a *Her name is Helen.*
> b *She's from Greece.*
> c *She's studying English.*

 a • Divide the class into pairs.
- Each pair copies the chart. (The chart should take about half a page.)

b • Tell students they will hear the cassette again, and while they listen they should complete the chart.
- Play the tape again.
- Students listen and complete the chart. (One student writes; the other helps give the information.)
- Check answers.
- Play cassette again as necessary.

 • Ask *What does Helen like and dislike about Britain?*
- Elicit answers.

> **Answer key**
> *Helen likes the people, the sweets and English breakfasts but she doesn't like the weather, the mealtimes or the closing time for shops, etc.*

> **Note**
> Make sure students use the 's' on likes and do not add 's' to *doesn't like.*

4 • Remind students that people from overseas also have opinions about their country.

- Ask *What things do you think people from overseas like and don't like about (your country)?*
- Students write these down.
- In pairs, students look at each other's ideas.

EXTRA ACTIVITY

Class discussion. Some students express their ideas to the class. Others agree or disagree. Students should give examples of opinions they have heard, if any.

FOLLOW UP

 • Students complete gaps in the dialogue using the chart.
- In pairs, students compare answers.
- Check answers.

> **Answer key**
> *about people What don't cold wrong do eat language lunch past hungry at have in I'm to closes shops all close o'clock at sweets are*

 Views of Britain

Interviewer Hello. I'm interviewing people about what they like or don't like about England. Can I ask you some questions?
Helen Yes, of course.
Interviewer Are you a tourist?
Helen No, I'm a student at a language school.
Interviewer And where are you from?
Helen Greece.
Interviewer What's your name?
Helen Helen Gogos.
Interviewer Thank you. Well, Helen, what do you like about England?
Helen I like the people. They are very friendly.
Interviewer What don't you like?
Helen I don't like the weather. It's too cold for me. And your times are all wrong.
Interviewer What do you mean?
Helen Well, you eat at the wrong times. At my language school, we have lunch at half past twelve. But I'm not hungry then. In my country, I eat at three o'clock and then I have a rest. Here in England I have lessons in the afternoon, but I'm tired and I want to sleep. And then everything closes very early. All the shops close at half past five and all the restaurants and pubs close at eleven o'clock or half past ten at night. But I love your sweets and English breakfasts are great.
Interviewer Thank you very much, Helen.

INTERACTION

The present simple tense 2

- Tell students to look at the words on each line.
- Say *Each line of words is mixed up. Sort out the words in each line to get a question. Write the questions in your book.*
- Students put the words in order and write down the questions.
- Check answers.

Answer key

Do you play tennis?
Where does Sue live?
What do they like about England?
Does Terry help his parents?
When do you do your homework?

BUILD UP

- Students complete the chart using four of the six words above it. (While they are doing this, draw the chart on the blackboard.)
- Elicit answers.
- One student writes these in the blackboard chart.
- Students correct answers as necessary.

Answer key

do   like or *play*
does   play or *like*

---

a • Students read the questionnaire.

- Put students into pairs.
- Say *In Column 1, write down what you **think** are the answers for your partner. Do not show your questionnaire to your partner, and definitely don't talk to him or her!*
- Students complete Column 1.

b • Read aloud instructions and example.

- In their exercise books, students list the questions they ask their partner to find the *true* answers. Walk round while they are doing this, explaining and correcting as necessary.

c • One student asks the other questions and writes the answers in the second column.

- Students change roles. Repeat.

d • Students compare the two sets of answers. They count how many they got right.

e • Students read the 'Scores' chart.

- Find out how many students are in each score group.

FOLLOW UP

- Students read the instructions and the examples.
- They write two sentences for each question. They give the answer for themselves and their partner.

EXTRA ACTIVITY

Find someone who

- Either produce a handout of the following *or* write it on the blackboard.

  Find someone in the class who:
  likes Michael Jackson
  gets up before you Monday to Friday
  doesn't like hamburgers
  wears blue pyjamas in bed
  stays in bed until ten o'clock on Saturdays
  plays a musical instrument
  helps his/her parents with the housework

- *Under* each item, students write the *question* they should ask to find the answer, e.g. *Do you like Michael Jackson?*
- Students stand up. They ask other students their questions and write down the answers.
- When each student has asked each question three times, tell everyone to sit down again.
- Check the answers of the student who finished first with the class.
- If there is no disagreement, that person is the winner.

Note
If the student has got an answer wrong – e.g. if he or she *incorrectly* says someone wears blue pyjamas, and they don't – repeat with the student who finished second, and so on.

LISTENING

Views of Britain

🔊 We can learn a lot about ourselves from other people. Listen, you will hear someone talking about Britain.

1 First listen and find this information about the speaker.

a What is her name?

b Where is she from?

c Why is she in England?

2 Work in pairs.

a Make a chart like this.

likes	dislikes

b Listen again and fill in your chart.

3 Say what Helen likes and doesn't like.

4 What do you think people like or don't like about your country? Write down some ideas.

FOLLOW UP

5 Complete this.

Interviewer What do you like .... England?

Helen I like the .... They are very friendly.

Interviewer .... don't you like?

Helen I .... like the weather. It's too .... for me. And your times are all ....

Interviewer What .... you mean?

Helen Well, you .... at the wrong times. At my .... school we have .... at half .... twelve. But I'm not .... then. In my country I eat .... three o'clock and then I .... a rest. Here .... England I have lessons in the afternoon, but .... tired and I want .... sleep. And then everything .... very early. All the .... close at half past five and .... the restaurants and pubs .... at 11 .... or half past ten .... night. But I love your .... , and English breakfasts .... great.

16

INTERACTION

The present simple tense

1 **Look at the groups of words. Put them in the correct order to make questions.**

tennis you play do?

Sue does where live?

like they about England do what?

his help parents does Terry?

do homework when your you do?

BUILD UP

2 **Complete this chart. Use four of these words.**
do likes play does plays like

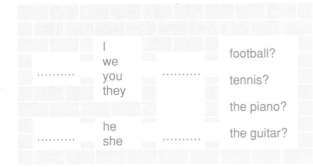

....	I we you they	....
		football? tennis? the piano?
....	he she	....
		the guitar?

3 **What do you know about your classmate?**

a Work in pairs. First try to answer the questions about your classmate. Write your guesses in Column 1, 'my guesses'. Don't show it to your partner!

b Write the questions you must ask your partner.

Example
What time do you get up?

c Now ask your partner the questions and write his/her answers in the second column.

d Change roles.

e Compare your answers. How many did you get right?

Scores
10–13	very good. You know your classmate very well.
5–9	average
2–4	poor
0–1	terrible. Your classmate is a stranger to you. You don't know him/her at all.

FOLLOW UP

4 **Write the answers to the questionnaire for yourself and your friend.**

Example
I have got two brothers and one sister. My friend has got two sisters.
I get up at seven o'clock. My friend gets up at seven o'clock, too.

QUESTIONNAIRE		
What do you know about your classmates?	my guesses	his/her answers
Has he/she got any brothers or sisters?		
When does he/she get up?		
How does he/she travel to school?		
What does he/she eat for breakfast?		
What TV programmes does he/she watch?		
What sports does he/she play?		
Can he/she play a musical instrument?		
What do his/her parents do?		
What is his/her favourite school subject?		
Has he/she got a pet?		
What does he/she want to do when he/she leaves school?		
What time does he/she go to bed?		
When is his/her birthday?		

PROJECT

Your life

> **Note**
> This can be done in class or for homework.

- Students write the heading 'My Daily Life' on a piece of paper.
- They write three paragraphs – one for each of **a**, **b** and **c**.

> **Note**
> In paragraph **c** you may wish the students to use *but*, e.g. *Terry ... but I ...* If so, go through this before they write.

- Students find photographs or do drawings to illustrate their work. They should attach these with paper clips.
- Correct and comment on work. Correct paragraphing as well as grammar and spelling. Make sure the writing makes sense.
- Return work. Students write out second draft and stick on illustrations securely.
- Display all pieces of writing. Provide a time for all students to look at them.
- Students stick their work into their project file.

▶ **Pronunciation: page T110**

LEARNING DIARY

- Students look at the list on the first page of Unit 1.

A Students complete the face next to each item to show how well they know it.

B In class or for homework, students do the self-check exercises in the Workbook.

C In pairs, students compare answers.

Check answers.

Explain any items or exercises which several students had problems with.

Refer students who want to know more to the relevant page of a pedagogic grammar.

Encourage any student who is still confused to come and talk to you.

D Students make a note of what they liked best about this unit.

Find out what were the most popular things.

List these on the board.

Try and find out why these were the most popular, and why other things were less popular. What does this tell you about the way your learners learn best?

CULTURE SPOT
Workbook page 14

- Divide the class into pairs or groups of three or four.
- Students look quickly at the Culture Spot.
- Ask *What is it about?*
- Students give their ideas.
- Ask *What do you already know about this topic?*
- Students give their ideas. Discuss these ideas.
- Say *Read the mealtime patterns. Note anything that you find interesting or unusual.*
- Explain any words that students need.
- Ask *Did you find anything interesting or unusual?*
- Students give their ideas.
- Read each comparison question in turn.
- Discuss each question. Encourage students to compare their situation to the one in the Culture Spot.

PROJECT

Your life

Write about your daily life.

a   Describe a typical day.

b   What do you do in your free time?

c   Compare your day to Terry's. What differences are there?

Illustrate your project with some pictures, photographs or drawings.

Learning diary

Look at the list on the first page of this unit.

A How well do you know each thing? Complete the circles to make faces.

B Try the self-check in the Workbook.

C Compare your self-check answers with a partner's. Do you understand everything? If you don't understand something, look in a grammar book or ask your teacher.

D What did you like best in this unit? Why?

1

2 the past

the past simple

Contents

Victoria Road: Sue teases Terry   20

Language work: The past simple tense   22

Reading: The King of Rock and Roll   24

Listening: Fans   26

Interaction: An interview with a pop star   27

Project: A biography of your
favourite pop star   28

Language work 😊 😐 🙁

Grammar

the past simple tense - to be
Terry was ill.
You were still in bed.

- regular verbs
I played football.
We painted my bedroom.

- irregular verbs
He went to a recording studio.
His mother bought him a guitar.

- questions with 'did'
When did you make your first record?
Did you have a good weekend?

- negatives with 'didn't'
I didn't want to get up.
She didn't go to London.

Word work

music

😊 😐 🙁 ## Learning objectives

In this unit you will learn how to:

talk about recent events

tell someone's life story

talk about pop music

ask people about their life story

talk about your favourite pop star

VICTORIA ROAD

Sue teases Terry

 • Ask *What happened to the people in 'Victoria Road' in Unit 1?*

• Students give answers.

• Refer back to page 10 to check.

Answer key
Terry was still in bed at eleven o'clock on Saturday morning. He was bored. His mother wanted him to get up and do something, like his friends. Terry secretly likes Sue, but he thinks she doesn't like him.

• Read the questions.

• Students look at the picture story and find the answers to the questions.

• Students give their answers.

• Ask *How do you know?* Students justify their answers with examples from the picture story.

Answer key
a *Kamala, Casey, Sue, Terry and two other girls*
b *At a bus stop and on the bus – on their way to school*
c *What they did at the weekend*
d *Monday*

Note
If students use an incorrect past tense form in answering **c**, do not correct it directly but rephrase the answer using the correct form.

• Students look at the picture story again. Ask *What happens in this episode?*

• Students give their ideas.

Answer key
(possible answer)
Sue teases Terry about being lazy. Terry gets annoyed. Casey asks Kamala what the problem is. Kamala says that Terry and Sue fancy each other, but don't want to show it.

 • Say *Now look at the full dialogue and listen.*

• Play the cassette.

• Say *Now look at the questions under the dialogue.*

• Ask *Does Terry like Sue?* Elicit answers.

• Repeat for the other two questions.

Answer key
Terry does like Sue: he was very apologetic when Sue got annoyed with him; he blushed when his mother mentioned her; he was drawing a heart with her name in; and he gets upset when Sue teases him.

Sue doesn't seem to like Terry: she complained to Kamala about how rude he was. However, she teases him, which suggests she is interested in him. Kamala thinks Sue fancies Terry.

• Students answer the questions.

• Check answers. Make sure the past tense is used correctly.

Answer key
a *Casey had a great weekend.*
b *He played football at the leisure centre, washed his father's car, and went swimming.*
c *Sue helped Kamala in her parents' shop.*
d *They weren't very busy.*
e *They painted Sue's bedroom.*
f *He watched a film on television and listened to his records.*
g *She teased him.*
h *He said it was for kids.*

▼4
- Students close their books.
- Say *Now listen carefully*.
- Play the cassette.
- Students listen carefully.

Notes

We painted my bedroom. Many people in Britain enjoy 'Do-It-Yourself' (sometimes called DIY). They often decorate their houses and even rebuild parts of them themselves.

I thought you worked in your parents' shop. Teenagers who are still at school often have a Saturday or other part-time job.

Oh, very funny. Terry is being sarcastic. He doesn't like Sue's joke.

I didn't get up, because I didn't want to. This is short for 'I didn't get up because I didn't want to get up.'

kidding means 'teasing'.

I'm fed up with ... means 'I'm bored with ...', 'I'm tired of ...', 'I've had too much of ...'

It's for kids. Terry means he thinks he's too adult to go to the leisure centre. This could of course be an excuse for not going ...

he fancies Sue means he likes Sue and finds her attractive. It is informal.

It's funny. Kamala here means 'It's strange'.

Sue teases Terry

1 **Look at the story.**

  a Who are the people?

  b Where are they?

  c What are they talking about?

  d What day is it?

> Did you have a good weekend?

> Yes, it was great.

2 📼 **Listen and follow in your books.**

Kamala Hi. Did you have a good weekend?

Casey Yes, it was great.

Kamala What did you do?

Casey I played football at the leisure centre on Saturday morning. In the afternoon I washed my dad's car and then I went swimming. What about you?

Sue We had a good time, too, didn't we, Kamala? We painted my bedroom. We had a good laugh.

Terry I thought you worked in your parents' shop on Saturdays, Kam.

Kamala Sue helped me in the shop in the morning, but we weren't very busy in the afternoon. So I helped her with her bedroom.

Casey Did you help, Tell?

Sue Oh no. Terry was ill, weren't you, Terry?

Terry No, I wasn't.

Sue That's strange. I phoned you at eleven o'clock and your mum said you were in bed. So I thought that you were ill.

> We painted my bedroom. We had a good laugh.

Kamala Don't tease him, Sue.

Terry Oh, very funny. I didn't get up, because I didn't want to. I wanted to stay in bed. Anyway, I watched a film on television and listened to my records. All right?

Casey What was wrong, Tell?

Kamala It's all right, Casey. Terry wasn't ill. Sue's only kidding.

Did you help, Tell?

Oh no. Terry was ill, weren't you, Terry?

4

What was wrong, Tell?

It's all right, Casey. Terry wasn't ill. Sue's only kidding.

Why didn't you come to the leisure centre?

I'm fed up with that stupid leisure centre. It's for kids.

5

Casey Why didn't you come to the leisure centre?

Terry I'm fed up with that stupid leisure centre. It's for kids.

Casey What's the matter with him?

Kamala I think he fancies Sue, but she teases him all the time. It's funny, because she likes him really.

What do you think?

- Does Terry like Sue?
- Does Sue like Terry?
- How can Casey and Kamala help?

3 **Answer these questions.**

a Who had a great weekend?

b What did he do?

c What did Sue do on Saturday morning?

d Why didn't Kamala work in the shop on Saturday afternoon?

e What did Sue and Kamala do on Saturday afternoon?

f What did Terry do at the weekend?

g What did Sue do to Terry?

h What did Terry say about the leisure centre?

4 **Close your book. Listen again.**

What's the matter with him?

I think he fancies Sue, but she teases him all time. It's funny, because she likes him really.

6

Useful expressions

- Students look at the 'Useful expressions'.
- Students write the mother-tongue equivalent of each item next to that item. While they are doing this, write the chart on the blackboard.
- In pairs, students compare charts.
- Elicit and discuss answers. If students are not sure, say *Go back to the story, and work it out from the situation.* Write expressions in your blackboard chart.
- Students correct and amend their own charts.

- Students get into groups of four.
- Students choose their roles: Sue, Casey, Kamala and Terry (or allocate the roles yourself).
- Students read the dialogue in their groups.
- Walk round the class. Note any serious errors in pronunciation.
- Correct serious pronunciation errors (if any).
- Choose one group (not the same group you asked in Unit 1) to read their dialogue aloud to the class.
- If time, students change roles and read the dialogue again.

- Students complete the diary.
- Ask one student to read out the part of the diary for Saturday.
- Students compare their own answers. If there are problems, students refer back to the dialogue to justify their answers.
- Repeat for Sunday and Monday with different students.

> **Answer key**
> **Saturday:** *worked   the   weren't   in   painted   had*
>
> **Sunday:** *up   my   phoned   leisure   played*
>
> **Monday:** *school   Terry   bus   at   weekend   didn't   stayed   watched   teased   He   fed   we   Terry   fancies   all   really*

LANGUAGE WORK

The past tense of *to be*

a
- Students complete the table with the words in the list. While they are doing this, write the table on the blackboard.
- Ask one student to complete the table on the blackboard. Students compare their tables.

> **Answer key**
> **I/He/She/It:** *was/was not/wasn't*
> **You/We/They:** *were/were not/weren't*

- Check answers. Write them on the board.
- Point out that the past tense of the verb *to be* is different from the past tense of other verbs since it has *two* forms: *was* and *were*. All other verbs have only one past tense form.

b
- Students put words in correct order.

> **Answer key**
> *He was ill.*   *Was he ill?*
> *You were busy.*   *Were you busy?*

c
- If necessary, check students know the meaning of *verb* and *subject*.
- Students complete the rule.
- Elicit rule.

> **Answer key**
> *verb   subject*

- Read the instructions aloud.
- Demonstrate with one pair.
- Students get into pairs.
- Student A asks *Where were you on Saturday morning?*
- Student B answers *I was . . . .* First student writes the answer down.
- Repeat until student A has asked about all six times.
- Students change roles and repeat.
- Ask around the class *Where was X on Sunday morning?* etc.

The past simple tense: regular verbs

BUILD UP

a • Students complete the table.

   • Tell them to complete the table – without looking back at *Victoria Road*. While they are doing this, copy the table on the blackboard.

   • In pairs, students compare tables.

b • Students look at *Victoria Road* on pages 20–21 and check their answers.

   • Ask one student to complete the table on the blackboard.

> **Answer key**
> play – played   tease – teased
> help – helped   want – wanted
> work – worked   paint – painted
> watch – watched   need – needed

c • Students complete the rule.

   • Check answers.

> **Answer key**
> *To make the regular past tense we add **-ed**.*

d • Say each past tense verb aloud.

   • Students repeat after you.

   • Ask *What is different about **wanted** and **painted**?*

   • Elicit answers.

> **Answer key**
> ***Wanted*** and ***painted*** end in / ɪd /. When verbs end in / d / or / t / the **-ed** is pronounced / ɪd /.

   • Chorus drill the verbs in the table. Correct if necessary.

   • Two or three students individually read aloud the verbs in the table.

The past tense: negative

BUILD UP

   • Students look at the two sentences.

   • Ask *How do we make the **negative** of the past tense?*

> **Answer key**
> *didn't + verb (with no **-ed**)*

   • Students complete table.

   • Students compare their tables in pairs.

   • Copy the table on the blackboard.

   • Ask one student to complete the table on the blackboard.

   • Students check their tables.

> **Answer key**
> play   tease   work   paint   want
> watch   help

   • Students look at the list.

   • Read the examples aloud.

   • Check students know what to do.

   • Ask one student to give the next answer.

   • Repeat for remaining items.

> **Answer key**
> *She helped Kamala.*
> *She didn't wash her hair.*
> *She cleaned her bedroom.*
> *She didn't watch a TV quiz show.*
> *She went to the cinema.*
> *She didn't iron her clothes.*
> *She painted her bedroom.*
> *She practised on the word processor.*
> *She didn't stay in bed late on Sunday.*

   • Students write a list like Sue's (9 items), e.g.
     clean my bike
     buy a new cassette
     go to the cafe

   • Under the list, students write what they did and didn't do.

   • Choose two or three different students to say what they *did*.

   • Choose two or three different students to say what they *didn't do*.

FOLLOW UP

   • Students do Exercise 7 in class or for homework.

Useful expressions

 5 How do you say these expressions in your language?

> Did you have a good weekend?
>
>
>
> It was great.
>
> We had a good laugh.
>
> That's strange.
>
> Oh, very funny.
>
> I didn't want to.
>
> She's only kidding.
>
> I'm fed up with …
>
> It's for kids.
>
> He fancies Sue.
>
> It's funny because …

 6 a Work in groups of four. Each person takes one of the parts.

   b Read the dialogue.

FOLLOW UP

7 Complete Kamala's diary.

Saturday

I _____ in the shop in _____ morning. Sue helped me. We _____ very busy _____ the afternoon, so Sue and I _____ her bedroom. We _____ a good laugh.

Sunday

I got _____ late and did _____ homework. After lunch Sue _____ . We went to the _____ centre and we _____ badminton.

Monday

I went to _____ with Sue. We met _____ and Casey at the _____ stop. Casey played football _____ the leisure centre at the _____ . Terry _____ do anything. He _____ in bed all morning and _____ television in the afternoon. Sue _____ him and Terry was angry. _____ said he was _____ up with the leisure centre. When _____ arrived at school, _____ walked away. I think he _____ Sue, but she teases him _____ the time. It's funny, because she likes him _____ .

LANGUAGE WORK

The past tense of 'to be'

BUILD UP

1 a Use the words to complete this table.

were   were not   was   wasn't   weren't   was not

I	....		
He	....		
She	... .	ill	yesterday.
It		busy	last week.
You	....	fed up	on Sunday.
We	....		
They	... .		

b Put the words in the correct order to make a statement and a question.

	statement	question
he ill was		
busy you were		

c Now complete this rule with these two words.

   verb   subject

> To make past tense questions with 'to be' we
> put the .... in front of the ....

 2 Ask your partner about his/her weekend. Ask about morning, afternoon, and evening for Saturday and Sunday.

   Example
   A 'Where were you on Saturday morning?'
   B 'I was at home.'

22

The past simple tense: regular verbs

BUILD UP

 a Complete this table.

present	past
play	....
help	....
work	....
watch	....

present	past
tease	....
want	....
paint	....
need	....

b Find the verbs in the Victoria Road story. Check your answers.

c Complete this rule.

> To make the past simple tense of regular verbs we add .... to the verb.

d Read the past tenses aloud. Note that 'wanted' and 'painted' are different from the others. Can you hear the difference?

The past tense: negative

BUILD UP

 4 Look at these sentences.

I **played** table tennis yesterday.

I **didn't play** football yesterday.

Complete this table with the correct part of the verbs in Exercise 3.

I		......	football	
He		......	Terry	
She		......	in the shop	yesterday.
It	didn't	......	the kitchen	
We		......	to get up	on Sunday.
You		......	television	
They		......	Kamala	

5 Here are the things Sue wanted to do last weekend. She didn't do all of them.

	THINGS TO DO	Done
1	Help Kamala	✓
2	Wash hair	✓
3	Clean bedroom	
4	Watch TV quiz show	✓
5	Go to cinema	
6	Iron clothes	✓
7	Paint bedroom	✓
8	Practise on the word processor	
9	Stay in bed late on Sunday	
10		
11		
12		

Say what Sue did and didn't do.

Example
She helped Kamala.
She didn't wash her hair.

 6 Make a list of the things you wanted to do at the weekend. Then say what you did and didn't do.

FOLLOW UP

 7 Write the answers to Exercise 5.

READING

The King of Rock and Roll

This section develops students' reading skills. Students read this text in a series of scanning activities:

- They use the pictures to establish who and what the text is about.
- They establish what they already know about the person.
- They scan the text to find the main stages of the text.
- They scan the text again to add more detail to the stages.
- They read the text in detail to learn new words.

It is important that they follow the activities and don't try to read the text in detail first.

Text notes
A white boy with a black voice. In the 1950s, American music was strictly segregated. There was black music (blues and gospel) and white music (country music). Rock and roll had the strong rhythms of black music, but as long as it was only black musicians who sang it, it wasn't acceptable to the whites. Elvis made it acceptable, because he was white.
Gladys Presley Elvis was devoted to his mother. He was heartbroken in 1958, when she died.

- Elvis married Priscilla Beaulieu in 1967. They had a daughter, Lisa Marie. But they were divorced in 1973.
- Elvis died of a heart attack. He didn't drink alcohol or smoke, but in his later years he ate a lot of junk food and became addicted to drugs. It is believed that the drugs caused his heart attack.

- Say *First, just look at the pictures.*
- Say *Now, what's the man's name?* Students look at the text if no one knows.
- Elicit answer.

Answer key
Elvis Presley

- Draw students' attention to the name *Elvis Presley* at the beginning of the text and on the gravestone.
- Ask how many people in the class have heard of Elvis Presley.

- Students close their books.
- In pairs, students do Exercise 2. They can write down anything they knew already, as well as anything they have learned from the pictures. (3 minutes)
- Students give their answers.
- Make a list on the blackboard.
- Continue until all known facts have been given.

- Students look at the list of places.
- Read the instructions aloud.
- Give students two minutes to read the story and list the place names in the correct order.
- Check answers.

Answer key
*Mississippi   Memphis
Sun Records recording studio   New York
Hollywood   Germany   Gracelands*

- Students make a table like this:

Date	Place	What Elvis did

- Copy the table on the blackboard.
- Students write the places in the correct order in the table.
- Say *Look at the list of dates. Find the correct dates in the story and add them to the table.*

Answer key

1935	*Mississippi*	1956	*Hollywood*
1948	*Memphis*	1958	*Germany*
1954	*Sun Records*	1977	*Gracelands*
1955	*New York*		

- Students read the text again and list the dates next to the correct places. (This time they do not have to read the text quickly.)
- Check answers.

Answer key

Date	Place	What Elvis did
1935	Mississippi	*born on January 8*
1948	Memphis	*moved here from Mississippi*
1954	Sun Records	*made a record for his mother's birthday*
1955	New York	*appeared on TV*
1956	Hollywood	*made his first film, 'Love Me Tender'*
1958	Germany	*went there with the army*
1977	Gracelands	*died in his mansion*

6
- Students write the heading 'Words Associated with Pop Music' in their exercise books.
- They look through the story for as many words associated with pop music as they can find, and write these in their books.
- Elicit the words students have found.

> **Answer key**
> (possible list)
>
> | | |
> | --- | --- |
> | rock and roll | groups |
> | guitar | Beatles |
> | recording studio | Rolling Stones |
> | record | stars |
> | single | millionaire |
> | radio stations | fans |
> | teenagers | albums |
> | disc jockeys | videos |
> | hit | electronic |

 7 a
- Say *What do you think about Elvis?* If necessary, ask more specific questions such as *Do you think you would have liked him? Do you think you would have bought his records?*, *Do you have any Elvis records?* and *Do you know any Elvis fans?*
- Elicit comments and ideas. (Encourage contributions here! Do not correct grammatical errors, as long as the contributions are comprehensible.)

b
- Ask *Do you think the story is fair?* If necessary, ask *Do you think the story talks about Elvis in a way which is too negative or too positive? Does it tell the truth about him?*
- Elicit opinions. Conduct discussion as for **7a**.

 8 a
- Students complete tables.
- Students compare their tables.
- While they are doing this, copy the tables on the blackboard.
- Ask one student to complete the tables on the blackboard.
- Students check their tables.

> **Answer key**
>
> | | | | |
> | --- | --- | --- | --- |
> | became | went | left | sang |
> | bought | was/were | made | told |
> | could | had | thought | |
> | came | heard | did | |

b
- Point out that these are called 'irregular verbs' because they are not formed by simply adding *-ed*. Many frequently used verbs are in fact 'irregular verbs'.
- Ask if students know any more irregular verbs.
- Elicit contributions. Add these to the table on the blackboard.
- Students add these to their table.

FOLLOW UP

 9
- Students use the information in their chart (see Exercise 4) to write a biography of Elvis. Encourage students to vary the sentence structure.

EXTRA ACTIVITY

The price of rock 'n' roll
Use the information for a discussion activity. Elicit comments and suggestions about why pop stars often die young. Ask if they know any other pop stars who have died young.

You may also use the information to revise dates. Use the following procedure:

- Give students two minutes to memorize the dates in The price of rock 'n' roll and the Elvis text.
- Divide the class into two teams.
- Books closed. Ask each team in turn a question.
  Example
  When did John Lennon die?
  When was Elvis born?
  What is today's date?
- One team member answers.
- Teams get one point for a correct date and one point for saying it correctly.
- Give each team four questions. The winning team is the one with the most points.

READING

1 Look at the pictures. Who is the text about? Find his name in the text.

2 Close your book. Work in pairs. Write down everything you know about him.

3 Look at this list of places. Read the story quickly and put them in the correct order. Don't worry if you don't understand everything.

Mississippi   Sun Records recording studio
Memphis   Hollywood
Germany   Gracelands
New York

The King of Rock and Roll

Elvis Presley came from a very poor family. He was born on 8 January 1935 in Mississippi.

Elvis loved music. He went to church every Sunday and sang in the choir. When he was 13, his mother bought him a guitar. (Elvis wanted a bicycle, but it was too expensive.) In the same year Elvis and his family left Mississippi. They moved to Memphis, Tennessee.

One day in 1954 he went to a recording studio called Sun Records. He wanted to make a record for his mother's birthday. The secretary at the studio, Marion Keisker, heard Elvis and she told her boss, Sam Phillips.

Elvis was Sam Phillips's dream – 'a white boy with a black voice'.

Phillips became Elvis's manager and Elvis made his first single – *That's All Right, Mama*. When disc jockeys played it on their radio stations, American teenagers went wild. Many American parents didn't like Elvis. He was too sexy.

In 1955, Elvis appeared on TV in New York. The following year he went to Hollywood and made his first film *Love Me Tender*. In the next two years he had many hit records – *Blue Suede Shoes, Heartbreak Hotel, All Shook Up, Jailhouse Rock, Teddy Bear*.

In 1958, Elvis joined the American army and went to Germany. When he returned to the United States in the early 60s, pop was not the same. British groups like the Beatles and the Rolling Stones were the new stars.

Elvis was a millionaire, but he was a very lonely man. In his last years he became fat and depressed. He died of a heart attack on 16 August 1977 in his mansion at Gracelands, Memphis.

But for his millions of fans, Elvis is still the King. Shane Lyons has got more than 250 albums by Elvis and videos of all his films. 'Man, he was great,' says Shane. 'Elvis could really sing. Not like these kids today with all their electronic machines. He was the King, Man, the King of Rock and Roll.'

24

8 **a** Look through the story about Elvis and the Victoria Road story on page 20. Find the past tenses of these verbs.

present	past
become	....
buy	....
can	....
come	....
go	....
be	....
have	....
hear	....
leave	....
make	....
think	....

present	past
do	....
sing	....
tell	....
	....
	....
	....
	....
	....
	....
	....
	....

b We call these verbs irregular verbs. Can you add any more verbs to the list?

FOLLOW UP

9 Use the information you have got to write a short biography of Elvis.

Example
In 1935 Elvis Presley was born in Mississippi.
In 1948...

4 Read the text again. Choose the correct dates and match them to the places in Exercise 3.

1932	1955	1965
1956	1951	1935
1948	1958	1980
1977	1954	1974

5 Read the text again. Write down what Elvis did at each place.

WORD WORK

6 Write down all the words associated with 'pop music'.

7 What do you think?

a What do you think about Elvis?

b Do you think the story is fair?

THE PRICE
OF ROCK 'N ROLL

Buddy Holly died in a
plane crash on 2 February 1959

Eddy Cochrane died in a car crash on
1 April 1960

Brian Jones, a guitarist with the Rolling Stones,
drowned in his swimming pool on 3 July 1969

Janis Joplin died from a drug overdose
on 4 October 1970

John Lennon was shot in New York
on 8 December 1980

LISTENING

Fans

 1 • Students look at the picture. Ask who they think
the people are.

> **Answer key**
> *Some of Elvis Presley's fans.*

 2 a • Students read the two lists.

• Check that students know the words.

b • Play the cassette. Students listen and draw
the connecting lines.

> **Answer key**
> Jane Asquith – *T-shirt*
> Shane Lyons – *holiday*
> Johanne Palmer – *teddy bear*

Fans

Interviewer Every Friday, the Elvis Presley Club
meets in the King's Head pub in Pond Road.
There are about twenty Presley fans here tonight.
Elvis fans are young and old. There's Jane
Asquith. Jane is eighteen and she works in a
bank. She's wearing a T-shirt with Elvis'
autograph on it.

Jane I collect anything with Elvis on it. At home,
I've got 360 albums and 25 Elvis videos. I've got
Elvis posters, Elvis mirrors, statues, books, pens,
clocks. If I see something with Elvis on it, I buy it.

Interviewer Elvis fans spend a lot of money on
their hero. Shane Lyons takes home £100 a week
and he spends a quarter of it on Elvis souvenirs.

Shane I spend most of the money on Elvis
holidays. I go to Memphis every August. Last
year, the holiday cost £1000.

Interviewer Elvis never came to England. Did
anyone in the club see him when he was alive?
Johanne Palmer did.

Johanne I went to his last show in Las Vegas. It
was fantastic. He sang all his old hits and when
he sang 'Teddy Bear' – you know 'I just want to
be your teddy bear' – he picked up this teddy
bear. He wiped it in the sweat on his chest and
then he threw it into the audience. And I caught
it. It was fantastic.

Interviewer The teddy bear is here tonight.
Johanne brings it every week.

Johanne It's like, well, you know, like Elvis is here
with us, when Teddy's here.

Interviewer What was so special about Elvis?

Johanne He was very sexy.

Shane Man, he was great. Elvis could really sing.
Not like these kids today with all their electronic
machines. He was the King, man, the King of
Rock and Roll.

• Ask these questions:
  a *What is the name of the pub?*
  b *How many albums has Jane got?*
  c *How much does Shane Lyons spend on Elvis
    things each week?*
  d *How much did the Memphis holiday cost last
    year?*
  e *When did Elvis visit England?*
  f *Where did Johanne see Elvis?*
  g *What did Elvis do with the teddy bear?*

• Students give their answers.

> **Answer key**
> a *the King's Head*
> b *360*
> c *£25*
> d *£1000*
> e *Never/He never came.*
> f *Las Vegas*
> g *Picked it up, wiped it in the sweat on his chest
>   and threw it into the audience*

3 a • In pairs, students write down everything they
can remember from the tape.

• Students give their answers.

• Make a list for each fan on the blackboard.

b • Play the cassette again. Students check
what they've written, and add anything else
they hear.

> **Answer key**
> **1 Jane Asquith**
> *18*
> *works in a bank*
> *collects anything with Elvis on it*
> *has 360 Elvis albums and 25 Elvis videos*
> *also has posters, mirrors, statues, books, pens and
>   clocks*
> **2 Shane Lyons**
> *takes home £100 a week*
> *spends a quarter on Elvis souvenirs*
> *spends most on Elvis holidays*
> *goes to Memphis every August*
> *last year holiday cost £1000*
> **3 Johanne Palmer**
> *went to Elvis' last show in Las Vegas*
> *caught the teddy bear when Elvis threw it into the
>   audience*
> *brings teddy bear to Elvis Presley Club every week.*

WORD WORK

4 a • Students read the list of words. They look up
the meaning of words they don't know in
their dictionaries and list the new words and
meanings in their exercise books.

b • Students tick each word in the list which was mentioned by a fan as a souvenir of Elvis.

• In pairs, students compare answers.

• Elicit answers. Make a list on the blackboard.

• Play the cassette again. Students check their ideas.

Answer key
poster	clock
statue	T-shirt
pen	teddy bear
mirror	video
album	book

5 a • Ask *Had you heard of Elvis Presley before reading about him here?* and *Have you heard his music?*

• Students read Shane's comment.

• Ask for comments on Shane's comment.

• Play 'Blue Suede Shoes' on page 28 – and one or two other Elvis songs, if you have them.

Note
'Blue Suede Shoes' is on the tape after the listening text. If you want to play it at this stage you need to wind the tape forward.

b • Read the question aloud.

• Students give their ideas.

FOLLOW UP

6 • Ask *Which fan said this?*

Answer key
Johanne Palmer

• Students fill in the gaps.

Answer key
went	was	sang	sang	want
picked	wiped	threw	caught	was

INTERACTION

The past simple tense: questions

1 • Students read the sentences. Ask *What do you notice about the verbs **play** and **go**?*

• Students complete Table B.

• In pairs, students compare tables.

• While they are doing this, copy Table B.

• Ask one student to complete the table on the blackboard.

• Students check their tables.

Answer key
eat   play   go   have   buy   see   feel   make

• Students complete the rule.

Answer key
*To make past tense questions, we put **did** in front of the subject.*

2 • Students look at the question–answer pairs.

• They also look at the gaps in the questions.

• Read aloud the example.

• Students fill in the gap in each question.

• Check answers.

Answer key
did the Presley family move
did Elvis Presley make
was he when he made his first record
didn't many American parents like
did he do
did he go
did he die

3 a • Divide the class into pairs.

• In pairs, students choose a famous pop singer.

b • Students write a list of questions to ask. They can use some of the questions in Exercise 2.

c • Students role play the interview, using the questions they have prepared.

• Walk round, answering questions if required, and remedying any serious problems of communication.

d • Students change roles and repeat.

• Get one or two pairs to act their dialogue in front of the class.

FOLLOW UP

4 • Students write their interview as a dialogue.

T27

LISTENING

Fans

1 Look at the picture. Who do you think the people are?

2 a Read the two lists below.

Jane Asquith	teddy bear
Shane Lyons	T-shirt
Johanne Palmer	holiday

b ▣ Now listen and connect the names with the things.

3 a What can you remember about each fan? Listen and write down your ideas.

b Listen again and check your ideas.

4 a Look at this list of words. Use a dictionary. Find the meaning of any word you don't know.

plate	statue	album	clock
poster	pen	radio	T-shirt
book	mirror	sweatshirt	teddy bear
bag	pencil	picture	video.

b Which of the words were mentioned as Elvis souvenirs?

5 What do you think?

a What do you know about Elvis's music? Do you agree with Shane?

> Man, he was great. Elvis could really sing. Not like these kids today with all their electronic machines. He was the King, man, the King of Rock and Roll.

b What kind of souvenirs do you collect of your favourite pop or sports stars?

FOLLOW UP

6 Complete this passage.

I .... to his last show in Las Vegas. It .... fantastic. He .... all his old hits and when he .... Teddy Bear – you know – 'I just .... to be your teddy bear'. He .... up this teddy bear. He .... it in the sweat on his chest and then he .... it into the audience. And I .... it. It .... fantastic.

INTERACTION

The past simple tense: questions

BUILD UP

1 **Look at these sentences.**

Did you **play** tennis yesterday?
Yes, I **played** tennis at the leisure centre.

Did you **go** to London last week?
Yes, I **went** to London on Tuesday.

Use the verbs from Table A. Complete Table B.

Table A

I	ate a lot	
He	played tennis	
She	went to the cinema	yesterday.
It	had a good time	
We	bought a new record	last week.
You	saw Susan	
They	felt ill	on Saturday.
	made him angry	

Table B

Did	I	...... a lot	
	you	...... tennis	
	we	...... to the cinema	yesterday?
	they	...... a good time	
	he	...... a new record	last week?
	she	...... Susan	
	it	 ill	on Saturday?
		...... him angry	

Now complete this rule.

> To make past tense questions, we put .... in front of the subject.

What must you do to join Dracula's fan club?
Just send your name, address and blood group.

2 **Here are some facts from Elvis Presley's life. Write the questions.**

Example
Where was he born?
He was born in Mississippi.

When .... to Memphis?
They moved there in 1948.

Where .... his first record?
He made it at Sun Records recording studio.

How old .... ?
He was 19.

Why .... Elvis?
They thought he was too sexy.

What .... in 1958?
He joined the army.

Where .... ?
He went to Germany.

How .... ?
He died of a heart attack.

3 **You are a DJ on a pop radio show. You are going to interview a famous singer about his/her life.**

a Work in pairs. Think of a person to interview.

b Write down the questions you will ask. Use Exercise 2 to help you.

c **A** is the DJ. **B** is the singer. Start like this.

A *This is .... , your DJ on your favourite radio programme. Today I'm going to interview .... .Hello .... Where were you born?*

B *I was born in .... on ....*

d When you have finished, change roles and do the interview again.

FOLLOW UP

4 **Write your interview from Exercise 3.**

EXTRA ACTIVITY
(to practise past tense questions)

- Put the following list of activities on the blackboard or on a handout:

  bought something new
  went to the cinema
  used a computer
  got into trouble
  was fed up
  had an argument with his/her parents
  ate something unusual
  received a present

a • In pairs, students ask each other these questions until they receive the answer *Yes*, e.g.

  A *Did you receive a present last week?*
  B *No, I didn't.*
  A *Did you have an argument with your parents last week?*
  B *No, I didn't.*
  A *Did you go to the cinema last week?*
  B *Yes, I did.*

- Having got the answer *Yes*, students continue by finding out more information, e.g.

  What film did you see?
  Did you enjoy it?
  Where was it on?
  Who was in it?
  When was it made?

b • Repeat, i.e. students move round the class asking the other questions to different students. They try to find someone who will say *Yes* to each question, and then find out more information about it.

c • In groups of four, students take it in turn to tell the group about someone who did each thing last week, e.g.

  Maria bought a new record. It was . . .

  Carlos went to the cinema . . .

PROJECT

Your life

- Students can work on this project individually, in pairs or in small groups.

- Go round the class finding out who students' favourite pop stars are. (If any student has no favourite pop star, he or she can choose a sportsman or sportswoman, or students can create an imaginary character.)

- Students look at the project about Madonna. Ask *Do you know any more information about her?*

- Read the questions.

- Students suggest other questions.

- Students write a rough draft of their biographies. They can do this in class or for homework.

- Look at rough drafts. Suggest improvements in paragraph organization. Correct grammar and spelling. Make sure the biographies make sense!

- Students rewrite their biographies and add illustrations, e.g. magazine pictures.

- Display the biographies for a day or two. Students look at each other's work.

- Students stick their biographies into their project file.

SONG: BLUE SUEDE SHOES

- Students look at the song.
- Students try to complete the gaps.
- Elicit ideas.
- ▣▣ Play the tape. Students listen.
- Students complete the gaps.
- Elicit answers.
- Play the tape again. Students check their songs.
- Play the tape again. Students sing along.

▣▣ Blue Suede Shoes

Well, it's one for the money
Two for the show
Three to get ready
Now go, cat, go. But don't you step on my Blue
    Suede Shoes.
You can do anything, but lay off of my Blue
    Suede Shoes.

Well you can knock me down,
Step on my face,
Slander my name all over the place
Do anything that you want to do.
But uh-huh Honey, lay off of my shoes
And don't you step on my Blue Suede Shoes.
You can do anything, but lay off of my Blue
    Suede Shoes.

Well, you can burn my house,
Steal my car,
Drink my liquor from an old fruit jar.
Do anything that you want to do.
But uh-huh Honey, lay off of my shoes
And don't you step on my Blue Suede Shoes.
You can do anything, but lay off of my Blue
    Suede Shoes.

Words and music by Carl Lee Perkins

▶ **Pronunciation: page T111**

LEARNING DIARY

- Students turn back to the list of items on the first page of Unit 2.

A Students draw a face on the symbols next to each item to indicate how well they know it.

B In class or for homework, students complete the self-check exercises in the Workbook.

C In pairs, students compare answers.

Elicit answers. Students correct as necessary. Identify 'common problem exercises' or items.

Spend a few minutes explaining 'common problem exercises' or items, if any.

Refer students who still do not fully understand (or who are simply interested) to the relevant page of a pedagogic grammar.

D Ask what students liked best in this unit, and why. (See procedure in Unit 1.)

CULTURE SPOT
Workbook page 23

- Divide the class into pairs or groups of three or four.
- Students look quickly at the text.
- Ask *What is the text about?*
- Students give their ideas.
- Ask *What do you already know about this topic?*
- Students give their ideas. Discuss these ideas.
- Say *Read the Culture Spot text. Note anything that you find interesting.*
- Ask comprehension questions about the text.
- Students give their answers. Explain any words that students need.
- Ask *Did you find anything interesting?*
- Students give their ideas.
- Read each comparison question in turn.
- Discuss each question.

PROJECT

Your life

Write a biography of your own favourite pop star.

- When was he/she born?
- Write about his/her early life.
- How did he/she become famous?
- What records has he/she made?
- Has he/she made any films or TV programmes?
- Has he/she got married?
- Has he/she changed during his/her career?
- Is there anything else interesting that you want to say about him/her?

Illustrate your project with pictures.

In July 1985, Madonna had her first No. 1 'Into the groove'.

Also in 1985, she married Sean Penn.

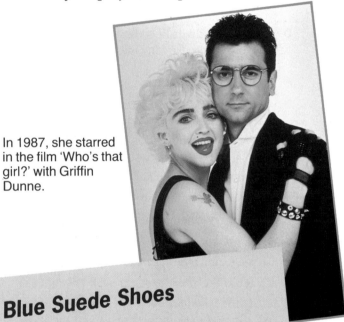

In 1987, she starred in the film 'Who's that girl?' with Griffin Dunne.

In 1990, she gave concerts all over the world on her 'Blond Ambition' tour.

Blue Suede Shoes

Well, it's one for the ....
Two for the ....
Three to get ....
Now go, cat, go. But don't you step on my .... Suede Shoes.
You can ..... anything, but lay off ..... Blue Suede Shoes.

Well you can knock me ......,
Step on my ......,
Slander my .... all over the place
Do .... that you want to do.
But uh–huh Honey, lay off of my ....
And don't you step on my .... Suede Shoes.
You can ..... anything, but lay off of ..... Blue Suede Shoes.

Well, you can .... my house,
Steal my .....,
.... my liquor from an old fruit jar.
Do .... that you want to do.
But uh–huh Honey, lay off of my ....
And don't you step on my .... Suede Shoes.
You can ..... anything, but lay off of ..... Blue Suede Shoes.

Words and music by Carl Lee Perkins

Learning diary

Look at the list on the first page of this unit.

A How well do you know each thing? Complete the circles to make faces.

B Try the self-check in the Workbook.

C Compare your self-check answers with a partner's. Do you understand everything? If you don't understand something, look in a grammar book or ask your teacher.

D What did you like best in this unit? Why?

2

▶ **Pronunciation: page 111**

3 places

the present continuous

Contents

Victoria Road: Jackie arrives 30

Language work: The present continuous tense 32

Reading: Hartfield 34

Listening: How observant are you? 36

Interaction: Giving directions 37

Project: Your neighbourhood 38

Language work :) :| :(

Grammar

the present continuous tense - statements
We're mending Casey's bike.
I'm going to the shop.

- negatives
The girl isn't going into the house.
I'm not doing anything.

- questions
What are you doing?
Is the boy wearing a red shirt?

the present continuous and the present simple
I play football every week.
I'm playing football now.

Word work

places

:) :| :(### Learning objectives

In this unit you will learn how to:

talk about what people are doing

contrast regular and current activities

describe a town

talk about what you can do in a town

ask for and give directions

VICTORIA ROAD

Jackie arrives

 • Say *Think back to Unit 2. What was wrong with Terry?*

• Elicit answer. If students cannot remember, tell them to look back at the story on page 20.

• Ask *What did Terry say about the leisure centre?*

• Repeat as above.

> **Answer key**
> *Terry was bored **and** he fancied Sue. He said the leisure centre was for kids.*

 • Say *In this unit, you'll find some new people in 'Victoria Road'. Look at the pictures and the story. Look for the names of the new people, and find out what they are doing in Victoria Road.*

• Students look for names and reasons.

> **Note**
> Students can get the answers by looking closely at the pictures or text, and/or by skimming and inferring what is happening.

> **Answer key**
> *Mrs Wright, Mr Wright and their daughter Jackie. They are looking at a house which is for sale. They want to buy it.*

• Students look at the picture story. Ask what happens.

• Elicit ideas.

> **Answer key**
> (possible answer)
> *Some people are looking at a house in Victoria Road. The girl comes over to talk to Sue, Vince, Casey and Terry. Terry thinks she is gorgeous and offers to show her round. Casey and Vince don't believe it. Sue is offended.*

 • Say *Now listen to the cassette and follow in your books.*

• ▄▄ Play the cassette.

• Students listen and read.

> **Notes**
> **You're up early.** Sue is being sarcastic, referring to Terry's habit of staying in bed late.
>
> **Go and ...** is often used in informal spoken English to mean 'Go + infinitive', e.g. *Go to talk*. Mrs Wright is using it to *suggest* that Jackie goes to talk to Sue, Terry and Casey. (*Come and ...* is used in the same way.)
>
> **over here** means 'to where we are'.
>
> **gorgeous** here means 'extremely attractive'. It can be used for boys and girls, men and women.
>
> **Are you doing anything at the moment?** means 'Are you busy now?'
>
> **I can show you around** means 'I can take you to see some of the different places in this area'.
>
> **I don't believe it!** Casey is *extremely* surprised because Terry has apparently completely changed his opinion about the town and the leisure centre.
>
> **in love** Explain this by translation; *in love* is usually followed by *with* and a name or a pronoun.
>
> **Hmph** is the sound someone makes if he or she is doubtful about, or annoyed by, something.
>
> • Most people in Britain live in houses, not flats. Most people also *own* their houses. (This usually means they have borrowed money to buy the house.)
>
> • Jackie and her parents are from Manchester, a large city in the north of England. They speak with northern accents. People with this accent don't use the /ʌ/ sound, e.g. /mʌst/ becomes /mʊst/. They often use /æ/ instead of /ɑː/, e.g. /bɑːθ/ becomes /bæθ/.

• Students read questions **a–h**.

- Ask question **a**.
- Elicit answer. (Students can look back.)
- Repeat with **b–h**.

Answer key

a *They are mending Casey's bike.*

b *It's Saturday. Terry says 'Why aren't you playing football today? You play football every Saturday, don't you?'*

c *He's hurt his knee.*

d *Terry usually stays in bed late. Sue is teasing him again.*

e *Her parents want to buy 23 Victoria Road.*

f *They come from Manchester. We know because Jackie says 'I want to stay in Manchester.'*

g *He thinks she's gorgeous.*

h *Terry says 'there's a really great leisure centre' and 'I go there a lot'. But he doesn't think it's great and he doesn't go there a lot!*

 • Say *Close your books. I'm going to play the cassette again. Listen carefully.*

- Play the cassette again. Students listen.

Useful expressions

• Students read 'Useful expressions'.

- Say *If you're not sure of the meaning of any of these, work it out from the story.*
- Students write first language equivalents in the chart.

Note

Remind students that they are looking for *phrases* with similar meanings, so they do not just want word-for-word equivalents. Give an example.

- In pairs, students compare answers.
- Elicit answers. (See **Note**.)

Jackie arrives

▼**1** Look back at page 20. What was wrong with Terry? What did he say about the leisure centre?

▼**2** Look at this story. Who are the new people? Find their names in the text. What are they doing?

▼**3** 📼 Listen and follow in your books.

Terry Hi. What are you doing?

Sue We're mending Casey's bike. You're up early, aren't you?

Terry Why aren't you playing football today, Casey? You play football every Saturday, don't you?

Casey I'm not playing this week. I've hurt my knee.

Sue Oh, look. I think we're getting new neighbours. Some people are looking at old Mrs Boswell's house.

Jackie Oh, why are we moving to this place? I want to stay in Manchester. All my friends are there.

Mrs Wright You can make some new friends here, dear. Go and talk to those young people over there.

Sue Oh, the girl isn't going into the house. She's crossing the road. I think she's coming over here.

Jackie Hi, I'm Jackie – Jackie Wright.

Terry Mmmm. She's gorgeous.

Sue Oh, hello. My name's Sue and thi . . .

Terry Hi, I'm Terry. Are you moving into number 23?

Jackie Well, we aren't moving in today, but my parents want to buy the house. Is there much to do round here?

Vince Well, Terry doesn't like . . .

Terry It's a great place. There's a cinema in town. And there are two good cafes and a park round the corner. And there's a really great leisure centre. I go there a lot.

Jackie Are you doing anything at the moment?

Sue Terry never does anything.

1 — Hi. What are you doing?

2 — Oh, look. I think we're getting new neighbours.

3 — Oh, the girl isn't going into the house. She's crossing the road.

Terry Well, er, actually I'm going to the shop. Do you want to come? I can show you around.

Casey I don't believe it!

Vince I think Terry's in love.

Sue Hmph.

We're mending Casey's bike.

Mmmm. She's gorgeous.

Hi, I'm Jackie – Jackie Wright.

Are you doing anything at the moment?

Terry never does anything.

Well, er, actually I'm going to the shop. Do you want to come?

Answer these questions.

a What are Sue, Vince and Casey doing?

b What day of the week is it? How do you know?

c Why isn't Casey playing football today?

d Why does Sue say 'You're up early'? What does she mean?

e Why is Jackie in Victoria Road?

f Where do Jackie and her family come from? How do you know?

g What does Terry think of Jackie?

h Why does Casey say 'I don't believe it'?

5 **Close your book. Listen again.**

Useful expressions

6 **How do you say these expressions in your language?**

You're up early.

I've hurt my …

Go and …

over there / over here

She's gorgeous.

Is there much to do round here?

It's a great place.

round the corner

Are you doing anything at the moment?

I can show you around.

I don't believe it.

He's in love (with) …

I don't believe it.

Hmph

I think Terry's in love.

31

7 **a** • Divide the class into groups of four.

• Each group decides parts.

b • Groups read the dialogue. Walk round, listen, answer questions, and note serious pronunciation errors.

• One group reads their dialogue aloud to the class.

8 • Ask *Who **didn't** see Jackie?*

Answer key
Kamala

• Point out that Casey, Terry, Sue or Vince would probably tell Kamala about Jackie.
  Kamala would probably ask *What's Jackie like?*

• Draw students' attention to the three different answers.

• Students read each speech bubble.

• They label each speech bubble with the name.

• Check answers. Students give their reasons.

Answer key
'Nothing special . . .' *Sue (or possibly Vince)*
'She's all right . . .' *Vince (or possibly Sue)*
'She's got beautiful blue eyes . . .' *Terry*

FOLLOW UP

9

Answer key
showing into Are No looking moment
She's great leisure lot Last the kids
Yes doing moment going come on

LANGUAGE WORK

The present continuous tense

BUILD UP

1 **a** • Read example sentence aloud.

• Say that the sentence *We're mending Casey's bike* describes what is happening *now*. The people are mending Casey's bike while they are speaking.

• Students look for more verbs like *We're mending* in the story.

• Elicit verbs.

• List these on the board.

Answer key	
are you doing	*aren't you playing*
we're getting	*are looking*
are we moving	*isn't going*
she's crossing	*she's coming*

b • Students look at the table.

• Students complete the table. (While they are doing this, copy the table on to the board.)

• Elicit answers. Write these in the table on the blackboard (or have a student do this).

• Students correct their tables as necessary.

Answer key		
	am	
	am not	
I	'm	*going to the . . .*
	'm not	
He	is	*crossing . . .*
She	is not	
It	's	
	isn't	*looking . . .*
We	are	
You	are not	*reading . . .*
They	're	
	aren't	

• Get students to make sentences using the table.
    Example
  He isn't reading a book.

2 **a** • Students look at the table.

• Students rearrange each set of words to make a statement and a question. While they are doing this, copy the table on to the blackboard.

• Elicit answers. One student writes these in the blackboard table.

• Students correct their tables as necessary.

Answer key
Jackie is crossing the street.
Is Jackie crossing the street?
They are looking at the house.
Are they looking at the house?

b • Students complete the rule.

• Elicit answer.

Answer key
*To make questions in the present continuous tense, we put **am**, **is** or **are** in front of the **subject**.*

3 • Tell students that Mr and Mrs Wright *do* buy the house and that they and Jackie are moving today.

• Say *Now I'm going to play the cassette. I want you to listen to what is happening, and write one sentence for each thing you hear.*

• Say *Look at the example.*

• Play the first example on the cassette.

• Check comprehension.

• Remind students to use the present continuous. They will hear things that are happening *at that moment.*

• Students look at the list of words.

• Say *These are clues about what you will hear.*

• Check understanding of words.

• Play the cassette.

• Students write the sentences.

• Play the cassette again. Students check their sentences and amend them as necessary.

• Check answers.

Mrs Wright Come on, Jackie. It's time to get up.
Jackie What time is it?
Mrs Wright It's five o'clock. We're moving today. Remember?
Jackie I don't want to go.

Mr Wright Put your clothes in this suitcase, Jackie.
Jackie What about these books?
Mr Wright There's a box for books downstairs.

Removal man Right, lift.

Removal man No, put it down a moment.
Mrs Wright Oh, please be careful!

Girl Goodbye, Jackie. We'll miss you.
Jackie Bye, everyone. Write to me.
Mr Wright Come on, Jackie. We're late.
Jackie I don't want to go.
Mrs Wright There, there, dear. Don't cry.

Jackie How much longer?
Mr Wright About two hours.
Jackie Oh.

Mr Wright Give me that spanner, Jackie.
Mr Wright Blast.

Mrs Wright Here we are. Our new home.
Jackie At last.

Removal man Where do you want this?
Mrs Wright Over there. No, I don't like it there. Can you take it downstairs into the dining room, please.

Mrs Moore Hello, are you the new people at number 23?
Mr Wright Yes.

Mrs Moore Pleased to meet you. My name's Pamela Moore and this . . .

Terry And this is our leisure centre.
Jackie Uh huh. It's not very big, is it?

> **Answer key**
> (possible answers)
> 1 *They are getting up.*
> 2 *They are packing.*
> 3 *The removal men are putting the piano in the van.*
> 4 *Jackie is saying goodbye to her friends.*
> 5 *They are driving to their new house.*
> 6 *Mr Wright is repairing the car.*
> 7 *They are arriving at their new house.*
> 8 *The removal men are moving the furniture into the house.*
> 9 *Mr and Mrs Moore are meeting Mr and Mrs Wright.*
> 10 *Terry is showing Jackie the leisure centre.*

The present continuous and present simple tenses

BUILD UP

4 • Read aloud the two sentences. Stress the time phrase in each, i.e. *at the moment* and *never.*

a • Ask *Now, which tense is in each sentence?*

• Students give answers.

> **Answer key**
> **First sentence:** *present continuous*
> **Second sentence:** *present simple*

b • Students read the gapped sentences.

• They look back at *Victoria Road* and complete the sentences, using the correct verb tense.

• Elicit answers.

> **Answer key**
> *play   'm not playing   go   I'm going*

c • Students complete the rule. (The sentences in **4b** will help them.)

• In pairs, students compare answers.

• Check answers.

> **Answer key**
> *We use the present continuous tense for something that is happening **now**.*
>
> *We use the present simple tense for something that happens **regularly**/**every day**.*

continued on T34

7 **a** Work in groups of four. One person is Terry, one is Sue, one is Jackie and one is all the other parts.

b Read the dialogue.

 8 Match the names to the answers. What's Jackie like?

Terry   Vince   Sue

> Nothing special. She's got a funny accent.

> She's got beautiful blue eyes. She's from Manchester.

> She's all right. She's quite tall and she's got blond hair.

FOLLOW UP

9 Complete this conversation.

Kamala Hi, Sue. Where's Terry?

Sue He's .... Jackie around.

Kamala Who's Jackie?

Sue Jackie Wright. She's moving .... old Mrs Boswell's house.

Kamala .... they moving in today?

Sue .... Jackie's parents are .... at the house at the ....

Kamala What's she like?

Sue .... nothing special. Terry thinks she's wonderful . He told her this is a .... place. 'There's a great .... centre. I go there a .... ,' he said.

Kamala I don't believe it. .... week he said .... leisure centre was for .... He called it stupid.

Sue .... , I know. Are you .... anything at the .... , Kam?

Kamala No.

Sue I'm .... to the cafe. Do you want to .... ?

Kamala Yes, OK. Come ....

The present continuous tense

BUILD UP

 1 **a** Look at this sentence.

We're mend**ing** Casey's bike.

> This is the 'present continuous' tense. It describes what is happening now.

Find more verbs like this in the Victoria Road story.

b Complete this table.

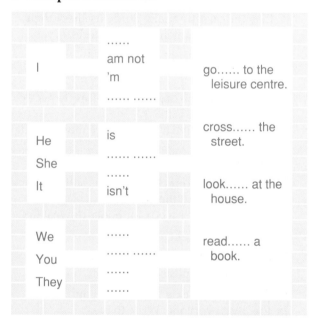

	......	
I	am not 'm	go...... to the leisure centre.
He She It	is .... isn't	cross...... the street. look...... at the house.
We You They	....	read...... a book.

 2 **a** Put these words in the correct order to make a statement and a question.

	statement	question
the crossing Jackie street is they house at looking the are		

b Complete this rule.

> To make questions in the present continuous tense, we put 'am', 'is' or .... in front of the ....

32

3 Moving day. Jackie and her parents are moving to Victoria Road today.

 Listen. Write down what is happening.

> Example
> *They are getting up.*

Here are some words to help you.

pack move furniture
van drive repair
meet arrive

The present continuous and present simple tenses

BUILD UP

4 Look at these two sentences.

Are you **doing** anything at the moment?
Terry never **does** anything.

a What tense is used in:

- the first sentence?
- the second sentence?

b Look at the Victoria Road story again and complete these sentences.

You .... football every Saturday.

I .... this week. I've hurt my knee.

There's a great leisure centre. I .... there a lot.

.... to the shop. Do you want to come?

c Complete this rule.

> We use the present continuous tense for
> something that is happening ....
> We use the present simple tense for
> something that happens ....

5 Terry and Jackie are talking. Put these verbs into the correct tense.

a We (go) to school at quarter to nine every day.

b What (do) your friends?
They (mend) Casey's bike.

c Casey (play) football every Saturday morning.

d Have you got any hobbies?
Yes, I (collect) stamps.

e What (do) your parents at the moment?
They (look) at the house.

f What (do) your father?
He (work) in an office.

g We (not move) in today.

h I (not do) anything at the moment.

i Kamala (work) in her parents' shop at the weekend.

FOLLOW UP

6 Write the answers to Exercise 5.

continued from T33

 5 • Read **a** aloud. Ask whether it is to do with something that is happening now, or something that happens regularly.

• Elicit answer.

> **Answer key**
> *Something that happens regularly*

• Repeat with **b–i**.

• For **a–i**, students, firstly, choose which tense should be used in each, and, secondly, decide what the form of the verb in brackets should be. (They can use short or long forms.)

• Check answers.

> **Answer key**
>
> **a** *go*   **f** *does ... do, works*
> **b** *are ... doing, 're mending*   **g** *aren't moving*
> **c** *plays*   **h** *'m not doing*
> **d** *collect*   **i** *works*
> **e** *are ... doing, 're looking*

FOLLOW UP

 6 • In class or for homework, students write the answers to Exercise 5, using full sentences.

READING

Hartfield

 1 • Students look at the map of Hartfield – the town where Victoria Road is, and the six texts.

• Say *Four of the texts are correct, and two are not. The map **is** correct. Look at each small text and decide whether it is correct.*

• Students identify the four correct texts.

• In pairs, students compare answers.

• Elicit answers.

> **Answer key**
> *2, 3, 4, 6*

• Ask *How do you know the other two are incorrect?*

• Students give their ideas.

> **Answer key**
> (possible answer)
> **1** *There isn't a tunnel under the river. It goes through the hill.*
> **2** *There are shops only on one side of King George Avenue. The petrol station is on the same side of the road as the library.*

 2 a • Students label the places on the map.

  • Check answers.

  b • Read aloud the list of places.

   • Check understanding.

   • Students underline the places *not* on the map.

   • Elicit answers.

> **Answer key**
> *a hospital*   *an island*
> *a forest*   *a canal*
> *a castle*   *the sea*
> *a bus station*   *a swimming pool*

 3 • Read the instructions and the example aloud.

• Check understanding.

• Students read the things Terry says and write a sentence, starting *They are ...* for each one.

• Check answers.

> **Answer key**
> *They are at the leisure centre.*
> *They are at the bus stop in King George Avenue.*
> *They are outside Kamala's parents' shop in King George Avenue.*
> *They are by the lake in the park near Victoria Road.*
> *They are at the cafe in King George Avenue.*
> *They are on East Hill above the shoe factory and the station.*

 4 • Ask questions. Students give answers.

> **Answer key**
> **a** *The river's name is the River Hart.*
> **b** *The two hills are called East Hill and West Hill.*
> **c** *Sue's father works in London.*
> **d** *Kamala's parents' shop sells newspapers, magazines, sweets, cigarettes and stamps.*
> **e** *Kamala lives in a flat above her parents' shop.*
> **f** *The name of the pub is the Red Lion.*
> **g** *Casey plays football in the park near Victoria Road.*

 5 • Students give their ideas.

W O R D   W O R K

 6 **a** • Students complete the table. (While they are doing this, copy the table onto the blackboard.)

• Elicit items. Write these on the blackboard.

Answer key
(possible words)
buildings

factory	shop
house	café
shopping centre	pub
cinema	petrol station
school	supermarket
leisure centre	hairdresser's
church	post office

man-made features

park	football pitch
bridge	road
tennis court	(lake)
swimming pool	tunnel

natural features

hill	valley
river	(lake)
marsh	

---

b • Students add words to the lists.

• Elicit words and write them in the table.

c • Read the question aloud.

• Students give their ideas.

 7 **a** • Students look at their maps for one minute.

b • Students close their books.

• Give the example *How many bridges are there on the map?*

• Elicit answer *There are three bridges.*

• Choose one student to ask a similar question to the class.

• He or she asks the question and chooses another student to answer.

• Questioner says *Yes* or *No*. If *No*, other students answer.

• Another student asks a different question.

• Continue until five or six questions have been asked and answered.

FOLLOW UP

8 • In class or for homework, students learn the words from Exercise 6 for a test.

• Ask ten questions about Hartfield.
Example
What is the Red Lion?
What is there in the middle of the park?

• Students write down the answers.

• Students exchange books and mark the test.

READING

1 Look at the map of Hartfield.
  - Here are six texts about the map.
    Only four are correct.
    Which are they?

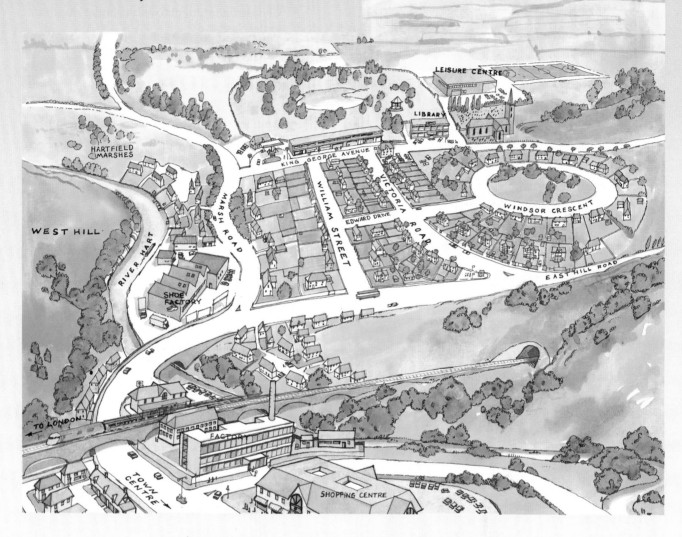

1 Hartfield lies in a valley between two hills. The town gets its name from the River Hart. The name means a field on the River Hart. Today there are two bridges over the river. There is also a railway tunnel under the river.

2 Many people from Hartfield work in offices in London. Sue's father travels up to London every day by train. But a lot of people work in Hartfield itself. There are two factories near the station and the town has a modern shopping centre.

3 All the young people from Victoria Road go to Hartfield Secondary School. Terry and his friends go to school by bus. The bus stop is in King George Avenue in front of the library.

4 There's a park near Victoria Road. There's a lake in the middle of the park. Next to the park there's a leisure centre with a football pitch. Casey plays football here every Saturday. The centre is behind the church near the entrance to the park.

5 There are some shops in King George Avenue. On one side of the street there is a newsagent's, a cafe and a library. The cafe is called the Fat Cat. On the opposite side of the street there is a petrol station, a supermarket and a hairdresser's.

6 At the end of Victoria Road there is a small parade of shops. Kamala's parents own the newsagent's. They sell newspapers and magazines, sweets and cigarettes. Kamala and her family live in a flat above the shop. On the corner of Victoria Road there is a pub called the Red Lion.

2 a Label these things on the map.

the bus stop   the Red Lion
the church   the lake
the station   the railway tunnel

b Which of these are not on the map?

a bridge   a river   a park
a hospital   a castle   a swimming pool
a railway line a lake   the sea
a forest   an island
a bus station   a canal

3 Terry is showing Jackie around. Read what Terry says.

- Where are they?

Example
We have a disco here every Friday night.
They are at the leisure centre.

This is where we get the bus to school or the centre of town. The buses go every twenty minutes.

Sue's friend, Kamala, lives up there.

In the summer they have boats here.

What do you want to drink?

My mum works there. They make shoes.

4 Answer these questions.

a What is the name of the river?

b What are the two hills called?

c Where does Sue's father work?

d What does Kamala's parents' shop sell?

e Where does Kamala live?

f What is the name of the pub?

g Where does Casey play football?

5 What do you think of the Victoria Road neighbourhood? Would you like to live there? What would you like? What wouldn't you like?

W O R D   W O R K

6 a Find as many words as possible to complete this table.

buildings	man-made features	natural features
factory	*park*	*hill*

b Use a dictionary. Find two or more words for each list.

c Which of these things are there in your neighbourhood?

7 A Game. How good is your memory?

a Look at the map for one minute.

b A Close your book.

   B Ask 'How many .... are there on the map?
   A Give the answer.

   Example
   A *How many bridges are there on the map?*
   B *There are three bridges.*

FOLLOW UP

8 Learn the words in your lists for Exercise 6.

LISTENING

How observant are you?

1
- Say *Look at this picture. Ask me if you don't know the English word for any of the things in the picture.* Answer questions.
- Students look at the picture for two minutes.
- Say *Time's up!*

2
- Students close their books.
- Students number 1–20 in their exercise books.
- Say *You are now going to hear twenty questions about the picture. Write the answers in your books. These should be **short** answers – not full sentences.*
- Play the cassette. Pause after each example.
- Students answer the questions.

 How observant are you?
1. Where is the baby playing?
2. What is the woman ironing?
3. What is the man on the ladder doing?
4. What time is it?
5. What are the children watching on TV?
6. Are the two girls coming into or going out of the house?
7. Where is the cat sitting?
8. What is the old man in the garden doing?
9. What is the boy in red trousers doing?
10. What is lying on the bed in the bedroom?
11. What is the boy in the bathroom doing?
12. What colour pyjamas is he wearing?
13. What is the girl in the bedroom doing?
14. How many people are there in the kitchen?
15. What is the dog doing?
16. How many women are there in the picture?
17. What is the woman in the hall doing?
18. What is the woman in the bedroom doing?
19. What are the men carrying from the van?
20. How many rooms of the house can you see?

3
- Say *You now have a second chance to get the answers. I'm going to play the cassette again. Listen carefully and check your answers.*
- Play the cassette again.
- Students check their answers and amend as necessary.

4
- In pairs, students compare answers.

5
- Students open their books at the picture.
- They check their own answers and add up their score (out of 20).
- Students read the 'interpretation' of their score.

- Find out how many students scored 17–20, and then how many scored 11–16 and so on.
- Play the cassette again. Pause after each question and elicit the answer. (This allows all students to have the right answer to each question.)

Answer key
1	*under the table*	11	*cleaning his teeth*
2	*a shirt*	12	*blue*
3	*cleaning windows*	13	*writing a letter*
4	*twenty-five past nine*	14	*three*
5	*Black Beauty*	15	*eating a bone*
6	*coming out*	16	*three*
7	*in an armchair*	17	*telephoning*
8	*drinking a cup of tea*	18	*combing her hair*
9	*riding a bicycle*	19	*a settee*
10	*a dress*	20	*six*

6 a
- Students look again at the picture.
- Ask for names of *furniture* in the picture.
- Elicit names.
- Say *Use your dictionary to find the English for any pieces of furniture you don't know the word for.*
- Students look up words.

b
- Students label the furniture in the picture.
- Check labels.

7
- Tell students they are now going to ask each other questions about what is in the picture. These questions should be similar to those on the cassette. Use the example in the Student's Book to illustrate.
- Add *If you can, use some of your new furniture words in your questions.*
- Elicit one or two further examples of questions.
- In pairs, students ask and answer questions about the picture.
- Walk round the class. Listen, observe, and answer questions.
- Point out and correct any serious common errors (of vocabulary, syntax or pronunciation).

Note
The questions should be about the content of the picture, not about the English words for things in the picture. However, students can use their new words for furniture as part of the questions. Thus *What do you call (x) in English?* is not a good question, but *What colour is the ironing board?* is.

• Students open their exercise books at the page where they wrote answers to Exercise 2.

• They list each *question* they were asked to get each answer.

• Say *I'm now going to play the cassette again. Listen, check **your** questions, and correct them if necessary.*

• Play the cassette.

• Students listen and correct their questions as necessary.

INTERACTION

Giving directions

 a • Students look at the map on page 34.

• They read the gapped dialogue.

• Students look again at the map on page 34. They try to complete the dialogue. Some gaps need one word; others need more than one.

• Say *I'm now going to play the cassette. Listen. Check your ideas and complete the dialogue.*

• Play the cassette.

• Students complete the dialogue.

• Elicit answers.

Excuse me. Can you tell me how to get to the library?
Yes. It's in King George Avenue. Go down here. Take the second turning on the right. That's King George Avenue. The library is on the left.
On the left?
Yes, behind the bus stop.
Thank you.

b • Read the question aloud.

• Say *What's the answer?*

• Students use the map and the dialogue to work out where the people are.

• Elicit answer.

> **Answer key**
> *At the station or at the junction of East Hill Road and Victoria Road.*

c • In pairs, students read the completed dialogue. Encourage them to use gestures, e.g. for *down here, turn right.*

• Students change roles and repeat.

 2 • Students look again at the map on page 34.

• They find the station on the map.

• They find Edward Drive on the map.

• They find the Hartfield Leisure Centre on the map.

• In pairs, students work out the two dialogues. (They can make notes if they wish, but should not write out the dialogues in full.)

• Students role play their dialogues.

• Ask for volunteer pairs (different from the pairs in Exercise 1) to 'perform' their role play for the class – without notes.

 3 • Write any necessary but unfamiliar vocabulary on the board, e.g. important local landmarks (*the statue of . . ., the fountain*).

• In pairs, students plan the two dialogues. (Again, they may make notes, but should not write the dialogues out in full.)

• Students role play their dialogues.

• Say *Now we'll hear some of these conversations. Listen carefully and decide whether the directions are accurate and sensible.*

• Volunteer pairs (different from before, if possible) 'perform' their role plays.

• Class listens carefully.

• Elicit comments from the class about each dialogue. Give feedback yourself.

FOLLOW UP

4 • Each student chooses one of the dialogues and writes it out in full.

LISTENING

HOW OBSERVANT ARE YOU?

1 Study this picture for two minutes. Ask your teacher for any words you want.

2  Close your books. Listen and answer the questions.

3 Listen again and check your answers.

4 Work in pairs. Compare your answers with your partner.

5 Look at the picture and check your answers. What did you score?

17–20	excellent. (You have a very good memory.)
11–16	good
8–16	average
4–7	poor
0–3	terrible. (You need glasses.)

W O R D   W O R K

6 a What are the names of all the pieces of furniture in the picture? Use a dictionary to find any that you don't know in English.

b Label them.

7 Ask your partner questions about the picture.

Example
How many adults are there?
What is the man in the kitchen doing?

FOLLOW UP

8 Look at your answers to Exercise 2. What were the questions on the tape? Write them down.

A mime game

A Mime an activity.
B Guess what A is doing.

INTERACTION

Giving directions

1 a  Look at the map on page 34. Listen and complete the dialogue.

Excuse me. Can you tell me how to get to the library?

Yes. It's .... King George Avenue. .... down here. Take the .... turning .... the right. That's ....

The library is ....

On the left?

Yes, ... the bus stop.

Thank you.

b Where are the people on the map?

c Work in pairs. Role play your completed dialogue.

2 Work in pairs. You are at the station. Make the dialogues for getting to:
● Edward Drive.
● the Hartfield leisure centre.

3 You are outside your school. Someone asks you the way to these places.
● the bus station
● the town centre
Make the conversations.

FOLLOW UP

4 Write one of your dialogues from Exercise 3.

PROJECT

Your life

Students can work on this in pairs, small groups or individually.

- Students read the instructions.
- Ask *What's our (your) neighbourhood like?*
- Elicit suggestions.
- Ask *What's particularly interesting about our (your) neighbourhood?*
- Elicit ideas.
- Ask *What would you put on a map of our (your) neighbourhood?*
- Elicit names of buildings, man-made features and natural features. Write these on the board.

a • Students take a clean sheet of paper and head it *(Name of neighbourhood)*.
  - *You* write the name of the neighbourhood on the blackboard. Draw and label the most important road and one or two landmarks.
  - Students copy this on to their paper.

b • Students add and label any other features they think are important.
  - Students compare maps.
  - Students complete their maps. They look at the map of Hartfield for ideas.

> **Note**
> If all the students come from different neighbourhoods, do the above for one that the greatest number of students live in. For the others, this will then be an example.

c • In class or for homework, students write three paragraphs about their neighbourhood, as follows. (They should leave spaces between the paragraphs.)

  Paragraph 1: *My street*
  Paragraph 2: *My local shops and what you can buy there.*
  Paragraph 3: *My school*

d • Students add *What you can do and where you can go* as a fourth paragraph.
  - They illustrate this, as above.
  - Take in the project work and comment on the organization, clarity and accuracy. Be as positive as you can.
  - Return the work.
  - Students write a second draft correctly. (This time all illustrations can be stuck on securely.)
  - Display all pieces of work.

- All students look at each other's work.
- After one or two days, students take their work down and stick it in their project file.

▶ **Pronunciation: page T111**

LEARNING DIARY

- Students turn to the first page of Unit 3.

A Students draw faces on the symbols next to each item to indicate how well they think they know it.

B In class or for homework, students complete the self-check exercises in the Workbook.

C In pairs, students compare answers. Check answers.

  Identify which things students had problems with. Refer students to the relevant section of their grammar book.

  Encourage confused students to come and talk to you, and set aside a time for this.

D In pairs, students discuss what they liked and didn't like about Unit 3.

  Elicit ideas. Consider: *language, content, activities.*

CULTURE SPOT
Workbook page 33

- Divide the class into pairs or groups of three or four.
- Students look quickly at the text.
- Ask *What is the text about?*
- Students give their ideas.
- Ask *What do you already know about this topic?*
- Students give their ideas. Discuss these ideas.
- Say *Read the Culture Spot text. Note anything that you find interesting or unusual.*
- Ask comprehension questions about the text.
- Students give their answers. Explain any words that students need.
- Ask *Did you find anything interesting or unusual?*
- Students give their ideas.
- Read each comparison question in turn.
- Discuss each question. Encourage students to compare their situation to the one in the text.

READING

 a
- Students read headlines.
- Choose one student to read headlines aloud.
- Say *Now, read the newspaper article. Read it **quickly**. Choose which headline goes with the article. You have one minute.*
- Students read article quickly and decide on headline. Time them!
- In pairs, students compare answers.
- Elicit answers.

Answer key
Famous people work in shops for a day.

b, c, d
- Read aloud questions **b–d**.
- Students read text quickly again.
- They look for answers to questions and note them down.
- Elicit answers.

Answer key
b *Kelly Hunter organized the event.*
c *It happened in Covent Garden, in London.*
d *It was to earn money for charity.*

- Students read the list of people who worked in the shops.
- Ask students which of the people they have heard of (if any).
- Elicit names.
- Ask what they know about them.

Note
All the people listed are famous except Joanne Walker.

- Elicit information and indicate if this is correct where possible.
- Students will probably not know very much about these people already. The purpose of the activity is to get students to interpret from the text. They may already know:
  Boy George: pop singer with a group called Culture Club; famous for wearing makeup and extravagant clothes.
  Frank Bruno: boxer; former European champion.
  Jeremy Irons: actor; appeared in 'The French Lieutenant's Woman', and 'Brideshead Revisited'.
  Uri Geller: illusionist; bends metal things by stroking them.
- Say *Now, read the article again. Read it carefully this time. Find out more information about these people.*
- Give the example of Jeremy Irons:
  Jeremy Irons:
  actor
  sold flowers
- Students read the article and note down or underline the information.
- In pairs, students compare answers.
- Elicit information. Write this on the blackboard.

Answer key
Boy George: *worked in a shop   sold kisses for £5 usually stays in bed on Saturdays*
Uri Geller: *sold knives and forks*
Frank Bruno: *boxer*
Joanne Walker: *young secretary visited hairdresser who was Eartha Kitt   paid £50*
Delia Smith: *TV cook (i.e. she presents a cookery programme on TV)*
Eartha Kitt: *actress and singer worked as a hairdresser*

- Ask students *What do you think Uri Geller does? Why does it say he didn't bend them?*

Answer key
He is an illusionist who bends metal objects by stroking them.

PROJECT

Your life

Imagine someone is coming to live in your neighbourhood. What would you tell them? Describe your neighbourhood.

a Draw a map of your neighbourhood.

b Label on your map:
- the important buildings.
- the streets.
- your house.
- your friends' houses.
- the places where you meet your friends.
- the local shops.

c Write about:
- your street.
- the local shops.
- what you can buy there.
- your school.

d What can you do in your neighbourhood? Describe what you can do and places to go.

e Add some pictures.

Learning diary

Look at the list on the first page of this unit.

A How well do you know each thing? Complete the circles to make faces.

B Try the self-check in the Workbook.

C Compare your self-check answers with a partner's. Do you understand everything? If you don't understand something, look in a grammar book or ask your teacher.

D What did you like best in this unit? Why?

3

▶ **Pronunciation: page 111**

4 revision

READING

1 Look at the newspaper article.

a Find out what happened and choose the correct headline.

> ### Famous people go shopping in Covent Garden
>
> ### Boy George buys a clothes shop
>
> ### Pop festival in London
>
> ### Famous people work in shops for a day
>
> ### Pop stars invite people to visit their gardens

b Who organized the event?

c Where did it happen?

d What was it for?

2 Read the article. Find out as much as possible about these people.

Jeremy Irons   Joanne Walker
Boy George   Delia Smith
Uri Geller   Eartha Kitt
Frank Bruno

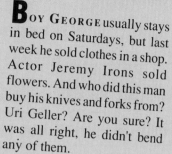

BOY GEORGE usually stays in bed on Saturdays, but last week he sold clothes in a shop. Actor Jeremy Irons sold flowers. And who did this man buy his knives and forks from? Uri Geller? Are you sure? It was all right, he didn't bend any of them.

Last Saturday, shoppers in Covent Garden in London had an unusual day. For 12 hours over 300 stars from television, pop music, sport and the cinema worked in the shops, pubs, cafes and restaurants in Covent Garden. More than 100,000 customers came to see them.

Actress Kelly Hunter organized everything. The idea was simple. People came to see the stars, they bought things and the shop owners gave 5 per cent of the money to charity. But the stars didn't only sell things. They signed thousands of autographs and gave kisses to their fans. (A kiss from Boy George cost £5.)

A young secretary, Joanne Walker, went to the hairdressers. The hairdresser on Saturday was the actress and singer, Eartha Kitt. Joanne paid her £50, the till rang and £2.50 went to charity. 'Next customer, please.' In other shops, customers met boxer Frank Bruno, the Bishop of California, TV cook Delia Smith and many others.

One hundred policemen and women were there, but there was no trouble. It was a good day for everyone. Fans got autographs and kisses from their favourite stars, the shops got a lot of new customers and at the end of the day more than £100,000 went to charity.

3 • Students read the list of statements.
• They tick the appropriate box next to each statement.
• In pairs, students compare answers.
• Elicit answers.
• Students justify their answers.

Answer key
a *R*   b *W*   c *W*   d *W*
e *D*   f *W*   g *D*   h *W*

---

4 a • Say *All the famous people worked in shops which had something to do with their own profession or their appearance.*
• Students draw lines connecting each person with the shop they think he or she worked in.
• In pairs, students compare answers.
• Check answers.

Answer key
(See **b**, below.)

---

b • Read aloud the example sentence.
• Elicit sentences saying where each famous person worked in Covent Garden and what they did.

Note
Students can imagine or work out the second. Many different answers are possible.

Answer key
(possible answers)
Sue Pollard worked in the optician's and sold glasses.
Frank Bruno worked in the sports shop and sold sports equipment.
Rick Astley worked in the record shop and sold records and cassette tapes.
Delia Smith worked in the kitchen shop and sold cooking equipment.
Barbara Cartland worked in the bookshop and sold books.
Gorden Kaye worked in the cafe and served lunches.

---

5 • Choose a student to read the first sentence.
• Ask *Why did £2.50 of the £50 Joanne paid go to charity?*

Answer key
The shop owners had agreed to give 5% of the money people paid to charity; 5% of £50 is £2.50.

---

a • Students read list of items and prices and work out the amounts.
• Elicit answers. (Students use 'pounds' and 'p', for example, *Four pounds twenty-five p.*)

Answer key
£4.25   7p/8p   £1.60   40p   60p
£5 (presumably – since a kiss is not an item which the shop owners had in stock)

---

b • Students read the list of items and amounts that went to charity.
• On the blackboard, work out the cost of the first item: *a record 35p*
i.e. 35p is 5% of cost
    Cost = 20 × 35p
        = £7.00
• They work out the price of the other items.
• In pairs, students compare answers.
• Elicit answers.

Answer key
record: *£7.00*   shirt: *£16.00*   video: *£12.00*
bicycle: *£235.00*

---

6 a • Students turn back to the text and list all the words they can find connected with 'star'.

   • Elicit words. List them on the board.

> **Answer key**
> (possible words)
> *charity   actor   television   pop music   sport*
> *cinema   actress   autographs   fans   singer*
> *policemen and women   £100,000*

   • Check understanding of the words.

   • Students suggest stars from their own country.

b • Say *Now, an easy one. Go back to the text again. This time, list all the words you can find connected with* **shop**.

   • Students reread text quickly and list words.

   • In pairs, students compare lists.

   • Elicit words. List them on the board.

> **Answer key**
> *sold   buy   shoppers   worked   customer(s)*
> *bought   shop owners   sell   till*

   • Check understanding of the words.

FOLLOW UP

 7 a • Say *Read the dialogue again and find out who is being interviewed. Look back at the text if necessary.*

   • Students read the incomplete dialogue and decide who the interviewee is.

   • Elicit answer.

> **Answer key**
> *Boy George*

b • Ask *What questions did the interviewer ask? Try to work out the question the interviewer asked to get each answer.*

   • Give students two minutes to do this.

   • Elicit each question in turn.

> **Answer key**
> *What do you usually do on Saturdays?*
> *What did you do last Saturday?/Where did you work last Saturday?*
> *What was the shop called?/What shop was it?*
> *What did you do there?/What did you sell?*
> *How much did a kiss cost?/How much was a kiss?*
> *Was there any trouble?*
> *How much (money) went to charity?*

LISTENING

 1 • Students read the article again.

 2 • Tell students they are now going to hear another interview. This also took place in Covent Garden last Saturday.

   • Students read questions **a–e**.

   • ▪▪ Play the cassette. Students listen carefully and note down answers.

   • Rewind tape.

   • Elicit answers to **a–e**.

> **Answer key**
> **a** *outside a large record shop*
> **b** *Karen Woods*
> **c** *Birmingham*
> **d** *Rick Astley*
> **e** *his autograph*

continued on T42

3

Right, Wrong or Don't know?

		✓	✗	?
a	Covent Garden is in London.	❑	❑	❑
b	Boy George works in a clothes shop every Saturday.	❑	❑	❑
c	There are only clothes shops in Covent Garden.	❑	❑	❑
d	All the stars were actors and actresses.	❑	❑	❑
e	Kelly Hunter lives near Covent Garden.	❑	❑	❑
f	The shop owners gave all their money to charity.	❑	❑	❑
g	Frank Bruno signed 300 autographs.	❑	❑	❑
h	The police arrested two people.	❑	❑	❑

4 Where do you think these people worked?

a Match them to the places.

kitchen shop   cafe   bookshop
sports shop   optician's   record shop

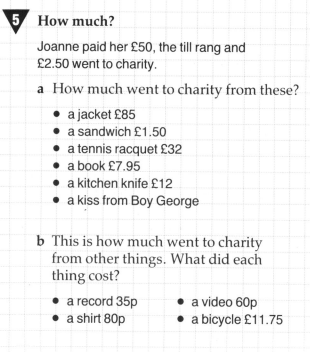

Rick Astley *pop singer*

Gorden Kaye *actor*

Barbara Cartland *writer*

Su Pollard *actress*

Delia Smith *TV cook*

Frank Bruno *boxer*

b Say what the people did.

> **Example**
> *Su Pollard worked in the optician's and sold glasses.*

5 How much?

Joanne paid her £50, the till rang and £2.50 went to charity.

a How much went to charity from these?

- a jacket £85
- a sandwich £1.50
- a tennis racquet £32
- a book £7.95
- a kitchen knife £12
- a kiss from Boy George

b This is how much went to charity from other things. What did each thing cost?

- a record 35p
- a shirt 80p
- a video 60p
- a bicycle £11.75

W O R D W O R K

6

a Write down all the words connected with 'stars'. Give examples of stars from your own country.

b Write down all the words connected with 'shop'.

FOLLOW UP

7 Here is some information from the text.

a Who is talking?

b What were the interviewer's questions?

.... ?
I stay in bed.

.... ?
I worked in a clothes shop.

.... ?
It was called 'Tops and Bottoms'.

.... ?
I sold clothes, I signed autographs and I sold kisses to my fans.

.... ?
£5.

.... ?
No, there were a lot of police there, but there was no trouble.

.... ?
I don't know, but more than £100,000, I think.

LISTENING

 1 Read the article again.

 2 Listen to the interview. Find the answers to these questions.

a Where is the interviewer?

b Who is he talking to?

c Where is the girl from?

d Who is she waiting to see?

e What does she want?

3 Now listen again and complete the dialogue.

Interviewer There .... thousands of people

here today. I'm .... a ....

and a lot of people ....

the shop. Excuse me, what's your name?

Girl ....

Interviewer And .... , Karen?

Girl I'm from Birmingham.

Interviewer You'................ outside this record

shop. Who .... here?

Girl ....

Interviewer .... you a Rick Astley .... ?

Girl Oh, ... fabulous.

Interviewer .... to buy anything?

Girl No, I just want to ....

on this ....

Interviewer And a .... , too?

Girl Ooh, don't.

4 Work in pairs. Act the dialogue with your partner.

5 Make up an interview with another customer. Act your dialogue.

FOLLOW UP

6 Write your dialogue from Exercise 5.

continued from T41

 3
- Students read through the gapped dialogue.
- Say *Now, fill in as many of the gaps as you can. Some gaps need only one word, but others need more.*
- Students fill in as many of the gaps as they can.
- Elicit suggestions.
- Say *Now, I'm going to play the cassette again. Check your answers, and fill in the rest of the gaps.*
- Play the cassette.
- Students check and fill in remaining gaps.
- In pairs, students compare answers.
- Check answers.

In the crowd

Interviewer Hello. This is Mike Moon. It's Saturday 30th July and I'm in Covent Garden in London. It's an unusual day here in the Garden because, today, over three hundred stars from the worlds of pop music, television and sport are working in the shops and cafes of Covent Garden. And it's all for charity. There are thousands of people here today. I'm outside a large record shop and a lot of people are standing in front of the shop. Excuse me, what's your name?

Girl Karen Woods.

Interviewer And where are you from, Karen?

Girl I'm from Birmingham.

Interviewer You're waiting outside this record shop. Who is working here?

Girl Rick Astley.

Interviewer Are you a Rick Astley fan?

Girl Oh, he's fabulous.

Interviewer Do you want to buy anything?

Girl No, I just want to get his autograph on this album.

Interviewer And a kiss, too?

Girl Ooh, don't.

 4
- In pairs, students read the dialogue.
- Walk round checking pronunciation. Answer any questions students ask.
- Correct any serious errors of pronunciation.
- Students change roles. Repeat.

5
- In the same pairs, students work out an interview with another customer. (This customer is in a different part of Covent Garden.) They may make notes, but should not write the dialogue out in full.
- Walk round. Answer questions and make suggestions or comments as necessary.

- Choose two or three pairs to 'perform' their dialogues for the class.

FOLLOW UP

6
- Students write out their dialogues from Exercise 5 in their exercise books.

PROJECT

Helping others

- Tell students that in this project they will plan their own event for charity – with, if they wish, stars of their choice.

a
- Students look at the pictures.
- Elicit ideas of what *cause* each represents.

> **Answer key**
> *helping old people*
> *caring for animals*
> *helping people in the third world*
> *cleaning up pollution*

- List causes on the board.
- Divide class into groups of three or four.
- Each group elects a secretary.
- Each group decides which cause they would like to raise money for, and why. (The cause might be one in the pictures, or not.)
- Secretary records cause and reason for choice.

b
- Students read the list of events which can be held to raise money.
- Elicit suggestions for other money-raising events.
- In their groups, students decide on the kind of event they will hold.
- The secretary records the event.

c
- Remind students how the event in Covent Garden raised money for charity.
- Read aloud the example given here.
- Groups decide how their event would raise money for their chosen cause.
- The secretary notes down the details.
- Students make posters advertising their event.
- Display posters.

- Everyone walks round and looks at all the posters.
- Be encouraging about all the posters, but single out one or two really good ones for general comment.
- Point out that large charity events are covered in newspapers as well as on radio and TV. Theirs is no exception!
- Each group decides on a newspaper headline to begin an article covering their event.
- In the same groups, students plan an article covering the event. They should use:
  a the headline;
  b the notes made by their group secretary; and
  c the Covent Garden text, as an example of a way to organize the article.
- Students write their articles.
- Take in articles. Correct and comment as necessary. (Consider text and paragraph organization as well as grammar, spelling and punctuation.)
- Return articles.
- Students rewrite their articles correctly.
- Display articles.
- Students stick/put the correct version into their project file or folder.

A QUIZ

- Students close their copy of *Hotline*.
- Tell students they are going to find out how much they remember from Units 1, 2 and 3. They will do a quiz, in pairs.
- Divide class into pairs.
- Say *When I say* **Now***, open your books at page 42. Find 'A Quiz, Exercise 1' – and do the quiz. You have* **two minutes***. Don't look back.*
- Write *page 42 – a Quiz, Exercise 1* on the board.
- Say *Now!*
- Students find the Quiz and answer **a–e** in their pairs. Do not let them turn back.
- After two minutes say *Stop!*
- Alternatively, you can read out the questions. Students have their books closed.
- Elicit answers.

- Ask who got 5, 4 and 3 etc.

MAKE YOUR OWN QUIZ

 a • Put students into groups of four. Each group elects a secretary.

b • Groups each work out five questions from Units 1–3. (These questions should be factual, like the Quiz questions in Exercise 1.)

- The secretary notes these down.
- While they are doing this, go round and check that the questions are reasonable.
- The secretary then rewrites the five questions neatly on a sheet of paper, leaving a place for the answer to each.

c • Pairs of groups exchange question papers.

- Each group tries to answer the questions together. Do not set a time limit at the start, but say *One more minute* if the activity is going on too long.
- The secretary writes the group's answers in the space provided on the question paper. These should be *short* answers only.
- Groups return question papers, with the answers written on.
- Groups mark each other's answers, give a mark out of 5, and give the question paper back again.
- Again, find out which groups got 5, 4 and 3.

FOLLOW UP

- In class or for homework, students write the answer to each question in a full sentence in their exercise books.

▶ **Pronunciation: page T111**

PROJECT

Helping others

In many countries people organise charity events to raise money for good causes. Imagine you are arranging a charity event.

First think about what you could do.

a What cause would you like to raise money for? Look at the pictures on this page for ideas or think of your own ideas.

b What kind of event could you hold? Here are some possible ideas.

- a race
- a pop concert
- a sale
- a fashion show

c How would your event help your good cause? For example, people pay to enter the race or people give some of their own clothes for the fashion show.

Make a poster to advertise your event.

Write a newspaper article about your event. Describe what happened. How much money did you make? What will happen to the money?

A QUIZ

What can you remember?

 Work in pairs. Do the quiz.

a What was Elvis Presley's first hit record?

b What are the two kinds of sleep called?

c What number in Victoria Road is Jackie moving into?

d What is Terry's family name?

e What kind of shop do Kamala's parents own?

2 Make your own quiz.

a Work in groups of four.

b Write five questions about things in Units 1–3.

c Exchange your quiz with another group. Answer their quiz.

FOLLOW UP

3 Write the answers to the quiz in Exercise 1 in full.

▶ Pronunciation: page 111

42

Contents

Victoria Road: Sue goes to Spain   44
Language work: The future simple   46
Reading: A long way to travel for your dinner   48
Listening: A day at the seaside   50
Interaction: At the station   51
Project: Your dream holiday   52

5 travel

Language work

Grammar

the future simple - statements
Carmen and her father will meet me.
I'll love you forever.

- negatives
We won't be in Madrid.

- questions
Where will you stay?
Will you be all right?
Shall we go to the seaside?

if clauses
If you get the 10.54 train,
you'll get to London at 14.14.

must, mustn't, needn't
We must be at the station by ten past eight.
You mustn't be late.
You needn't come to the station.

Word work

geographical names
seasons

Learning objectives

In this unit you will learn how to:

talk about future plans

make suggestions

express conditions

describe a route

make arrangements for a journey

buy a train ticket

ask about train times

describe a holiday

the future simple

VICTORIA ROAD

Sue goes to Spain

- Say *Look at the questions.* Read them out.
- Students look at the pictures and find the answers.
- Elicit answers.

> **Answer key**
> a *It's from Carmen.*
> b *Carmen invites Sue to Spain.*
> c *She suggests a trip to the seaside next Sunday. She may want to go somewhere with Terry – and without Sue.*
> d *Aunt Ada is ill, so Mr Scott can't take Sue to the airport.*

- Say *Now I'll play the cassette. Listen and follow in your books.*
- Play the cassette. Students listen and read.
- Check understanding.
- Ask *What do you think Vince and Terry will do?*
- Elicit suggestions.

> **Answer key**
> (possible answers)
> *go to the airport with Sue*
> *say they can't go with Sue because they've made other plans*
> *one of them (probably Vince) will go with Sue; the other (probably Terry) will go to the seaside with Jackie*

- Rewind the cassette.

- Students look at the 'Right, Wrong or Don't Know' chart.
- Check understanding of symbols.
- Students tick one box next to each statement to indicate whether the statement is right, wrong, or that they don't know.
- In pairs, students compare answers.
- Check answers.

> **Answer key**
> a *R*   b *R*   c *R*   d *W*   e *W*   f *W*
> g *W*   h *D*   i *D*   j *W*

- Play the cassette again. Students listen carefully.

> **Notes**
> • Mr Scott is worried about the heat because Spain can be much hotter than Britain.
>
> • Sue is leaving from Heathrow Airport, one of the four airports in London. She can get a train into London and then an underground train from the centre of London to the airport.
>
> **in the country** here means 'in the country*side*', i.e. not in a town or a city.
>
> **I'm so excited** means 'I'm very excited'.
>
> **what a pity.** This is another way of saying 'that's a pity' or 'that's a shame'. It's often used in an ironic way, as Jackie is doing here.
>
> **on my own** means 'alone' or 'without any help'.

Sue goes to Spain

1 Look at the pictures.

a Who is Sue's letter from?

b What is it about?

c What does Jackie suggest?

d What is the telephone call about?

2 🔊 Listen and follow in your books.

Sue Listen to this. It's from Carmen. 'Would you like to come and stay with us next month?' Oh, Dad. Can I go, oh, please, please, can I, Dad, can I?

Mr Scott Where will you stay? It will be very hot in Madrid in August.

Sue We won't be in Madrid. We'll be at Carmen's uncle's house in the country. It's near the coast.

Mrs Scott But, how will you get there?

Sue I'll fly to Madrid. Carmen and her father will meet me at the airport and then we'll drive to the country. Oh, come on, please. I'll be all right.

Mr Scott Well, all right, then, but . . .

Sue Oh, thank you, Dad. I'll love you forever. Oh, it will be wonderful. Three weeks in Spain. I'll go swimming in the sea and sunbathe on the beach and I'll . . . Oh, I'm so excited.

Later

Jackie Shall we all go to the seaside next Sunday?

Terry Oh, yes, that's a great idea.

Vince Sue can't come. She'll be at the airport. She's going to Spain next Sunday.

Jackie Oh, what a pity.

Saturday evening

Mrs Scott Have you got your passport, your tickets, your Spanish money and all your clothes?

Sue Yes, Mum. Don't panic.

Mr Scott I'm sorry, Sue, but I can't take you to the airport by car tomorrow. Aunt Ada is very ill. Your Mum and I must go and see her.

Sue Oh, Dad. How will I get to the airport? I can't carry all this luggage on my own.

Mr Scott That's all right. You can go by train. Vince and Terry will help you, won't you, boys?

What do you think? What will Vince and Terry do?

▼3

Right, Wrong or Don't know?

		✓	✗	?
a	Carmen wrote the letter in July.	❏	❏	❏
b	Sue's parents are worried.	❏	❏	❏
c	Sue will travel to Spain by plane.	❏	❏	❏
d	Carmen's parents will meet Sue at the airport.	❏	❏	❏
e	Sue will be in Spain for a month.	❏	❏	❏
f	Jackie wants to go to London next Sunday.	❏	❏	❏
g	Jackie is disappointed because Sue can't go to the coast.	❏	❏	❏
h	Casey will go with Jackie.	❏	❏	❏
i	Sue has got three suitcases.	❏	❏	❏
j	Sue must take a taxi to the airport.	❏	❏	❏

▼4 **Close your book. Listen again.**

Shall we all go to the seaside next Sunday?

Oh, yes, that's a great idea.

3

Aunt Ada is very ill. Your mum and I must go and see her.

Oh, Dad. How will I get to the airport? I can't carry all this luggage on my own.

5

Vince and Terry will help you, won't you boys?

6

45

Useful expressions

- Students look at the 'Useful expressions' chart.
- Students write down the phrase in their own language which is nearest in meaning to the English phrase. Say *Go back to the story. Look at the situation in which the phrase is used.*
- In pairs, students compare answers.
- Check answers.

a
- Put students into groups of three.
- Students go back to the story on page 44.
- Write the characters for each part of the dialogue on the board:
  Dialogue 1: Sue, Mrs Scott and Mr Scott
  Dialogue 2: Jackie, Terry and Vince
  Dialogue 3: Mrs Scott, Mr Scott and Sue
  (Vince and Terry are also in the room)
- In their groups, students give themselves parts for each dialogue.

> **Note**
> If you wish, students can keep their roles for all three dialogues where possible, e.g. the same student can be Sue in Dialogue 1 and Dialogue 3.

b
- Students role play the dialogue.
- Walk round the class. Answer questions, and correct any serious errors in pronunciation (including stress, rhythm and intonation).
- Students change roles.
- Repeat as above.
- Select students from different groups to read each part of the dialogue to the class.

FOLLOW UP

- Students complete Carmen's letter. They look back at the dialogue if necessary.

> **Answer key**
> *are   in   like   month   won't   at   country*
> *fly   father   meet   at   we'll   to   uncle's*
> *weeks   is   coast   swimming   sunbathe   can*

> **Note**
> We use *in* before countries and cities. We usually use *at* before buildings and places. Exceptions: *in hospital* (when you are a patient), *in prison* (when you have been put in prison for breaking the law).

LANGUAGE WORK

The future simple

BUILD UP

a
- Draw students' attention to the table. Read the instruction.
- Students complete the table.
- Copy the table on to the blackboard.
- In pairs, students compare answers.
- Choose one student to complete the table on the blackboard.
- Check answers.

> **Answer key**
> *'ll   won't*

b
- Students complete the rule by filling in the gaps.
- Elicit answers.

> **Answer key**
> *To make the future tense, we put **will** or **'ll** in front of the verb. For the negative, we put **will not** or **won't** in front of the verb.*

- Draw student's attention to the **Note** on *shall*.
- Ask them to find an example of *shall* in the story.

> **Answer key**
> *Shall we all go to the seaside next Sunday?*

- Point out that this is a question, and the subject is *we*.
- Give other examples, e.g.
  Shall I do it?
  Shan't we be able to visit them?
  (See **Note** on *shan't* on T47.)

c
- Give students the sentence *I'll do it, shall I?*
- Ask what *I'll* is short for. (It could be *shall* or *will*.)
- Then ask *So what is the short form of **shall**?*

> **Answer key**
> *'ll*

• Students read the list of Sue's possible holiday activities.

• Check comprehension.

• Ask for suggestions about what Sue will do.

• Students make suggestions.

• Ask for suggestions of what Sue won't do.

• Students make suggestions.

Note
There are no set answers to this. For example, Sue may or may not feel homesick. So get different suggestions. It does not matter if students disagree. However, it is *unlikely* that Sue will do the following:

go to school   work on the farm
stay in Madrid   do her homework
go skiing

• In class or for homework, students write out their suggestions about what Sue will do and won't do on her holiday.

• Students make questions in the future tense by putting the words in the correct order.

• In pairs, students compare answers.

• Check answers.

Answer key
Where will you stay?   *Will he be all right?*

• Students complete the rule.

• Check answer.

Answer key
To make questions in the future simple we put 'will' in front of the subject.

• Remind students of the use of *shall*. As they have seen, this can also be used to form questions with *I* and *we*.

• Students reread the story on page 44.

• Draw students' attention to the question–answer pairs below. Point out that the first word of each question is given.

• In pairs, without looking back, students decide what each question is (1 or 2 minutes). They should not write anything down.

• In pairs, one student asks the questions and the other answers.

• Pairs change roles.

• Ask one pair to 'perform' their dialogue.

• Students write out the question–answer pairs.

• Check answers.

Answer key
How will you get to the airport?
How will you carry all your luggage?
Where will you stay?
How long will you stay?
What will you do?

FOLLOW UP

• Students read the instructions and the examples.

• Students write six sentences about what they will do next weekend using *I'll*.

• Students write six questions asking what their partners will do next weekend (same partners as Exercise 4).

• Select one pair. Student A asks his/her six questions. Student B answers each with *Yes, I will*; *No, I won't*; *Yes* or *No*.

• All pairs ask and answer their questions.

Note
We do not use the short form *'ll* in the short answer to a *will* question, i.e. we can say *Yes, I will*, but not *Yes, I'll*. However, we do say *No, I won't*.

Useful expressions

 5 How do you say these expressions in your language?

Would you like to ...?	
in the country	
near the coast	
I'm so excited.	
Oh, what a pity.	
Don't panic.	
How will I get to ... ?	
on my own	

6 a Work in groups of three. One person is Sue and Jackie, one is Mr Scott and Terry, and one is Mrs Scott and Vince.

b Role play the dialogue.

FOLLOW UP

 7 Complete Carmen's letter.

5th July

Dear Sue

Hi. How _____ you? It is very hot _____ Spain now. Would you _____ to come and stay with us next _____? We _____ be in Madrid. We'll be ___ my uncle's house in the _____. If you _____ to Madrid, my _____ and I will _____ you ___ the airport and then _____ drive ___ the country. We'll be at my _____ house for three _____. My uncle's house _____ near the _____ so we can go _____ every day and we can _____ on the beach. I hope you _____ come....

LANGUAGE WORK

The future simple: will

BUILD UP

1 a Complete this table with the short forms.

I He She It We You They	will ...... will not	go to the seaside catch the 7.15 train be late have a great time fly to Greece	tomorrow. next week.

We call this the **future simple**.

b Complete this rule.

> To make the future simple we put .... or .... in front of the verb. For the negative we put .... or .... in front of the verb.

Note: With **I** and **We** we can also say **shall/shan't**, especially in questions. Find an example in the story.

c What is the short form of 'shall'?

2 Look at this list of things. What do you think Sue will or won't do on her holiday in Spain?

Example
She will meet Carmen's family.
She won't go to school.

meet Carmen's family	eat English food
go to school	write some postcards
swim in the sea	do her homework
sunbathe on the beach	feel homesick
make new friends	go to a disco
learn Spanish	go skiing
stay in Madrid	work on the farm

3 Put these words in the correct order to make questions in the future simple.

stay   where   you   will   ....

right   will   he   all   be   ....

Complete this rule.

> To make questions in the future simple we put
>
> will .... the subject.

4 Look at the story on page 44 again. Here are Sue's answers. What were the questions?

Example
How will you travel to Spain?
By plane.

How ....?
I'll get the train.

How ....?
Vince and Terry will help me.

Where ....?
At Carmen's uncle's house in the country.

How long ....?
Three weeks.

What ....?
I'll sunbathe on the beach and visit lots of places. I'll have a great time.

FOLLOW UP

5 What will you do next weekend? Write six sentences about what you will do. Write six questions to ask your friend what he/she will do.

Example
I'll tidy my room.   Will you tidy your room?
I'll help my father.   Will you . . . ?

THINGS TO DO

☐ Tidy room
☐ Help father
☐ Wash car
☐ _____
☐ _____
☐ _____
☐ _____
☐ _____

47

READING

A long way to travel for your dinner

This reading activity has two aims:

a Students first look for specific information in the text. They probably won't understand everything when they do this. The activity will encourage them to tackle a difficult text. In each activity the students look for more information and so gradually build up a picture of the whole text.

b Students use the context they have established to work out the meanings of particular words (Exercise 5).

1
- Students look at the title and pictures.
- Elicit suggestions for what the text is about.
- Continue until someone suggests *migration* (in any language/words).

2
- Read questions **a–e** aloud.
- Give students one minute to read the text. Remind them that they do not need to understand every word. Say *Make a note of the answers.*
- Students look quickly through the text for the answers and note them down. (They should not use dictionaries.)
- Elicit answers.

> **Answer key**
> a *arctic tern*
> b *six inches/16 centimetres long (beak to tail)*
> c *flies from one end of the Earth to the other*
> d *over sea (mostly)*
> e *we don't know (but perhaps they use the sun, moon and stars as a compass)*

3 a
- Students look at the map.
- Students read the text carefully.
- They write the names on the map.
- In pairs, students compare answers.
- Check answers.

b
- Students draw the terns' routes on the map.

> **Note**
> If there is a world map or a globe in the classroom, use this for pointing out the routes and places.

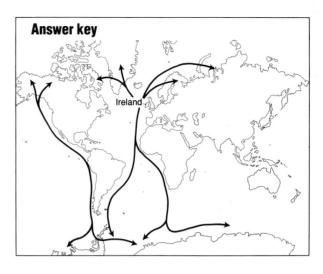

Answer key

Ireland

4
- Students read questions **a–g**.
- They write answers to the questions using full sentences.
- Check answers. Discuss as necessary.

> **Answer key**
> (possible answers)
> a *Terns can't spend winter in the Arctic because it is too cold and there is no food.*
> b *The terns fly to the Antarctic because it is summer there when it is winter in the Arctic.*
> c *A tern travels 24,000 miles (36,000 kilometres) in one year.*
> d *The Atlantic birds meet over the Atlantic Ocean, near Ireland.*
> e *One route is along the west coast of Africa. The other is along the east coast of South America.*
> f *The birds will not migrate in cloudy or foggy weather.*
> g *In its life, a tern travels as far as the moon and back.*

WORD WORK

5 **a**
- Draw students' attention to the chart.
- Students complete each list. All the words are in the text.
- In pairs, they compare answers.
- Elicit answers. Refer to the text, if necessary.
- Students complete their lists.

> ### Answer key
> *spring, summer, autumn, winter*
> *north, south, east, west*
> *Australasia, Europe, Africa, America, Asia, Antarctica*

b
- In pairs, students find other names for the Arctic and the Antarctic in the text.
- Elicit answers.

> ### Answer key
> *the North Pole   the South Pole*

'If' clauses

6 **a**
- Draw students' attention to the gapped sentence.
- Point out that it comes from the text.
- Students complete the sentence.

> ### Answer key
> *If the tern stays in the Arctic, it will die.*

b
- Students identify the tense in each clause.
- Elicit answers and compare with the mother tongue.

> ### Answer key
> *if* clause: *present simple tense*
> main clause: *future simple tense*

> ### Notes
> • The *meaning* of a first conditional sentence is to predict what, according to the speaker or writer, will happen in the future *if* something else (referred to in the *if* clause) happens.
>
> • When *if* is replaced by *when*, whatever is referred to in the *when* clause will definitely happen, and so the event referred to in the main clause will also definitely happen – again, according to the speaker or writer.
>
> • Clause order can be reversed with no change in sentence meaning, e.g. *If you're late, I'll go without you. I'll go without you if you're late.*
>
> • In writing, if the *if* clause comes second, we usually omit the comma.

7
- Say *We are now going to practise **if** sentences using these two tenses.*
- Students complete the sentences with the words in brackets.
- In pairs, students compare sentences.
- Check answers.

> ### Answer key
> **a** *If the birds live in Europe, they will travel over the Atlantic Ocean.*
> **b** *If the terns come from Alaska, they will fly along the Pacific coast.*
> **c** *If the weather is cloudy, the birds will not migrate.*
> **d** *If the birds cannot see the sun, they will not fly.*
> **e** *If you go to the Arctic in winter, you will not see any terns.*
> **f** *If the terns do not leave the Arctic, they will die.*
> **g** *If a tern lives for five years, it will travel 120,000 miles.*

EXTRA ACTIVITY
Quiz
- Students close their books and write down as many facts about the arctic tern as they can remember.
- In pairs, students combine lists and make a new list.
- Ask one student to read out his/her list.
- Ask if anyone has a longer list. Ask him/her to read it out.
- Continue until you find the pair with the most facts.

FOLLOW UP
8
- Draw students' attention to the instructions. Read them out.
- Students suggest other animals, fish or birds that migrate. Translate into English any suggestions made in the students' own language.
- Write these on the blackboard.
- Add others yourself.
- Each student chooses a bird/fish/animal which migrates.
- Advise about an encyclopaedia and other resources.
- Students find facts about the bird/fish/animal. They list them (in class or for homework).
- Students report their facts to the class.

READING

1 Look at the title and the picture. What do you think the text is about?

2 Look quickly through the text. Find answers to these questions.

a What is the name of the bird?

b How big is the bird?

c What does it do every year?

d Does it travel over land or over the sea?

e How does the bird do it?

Remember: You don't have to understand every word.

A long way to travel for your dinner

This is an arctic tern. It is not a very big bird. It is only about six inches (16 centimetres) from its bright red beak to its tail. But soon this small bird will begin an incredible journey. It will fly from one end of the Earth to the other – a journey of about 12,000 miles (18,000 kilometres).

The tern spends the summer in the Arctic, but it cannot spend the winter there. It is too cold and there is no food. If the tern stays in the Arctic, it will die. But when it is winter in the northern hemisphere, it is summer in the southern hemisphere. In autumn the arctic tern will leave the North Pole and fly south across the equator to the South Pole. When spring comes again in the northern hemisphere, the tern will return to the Arctic.

When the terns migrate, birds from Europe, America and Asia meet over the Atlantic Ocean near Ireland. From here some of the birds will fly along the west coast of Africa. Other terns will follow the east coast of South America. At the same time birds from Alaska will travel down the Pacific coast of America to Antarctica.

How do these small birds make this incredible journey? We don't know the answer. Perhaps they use the sun, the moon and the stars as a compass. If it is cloudy or foggy, the birds will not migrate. In its life, an arctic tern travels as far as the moon and back. That's a long way to travel for your dinner!

3 Look at the map. Now read the text carefully.

a Fill in these names.

the Arctic	the Pacific Ocean
the Antarctic	America
the equator	Europe
the Atlantic Ocean	Africa

b Draw the terns' routes on the map.

4 Answer these questions.

a Why can't the terns spend winter in the Arctic?

b Why do the terns fly to the Antarctic?

c How far does a tern travel in one year?

d Where do the Atlantic birds meet?

e What are the two Atlantic routes?

f Why do people think the birds use the sun, moon and stars to guide them?

g How far does a tern travel in its life?

Alaska

Ireland

Why do birds fly south in winter?

Because it's too far to walk.

WORD WORK

5 **a** Complete these lists.

> **the four seasons:**
>
> spring, ..., ..., ...
>
> **the four points of the compass:**
>
> north, ..., ...
>
> **the six continents:**
>
> Australasia, ..., ...
>
> ...., ..., ...

b Find other names for the Arctic and the Antarctic.

'If' clauses

6 **a** Complete this sentence from the text.

If the tern .... in the Arctic, it ....

b What tense is used in:

- the if clause?
- the main clause?

7 Complete these sentences with the verbs in brackets.

a If the birds .... in Europe, they .... over the Atlantic Ocean. (live/travel)

b If the terns .... from Alaska, they .... along the Pacific coast. (come/fly)

c If the weather .... cloudy, the birds .... (be/not migrate)

d If the birds .... see the sun, they .... (cannot/not fly).

e If you .... to the Arctic in winter, you .... any terns. (go/not see)

f If the terns .... the Arctic, they .... (not leave/die)

g If a tern .... for five years, it .... 120,000 miles. (live/travel)

FOLLOW UP

8 Use an encyclopaedia to find out about another bird, fish or animal that migrates, for example, the salmon or the African elephant. Write some interesting facts about it. Report your facts to the class.

LISTENING

A day at the seaside

- Revise the Victoria Road story on pages 44–5. Ask students question **a**.
- Elicit answer.
- Read **b**, **c**, **d** aloud.
- Tell students you are going to play the cassette. They listen for the answers. They should not worry if they don't understand every word.
- 📼 Play the cassette.
- Elicit answers.
- Rewind cassette.

Answer key

a *A trip to the seaside*
b *By train*
c *Ten past eight*
d *Buy the tickets*

- Students read the gapped conversation.
- Students guess what the missing words are.
- Elicit answers.
- Tell students you are going to play the cassette again.
- Say *As I play it, fill in the gaps. Some gaps need only one word, others need more than one.*
- Add that you will pause the cassette in several places.
- 📼 Play the cassette. Pause at the end of sentences containing gaps which require more than one word.
- Students fill in the gaps (or check their guesses).
- Play the cassette again, without pausing. Students check their answers.
- Students compare answers in pairs.
- Check answers.

📼 **A day at the seaside**

Terry Vince and the others can't come. They'll be at the airport with Sue.
Jackie Well, that's their hard luck. So it will be just <u>you and me</u>, Terry.
Terry What time <u>must</u> we meet?
Jackie The train goes at a <u>quarter</u> past <u>eight</u>. I'll <u>buy</u> the tickets today. Then we needn't be <u>at the</u> station too early.
Terry <u>How much will it</u> cost?
Jackie The fare will be <u>£9</u> return. You needn't come to the station. If you <u>give</u> me the money, I'll get the <u>tickets</u>.
Terry OK. So we <u>must</u> be at the station by <u>ten</u> past eight.

Jackie Yes. And remember I'll <u>have</u> your ticket. So, you mustn't <u>be</u> late. If you're late, <u>I'll</u> go <u>on my own</u>.
Terry Don't panic, Jack. I'll <u>be</u> there. <u>What time will we get home?</u>
Jackie The <u>last train</u> is at half past six. So we <u>mustn't</u> miss it. Oh, it'll be <u>great</u>. We'll <u>sunbathe on the beach</u>.
Terry We'll go <u>to</u> the fun fair. And we'll hire a <u>boat</u> and go sailing on the boating lake. <u>We'll have a really good time.</u>

must, mustn't, needn't

 a
- Students look at their completed dialogue between Jackie and Terry.
- They find the sentences containing *must*, *mustn't* and *needn't* and underline them.
- Check answers.

Answer key

*What time **must** we meet?*
*So we **must** be at the station before eight o'clock.*
*We **needn't** both go to the station.*
*So, you **mustn't** be late.*

---

b
- In pairs, students translate the sentences into their own language.
- Ask students how the English *must* and *mustn't* compare with how these ideas are expressed in their own language.
- Elicit ideas.
- Discuss and explain as necessary.

Answer key

must *means that doing something is compulsory*
mustn't *means that **not** doing something is compulsory*
needn't *means that something is not compulsory*

Notes

- *must* (and *mustn't*) are never followed by *to*, just by the verb.

- *must* has no past tense form – we say *had to* instead.

- *must* usually refers to an obligation one imposes on oneself (*I must*) or on other people (*you must*). When referring to an obligation imposed on oneself or another person *by* another person, we usually use *has/have to*.

• Students read questions **a–i**.

• Ask for *short* answers for each.

• Elicit answers.

Answer key

a *To the seaside*
b *A quarter past eight*
c *Ten past eight*
d *So they needn't be at the station too early tomorrow*
e *Go to the station*
f *£9*
g *Be late*
h *It's the last train back.*
i *Sunbathe on the beach, go to the funfair, and hire a boat and go sailing on the boating lake*

 • Read instruction from *We'll have ... to ... happen.*

• Read the example aloud.

a • Students have five minutes to write down what they think will go wrong (full sentences using the *will* form).

b • In pairs, students compare answers.

• Elicit suggestions. Do not comment on these!

6 • Tell students you are now going to play a cassette of what actually happened to Jackie and Terry.

• Say *Listen to see if you were right.*

• 🔲 Play the cassette.

• Ask who guessed what went wrong. Any student who *did* guess tells the class about the event.

• Elicit what else went wrong.

Answer key

Terry was late and they missed the eight fifteen train.
Jackie got sunburnt on her nose and back.
Terry felt sick because he went on the Octopus.
Terry fell in the boating lake.
Jackie lost the train tickets and they had to buy new ones.

🔲 At the station

Jackie Now we won't be there till eleven thirty.
Terry Look, I'm sorry. All right? I got up late.

On the beach

Terry Hey, Jack, you're all sunburnt. Your nose is bright red. Ha, ha.
Jackie It's not funny. It hurts. Ow. My back.
Terry Sorry, Jack.
Jackie And don't call me Jack. My name's Jackie.
Terry Sorry, Jack, I mean Jackie.

At the funfair

Jackie Whee, the Octopus was great. Let's go on it again.
Terry I think I'll sit on the beach. I feel sick.

On the boating lake

Terry Ahoy, there. This is Captain Blood and his pirate ship.
Jackie Don't do that. Sit down. You'll fall.
Terry No, I wooooooon't ...

At the station

Jackie But we bought tickets. I think I lost them in a cafe.
Ticket clerk I'm sorry, love, but you'll have to buy another ticket.

FOLLOW UP

 • Students read example.

• Students suggest how the second sentence continues.

Answer key

... Terry got up late and so they missed it.
or
... they missed it because Terry got up late.

• Students write the heading 'Terry and Jackie's day at the seaside'.

• They copy the first two sentences of the description under the heading.

• They continue the description of Terry and Jackie's day at the seaside in class or for homework.

Note

If necessary, revise irregular past tense forms before doing Exercise 7.

continued on T52

LISTENING

A day at the seaside

1 📼 **Listen to the conversation.**

a Where are Terry and Jackie going?

b How will they travel?

c What time must they meet?

d What will Jackie do later today?

2 **Listen again and complete the conversation.**

Terry Vince and the others can't come. They'll be at the airport with Sue.

Jackie Well, that's their hard luck. So it will be just ...., Terry.

Terry What time .... we meet?

Jackie The train goes at a .... past .... I'll .... the tickets today. Then we needn't be .... station too early.

Terry .... cost?

Jackie The fare will be ...... return. You needn't come to the station. If you .... me the money, I'll get the ....

Terry OK. So we .... be at the station by .... past eight.

Jackie Yes. And remember I'll .... your ticket. So, you mustn't .... late. If you're late, I .... go ....

Terry Don't panic, Jack. I'll .... there. ....?

Jackie The .... is at half past six. So we .... miss it. Oh, it'll be .... We'll ....

Terry We'll go .... the fun fair. And we'll hire a .... and go sailing on the boating lake. ....

50

must, mustn't, needn't

 3

a Find the sentences with these words.

must   mustn't   needn't

Underline them.

b Translate the sentences into your own language. Do you notice any differences? What do you notice about the meaning of 'must' and 'mustn't' in English?

 4 Answer these questions.

a Where are Terry and Jackie going?

b What time does the train leave?

c When must they be at the station?

d Why will they buy the tickets today?

e What needn't Terry do today?

f How much will the fare be?

g What mustn't Terry do tomorrow?

h Why mustn't they miss the half past six train back?

i What will they do at the seaside?

 5

We'll have a really good time.

The day at the seaside wasn't so great. Look at the pictures of the places on page 50. What do you think will happen?

a Write down your ideas.

Example
Terry will be late and they'll miss their train.

b Work in pairs. Compare your answers with your partner.

 6 Listen. What happened at the seaside? Were you right?

FOLLOW UP

 7 Describe Terry and Jackie's day at the seaside.

Example
Terry and Jackie bought their tickets the day before. They wanted to get the 8.15 train but . . .

INTERACTION

At the station

 1 Listen to the dialogue at the railway station.

 2 Now listen again and fill in the passenger's part.

Passenger ....

Ticket clerk Single or return?

Passenger ....

Ticket clerk That will be £18.

Passenger .... ?

Ticket clerk If you get the 10.54 train, you'll get to London at 14.14.

Passenger ....

 3 Work in pairs. Role play your dialogue with your partner.

4 Make dialogues for these situations. Use the timetable. You are in Lancaster.

Lancaster → London

Mondays to Saturdays		Sundays	
Lancaster depart	London Euston arrive	Lancaster depart	London Euston arrive
0534	0904	1509	1849
0625 **sx**	0945	1624	2014
0625 **so**	0945	1658	2044
0707	1016	1701	2044
0805	1135	1708	2103
0855	1204	1806	2206
0938 **sx**	1244	1942	2311
0948 **so**	1244	2258	0448
1054	1414		
1154	1437		
1221	1635		
1422	1748		
1625	1923		
1636	2011		
1725	2130		
1824	2140		
1923 **so**	2225		
1923 **sx**	2230	**so** saturday only	
2257 **sx**	0448	**sx** except saturday	

a You want to travel to London with two friends. You must be there by 10 pm.

b You want to travel to London. You needn't be there till 5 pm.

c You want to travel to London. You must meet someone at 12 o'clock. You mustn't be late.

d You want to travel to London. You are travelling with a friend. You must be there by 2 o'clock on Saturday.

FOLLOW UP

 5 Write two of your dialogues from Exercise 4.

continued from T51

INTERACTION

At the station

- Tell students they are now going to listen to a dialogue at a station.
- Tell them to listen carefully to the dialogue on the cassette.
- Play the cassette.
- Rewind the cassette.

- Students read the gapped dialogue.
- Say *Now, I'm going to play the cassette again. I'm not going to stop it, but I shall play it twice. You fill in the passenger's words.*
- Play the cassette twice. Students complete the dialogue.
- Play the cassette a third time. Students check their answers.

At the station
Passenger London, please.
Ticket clerk Single or return?
Passenger Single, please.
Ticket clerk That will be £18.00.
Passenger What time will I arrive in London?
Ticket clerk If you get the 10.54 train, you'll get to London at 14.14.
Passenger Thank you.

- Pairs role play the dialogue twice.
- Students change roles. Repeat.
- Choose one or two pairs to 'perform' their dialogue (from memory if they can).

- Draw students' attention to the timetable.
- Students read **a–d**.
- In pairs, students work out how to role play each dialogue. They use the information in the chart.
- Pairs role play **a–d**, changing roles, e.g. one student is the clerk in **a** and **c**, and the passenger in **b** and **d**.
- Select two pairs to perform each dialogue.
- Class listens carefully. Say *Make sure they get it right*.
- Students comment on the accuracy of the information.
- Give feedback on the performance of each dialogue.

- Students choose two of their dialogues and write them in their exercise books.

PROJECT

Your life

- Read each question aloud.
- Class brainstorms vocabulary for answering each question.
- List words on board.
- Give students two minutes to think about their answers.
- Briefly revise *will, will not, won't, 'll, won't* and *shall*.
- Use questions as a plan and write the plan on the board, e.g.
  Paragraph 1 Where will you go? **etc.**
- In class or for homework, students write four short paragraphs on 'My Dream Holiday'.
- Take work in and correct as necessary.
- Students write a second draft.
- Students collect some travel brochures and select pictures to illustrate their 'Dream Holiday'.

> **Note**
> Students may be able to get travel brochures from Travel Agents or Tourist Information Centres. If not, bring some brochures yourself. Alternatively, students can send for brochures or other travel information, using advertisements in newspapers or magazines. Magazine pictures, postcards and photographs can also be illustrations for 'Dream Holidays'. Students can draw or paint their illustrations themselves, too.

- Students cut out the pictures and stick them above, under or around their 'Dream Holiday' text.
- Display work. Students look at each other's work.
- Students put or stick their project into their project files.

▶ **Pronunciation: page T112**

LEARNING DIARY

- Students look back at the list on the first page of Unit 5.

A Students draw faces on the symbols to indicate how well they know each item.

B In class or for homework, students do the self-check exercises in the Workbook.

C In pairs, students compare answers.

Check answers.

Do not ask for numbers of correct answers, but do find out which exercises caused problems. Go over these again carefully. Refer students who are still puzzled or who are particularly interested to the appropriate section of a grammar book. Remind students that these exercises are not 'tests'. They are one way they can find out about their progress, and about what they need practice with.

D Students make a chart with two columns, with headings.

They list which parts they liked best in one column, and why they liked each part in the other column. Walk round the class while they are doing this.

In pairs, students compare charts.

Repeat in different pairs.

From what you have seen, tell the class what you think they liked. Ask for confirmation or otherwise. Also get modifications and reasons. These will give you insights into the activities students like, and into the language items your students find easy and which they find difficult.

CULTURE SPOT
Workbook page 45

- Divide the class into pairs or groups of three or four.
- Students look quickly at the text.
- Ask *What is the text about?*
- Students give their ideas.
- Ask *What do you already know about this topic?*
- Students give their ideas. Discuss these ideas.
- Say *Read the Culture Spot text. Note anything that you find interesting or unusual.*
- Ask comprehension questions about the text.
- Students give their ideas.
- Read each comparison question in turn.
- Discuss each question. Encourage students to compare their situation to the one in the text.

PROJECT
Your life

Make plans for your dream holiday. Think about these questions.

- Where will you go?
- Who will you go with?
- How will you travel?
- What will you do?

Make a holiday brochure. Describe your holiday.

- Where will you go and what will you do?
- Where will you stay?
- What will your travel itinerary be?

Collect some travel brochures and find some pictures for your own brochure.

Learning diary

Look at the list on the first page of this unit.

5

A How well do you know each thing? Complete the circles to make faces.

B Try the self-check in the Workbook.

C Compare your self-check answers with a partner's. Do you understand everything? If you don't understand something, look in a grammar book or ask your teacher.

D What did you like best in this unit? Why?

6 problems

the past continuous

Contents

Victoria Road: Kamala's story   54
Language work: The past continuous tense   56
Reading: The brave village   58
Listening: The cat   60
Interaction: My scar   62
Project: A newspaper story   62

Language work 😊 😐 🙁

Grammar

the past continuous tense - statements
I was putting some things on the shelves.
They were walking in the fields.

- negatives
They weren't really doing anything.
He wasn't looking.

- questions
What were you doing?
Was she reading a magazine?

the past continuous and the past simple
As I was rescuing the cat, it scratched me.
When the cat scratched me, I dropped it.

Word work

disease

somebody, anybody, etc.

😊 😐 🙁 Learning objectives

In this unit you will learn how to:

tell a story

ask about a story

describe an historical event

talk about an event in your life

UNIT 6 Problems

VICTORIA ROAD

Kamala's story

- Ask *What happened in 'Victoria Road' in Unit 5?*
- Elicit ideas.
- If students are not sure, they look back at pages 44 and 45.

> **Answer key**
> *Sue went to Spain to stay with her penfriend Carmen.*
> *Jackie and Terry went to the seaside and had a terrible time.*

- Say *Now we're going to have a look at the next part of 'Victoria Road'. Look at it **quickly** and look at the pictures. Then answer these questions.*
- Read the two questions aloud.
- Students look at the story and the pictures.
- Stop them after one minute.
- Ask *Who are the people?*
- Elicit answer.

> **Answer key**
> *Kamala and Sue.*

- Ask *What are they talking about?*
- Elicit answer.

> **Answer key**
> *They're talking about Terry and Jackie. Terry tried to shoplift some cigarettes for Jackie.*

- Ask *What does **shoplift** mean?*
- Elicit answer.

> **Answer key**
> *steal from a shop*

- Students look at the picture story again. Ask *What do you think happens in this episode?*
- Students give their ideas.

> **Answer key**
> (possible answer)
> *Sue has just got back from her holiday. She meets Kamala. Kamala tells her Terry tried to steal some cigarettes from her parents' shop. Sue is very upset.*

> **Notes**
> **How are things here?** Sue means 'What's been happening here while I've been away?' (What she probably *really* means is 'What's been happening between Terry and Jackie?')
>
> **Don't talk to me about him** (i.e. *Terry*). Sue means she doesn't want to hear about Terry as she is annoyed with him.
>
> **You know who.** Kamala means *Jackie*. This expression suggests that they don't really like Jackie *and* that there is something secret happening – as there is.
>
> **Yes and no** means 'In one way yes, and in another way no'. Kamala means that, yes, he was *trying* to take them, but also no, because he did not succeed.
>
> **He went bright red** means 'he blushed'. Terry went bright red because he was very embarrassed when Kamala saw him try to take the cigarettes.
>
> **shoplifting** means 'stealing things from a shop'.
>
> **It serves him right** means 'he deserves the trouble he's in'. Sue means that if Terry is getting into trouble because of Jackie, it's his own fault.
>
> - Cigarettes are more expensive in Britain than in many other European countries.
> - It is illegal for shopkeepers to sell cigarettes to people under the age of 16.

3 • Say *Now listen to the cassette carefully and follow the story in your books.*

• Play the cassette. Students listen and read.

• Rewind the cassette.

• Read aloud the questions at the bottom of the conversation.

• Ask each question in turn and elicit ideas.

Answer key

Terry was stealing cigarettes for Jackie.

• *Perhaps she asked him to.*
• *Perhaps she 'dared' him to.*
• *Perhaps Terry wanted to impress Jackie.*

Sue feels upset and disappointed. She thought Terry was honest.

• *She knows Terry is lazy but she doesn't think he is a thief.*
• *She secretly likes Terry, and so she is disappointed with his behaviour.*
• *She feels Jackie is a bad influence on Terry. And she now knows Terry must really like Jackie.*
• *Terry was trying to steal from her best friend's parents' shop.*
• *She feels jealous because Terry was stealing the cigarettes for Jackie.*
• *She is worried that Terry may get into serious trouble.*

Kamala and Sue can:

• *talk to Terry (after all, Terry knows Kamala saw him trying to take the cigarettes).*
• *talk to Jackie.*
• *try to get him away from Jackie.*
• *tell Terry's parents.*

---

4 • Students read statements **a–j**.

• Students tick one box next to each statement to indicate whether the statement is right, wrong, or that they don't know.

• In pairs, students compare answers.

• Check answers.

• Students justify their answers.

Answer key

a D	b W	c W	d W	e R	f R
g D	h R	i W	j D		

---

5 • Say *Now I'm going to play the cassette again. Listen carefully. You should understand most of it now. Close your books.*

• Play the cassette. Students listen carefully.

Kamala's story

1 What do you remember? What happened in the last part of the story? Look back at pages 44 and 45. Check your ideas.

2 Look at this episode. Who are the people? What are they talking about?

3 Listen and follow in your books.

Kamala Hi, Sue. Did you have a good time in Spain?

Sue It was great! I had a wonderful time. How are things here?

Kamala Well, all right, but . . .

Sue But what?

Kamala Well, it's Terry.

Sue Huh! Don't talk to me about him. He didn't come to the airport with me. He went to the seaside with that Jackie.

Kamala That's the problem – Jackie. Jackie and Terry came into our shop last Saturday. I was putting some things on the shelves. So they didn't see me. Well, they were in the shop for a long time.

Sue What were they doing?

Kamala They weren't really doing anything. Jackie was reading the magazines and Terry was looking at the cigarettes.

Sue Cigarettes? Terry doesn't smoke.

Kamala No, but you know who does.

Sue Go on, what happened?

Kamala After about ten minutes, Jackie asked my father for something. While Dad wasn't looking, Terry picked up some packets of cigarettes and put them in his pocket.

Sue No! Was he stealing them?

Kamala Yes and no. You see, as he was taking them, he saw me.

Sue What did he do?

Kamala When he saw me, he went bright red. He put the cigarettes back and then they both left the shop.

Speech bubble: I had a wonderful time.

Speech bubble: Hi, Sue. Did you have a good time in Spain?

Sue Oh, I don't believe it. Terry was shoplifting – and for *her*, too. Well, it serves him right.

Kamala Do you really mean that, Sue?

Sue No, Kam, I don't. Oh, poor Terry. He's such an idiot.

Kamala Oh, Sue. Don't cry.

What do you think?

● Why was Terry stealing cigarettes?
● How does Sue feel?
● What can Kamala and Sue do?

Right, Wrong or Don't know?

	✓	✗	?
a Sue got back from Spain last night.	❑	❑	❑
b Terry went to the airport with Sue.	❑	❑	❑
c Terry and Jackie went to the seaside last Saturday.	❑	❑	❑
d Kamala wasn't working in the shop when Jackie and Terry came in.	❑	❑	❑
e Terry was standing next to the cigarettes.	❑	❑	❑
f Jackie smokes.	❑	❑	❑
g Terry picked up three packets of cigarettes.	❑	❑	❑
h Kamala was watching Terry.	❑	❑	❑
i Terry left the shop on his own.	❑	❑	❑
j Kamala told her father that Terry was shoplifting.	❑	❑	❑

5 Close your book. Listen again.

Useful expressions

- Students read 'Useful expressions'.
- Say *Write down how you think you say each expression in our/your language. If you're not sure of the meaning of any of the expressions, go back to the story and work out the meaning from the situation.*
- Students write the first language equivalent next to each English phrase or sentence.
- In pairs, students compare charts.
- Check answers. For each one, ask a student who got it right to explain *how* they arrived at the answer. Students correct and amend their charts as necessary.

- In pairs, students decide who plays each role.
- Pairs role play the dialogue.
- Students change roles and repeat.

FOLLOW UP

- Say *On Saturday evening, after Terry and Jackie had been in Kamala's parents' shop, Kamala wrote her diary.*
- Students fill in the gaps in the diary.

Answer key

came	putting	see	for	weren't
was	magazines	at	doesn't	
minutes	for	up	cigarettes	
putting	pocket	saw	bright	put
left	believe	shoplifting		was stealing
for	can			

LANGUAGE WORK

The past continuous tense

BUILD UP

- Read aloud the example.
- Students look for more examples of the past continuous tense in the story.
- Elicit examples.

Answer key
I was putting some things on the shelves.
What were they doing?
They weren't really doing anything.
Jackie was reading the magazines.
Terry was looking at the cigarettes.
While Dad wasn't looking …
Was he stealing them?
as he was taking them …
Terry was shoplifting …

Note
Accept the two examples in which the past continuous is used in a *question* but do not press students to suggest these.

- Students complete the table. (While they are doing this, copy the table onto the blackboard.)

Note
There should be positive, negative and short forms in the second column.

- In pairs, students compare answers.
- Elicit answers. Write these on your table on the blackboard. (Alternatively, a student can fill it in.)

Answer key

I		reading a book.
He	was	
She	was	looking in a shop window.
It	wasn't	watching television.
		putting something on the shelf.
We	were	
You	were not	crossing the street.
They	weren't	writing a letter.

- Students turn back to the picture on page 36.
- Remind them they have already talked about this picture.
- Students close their books.
- Students read the example.
- In pairs, students open *one* book at the picture.
- Students look at the picture together and memorize what the people are doing.
- After one minute, say *Close the book.*
- Say *Now, who can tell me what someone was doing?*
- Elicit one answer from a volunteer and write it on the board. *This should be a full sentence in the past continuous tense.*
- In pairs, students write down everything they can remember about who was doing what, using the past continuous tense.
- Each pair compares their list with another pair. They find out which pair remembered the most activities.
- Find out which pair out of the whole class remembered the most activities.
- One member of the 'winning' pair reads out their list of activities. Rest of the class listens carefully.
- Ask if any pairs remembered any additional activities, and elicit these.

Answer key

(possible answers)

A man was washing up in the kitchen.
A girl with long hair was carrying a record.
Some children were watching 'Black Beauty' on TV.
A woman was ironing a shirt.
A woman was making a telephone call.
Some men were carrying a settee into the house.
A baby was playing under the table.
A dog was eating a bone.
A girl was writing a letter.
A boy was riding a bicycle.
Two girls were coming out of the house.
A boy was cleaning his teeth.
An old man was drinking tea.
A man was cleaning the windows.

Answer key

What were you doing?
What were Jackie and Terry doing in the shop?
What was Jackie reading?
What was Terry looking at?
What were your parents doing?
Where was Terry putting the cigarettes?
Why wasn't your father looking?
What were they talking about?
Why was Terry stealing the cigarettes?

 4 a • Students look for the two past continuous questions in the story. They are:
What were they doing?
and
Was he stealing them?

    • Students rearrange the two groups of words to make a statement and a question for each.

    • They write these in the table.

    • In pairs, students compare tables.

    • Check answers.

Answer key

He was stealing the cigarettes.
Was he stealing the cigarettes?
They were reading the magazines.
Were they reading the magazines?

b • Students complete the rule.

    • Check answers carefully.

Answer key

To make questions in the past continuous, we put **was** *or* **were** *in front of the subject.*

 5 • Students look at Exercise 5.

    • Read the examples aloud.

    • Ask one student to do the next example.

    • Students make the questions.

    • Check answers (i.e. questions!).

    • In pairs, students role play the dialogue.

 6 • Read example aloud.

    • Students give the questions.

Answer key

(See Exercise 7 below.)

FOLLOW UP

 7 • Students write full questions and answers for Exercise 6.

Answer key

a *What was the man in the kitchen doing?*
   He was washing up.

b *What was the girl with long hair carrying?*
   She was carrying a record.

c *What (film) were the children watching?*
   They were watching 'Black Beauty'.

d *What was the woman in the kitchen ironing?*
   She was ironing a shirt.

e *What was the woman in the hall doing?*
   She was making a telephone call.

f *What were the two men carrying?*
   They were carrying a settee into the house.

g *Where was the baby playing?*
   It was playing under the table.

h *What was the dog eating?*
   It was eating a bone.

i *What was the girl writing?*
   She was writing a letter.

j *What was the boy on the bicycle wearing?*
   He was wearing red trousers.

Useful expressions

 How do you say these expressions in your language?

How are things here?	
Don't talk to me about …	
You know who does.	
He went bright red.	
He was shoplifting.	
It serves him right.	
Do you really mean that?	
He's such an idiot.	

 a Work in pairs. Each person takes one of the parts.

b Role play the dialogue.

FOLLOW UP

8 Complete Kamala's diary.

Saturday

Terry and Jackie .... into our shop today. I was .... some things on the shelves. So they didn't .... me. They were in the shop .... a long time, but they .... really doing anything. Jackie .... reading the .... and Terry was looking .... the cigarettes. That was strange, because Terry .... smoke. After about ten .... , Jackie asked my father .... something. While he was talking to Jackie, Terry picked .... some packets of .... As he was .... them in his ...., he .... me. He went .... red and he .... the cigarettes back. Then they both .... I couldn't .... it. Terry was .... He .... cigarettes .... Jackie. What .... I do?

LANGUAGE WORK

The past continuous tense

BUILD UP

1 Look at this sentence.

> I **was** putt**ing** some things on the shelves.

We call this the past continuous tense. It describes a continuous activity in the past. Find more sentences like this in the story.

 Complete this table.

I	was	reading a book.
He		
She	....	look...... in a shop window.
It	wasn't	
		watch...... television.
We	......	put...... something on the shelf.
You	were not	cross...... the street
They	......	writ...... a letter.

3 Test your memory.

a Work in pairs. Look at the picture on page 36 for one minute.

b Close the book. What were the people in the picture doing? Write down everything you can remember.

> Example
> *A man was washing up in the kitchen.*

c Compare your list to another pair's. Who remembered the most activities?

 a Put these words into the correct order to make a statement and a question.

	statement	question
cigarettes the was stealing he		
magazines reading they were the		

56

b Complete this rule.

To make questions in the past continuous
we put .... or .... in front of the
subject.

5 Make Sue's questions to complete the
dialogue. Use the cues provided.

Example
Sue *What were you doing?*
(What/you/do)
Kamala I was putting things on the shelves.

Sue Tell me about it again, Kamala.
....?
(What/you/do)
Kamala I was putting things on the shelves.

Sue ....?
(What/Jackie and Terry/do/in the shop)
Kamala They weren't really doing anything.

Sue ....?
(What/Jackie/read)
Kamala A magazine.

Sue ....?
(What/Terry/look at)
Kamala The cigarettes.

Sue ....?
(What/your parents/do)
Kamala My mum wasn't in the shop and my dad
was serving a customer.

Sue ....?
(Where/Terry/put/the cigarettes)
Kamala In his pocket.

Sue ....?
(Why/your father/not look)
Kamala He was talking to Jackie.

Sue ....?
(What/they/talk about)
Kamala Jackie was asking him for something.

Sue ....?
(Why/Terry/steal/the cigarettes)
Kamala I don't know, Sue.

6 Here are some answers about the picture on
page 36. What were the questions.

Example
What was the man in the kitchen doing?
washing up

a .... ?
washing up

b .... ?
a record

c .... ?
Black Beauty

d .... ?
a shirt

e .... ?
making a telephone call

f .... ?
a settee

g .... ?
under the table

h .... ?
a bone

i .... ?
a letter

j .... ?
red trousers

FOLLOW UP

7 Write the answers to Exercise 6 in full.

Example
What was the man in the kitchen doing?
He was washing up.
What was the girl with long hair carrying?
She was carrying a record.

My brother's in prison.
Why? What did he do?
He threw a policeman's helmet into the river.
That's not very serious.
No, but the policeman was still wearing it.

57

READING

The brave village

> **Note**
> This is a true story.

- Ask students if they know any fatal diseases which spread to large numbers of people in the past, either in their own or another country.
- Tell students they are going to read about such a disease.
- Students read questions **a–d**.
- Read questions aloud.
- Say *Look through the text quickly to find the answers. Don't read every word, and don't worry about words you don't understand. I'll stop you after two minutes!*
- Students look through the text quickly. Time them carefully. After two minutes say *Stop*.
- Elicit answers.

> **Answer key**
> a *Eyam.*
> b *A tailor received a parcel from London which carried the plague.*
> c *They stayed in the village.*
> d *262 people.*

- Read aloud the four names.
- In their exercise books, on a clean page, students write the four names down the left hand side, spacing them equally from the top to the bottom of the page.
- Students underline the names.
- They read the text again, and write down three facts about each person under the name of that person.
- In pairs, students compare answers.
- Elicit as many answers for each name as you can.

> **Answer key**
> (possible answers)
> **George Viccars**
> *He was a tailor.*
> *He received a parcel of cloth from London.*
> *He died from the plague a few days later.*
>
> **William Mompesson**
> *He was the vicar of Eyam.*
> *He told people to stay in Eyam.*
> *His wife's name was Katherine.*
> *He survived the plague, and lived for 44 years after his wife died.*
>
> **Emmott Sydall**
> *She was a girl from Eyam.*
> *She had a sweetheart in the next village.*
> *She died from the plague in 1666.*
> *Most of her family also died from the plague.*
>
> **Katherine Mompesson**
> *She was married to William Mompesson, the vicar of Eyam.*
> *She helped the villagers when their relatives died.*
> *She died from the plague in 1666.*

- Put students into groups of three or four.
- Students read the questions.
- Ask one student *What would you do?*
- Each group discusses the questions for five minutes.
- A spokesperson from each group reports to the class what the group would do.
- Write the different possibilities on the board.
- Find out which of these would be most popular. Count the number of individuals who would do each.
- Tell the class what you would do.

- Students read the example and the 'short form' answers.
- Point out that the questions and answers are all about George Viccars.
- Say *Now, decide what the other questions are. You will have to go back to the text to find the answers. There is more than one possible question for each answer.*
- Students decide what questions were asked and write these down.
- In pairs, students compare questions.
- Elicit questions. (Do not stop after one correct answer.)

T58

Answer key

(possible answers)

a *What was George Viccars' job?*
b *Where did he live?*
c *What did he receive?*
d *Where did it come from?*
e *What was in it?*
f *What did he do with the cloth?*
g *Why did he hang it in front of the fire?*
h *What happened the next day?*
i *When did he die?*
j *What were on his face and body?*

5 • Read the instructions aloud.

• Read **a** aloud.

• Draw students' attention to the answer to **a**, in the example.

• Students note down the speaker(s) in **a–f** and what he/she/they were doing when they said these words.

• Elicit answers.

Answer key

b *Rowland and Emmott Sydall.*
   They were calling to each other.
c *Someone from another village.*
   They were leaving clothes for the people of Eyam and taking the money.
d *George Viccars, the tailor.*
   He was hanging the cloth from London in front of the fire.
e *Rich people from Eyam.*
   They were leaving Eyam.
f *The doctor in Eyam and Mrs Viccars.*
   He was examining George Viccars.

W O R D   W O R K

6 a • Students read the story again and list all the words which have something to do with *disease*.

• In pairs, students compare lists.

• Elicit words. List these on the blackboard.

• Students add words to their lists.

• For homework, students learn the words.

Answer key

(possible words)

ill	died	purple ring(s)	plague
dying	doctors	cure	medicine
dead	sign		

---

b • Students look at the gapped lists of words headed:

   somebody   something   somewhere

• Students look back at the story and dialogues. They find words to complete the lists.

Answer key

somebody	something	somewhere
everybody	everything	everywhere
anybody	anything	anywhere
nobody	nothing	nowhere

• Students give examples from the story and dialogues with these words, e.g.
  Doctors could not help anybody.
  Everybody must stay in the village.

FOLLOW UP

7 • Read out the instructions and beginning of the story.

• Elicit suggestions for how the second sentence could continue.

• In class or for homework, students write the story from the point of view of William Mompesson. Tell them to consider *paragraph organization* carefully.

Rhyme

• Read the rhyme aloud.

• Explain that: *o'* is a short, old-fashioned, form of *of*; *posies* are small bunches of flowers; *atishoo* is a sound which represents a sneeze.

• Ask *What do you think 'We all fall down' refers to?*

• Elicit ideas.

• Ask what the *ring of roses* was.

• Elicit ideas.

Answer key

We all fall down: *people dying*
Ring of roses: *the purple rings on the victims' bodies*

1 Look at these questions.

a What is the name of the village?

b What happened there in 1665?

c What did the villagers do?

d How many people died?

Look through the text quickly and find the answers.

The brave village

GEORGE VICCARS was a tailor in the Derbyshire village of Eyam. One day in September 1665, he received a parcel from London. The cloth in the parcel was damp, so George Viccars hung it in front of the fire. The next day Viccars was very ill and a few days later he died. There were large purple rings on his face and his body.

In London, thousands of people were dying from the plague. Now the terrible disease was outside the city, too. Nowhere was safe.

When they heard the news a few rich people left Eyam, but the other people stayed. 'Everybody must stay in the village,' said the local vicar William Mompesson. In the next 13 months nobody left Eyam and 262 of the 350 villagers died. But the disease did not spread to other places.

People from other villages brought food, clothes and medicine to places near Eyam. The people from Eyam collected the things and left money there. They left the money in small holes full of vinegar.

One girl from Eyam, Emmott Sydall, had a sweetheart in the next village. When the plague started, they couldn't meet each other. Every evening they came to a place between their villages and called to each other. Then one evening in spring 1666 Rowland waited and waited, but Emmott did not arrive. Rowland came back to the place every evening, but he never saw Emmott again. She, her father, brother and three sisters were dead.

The vicar of Eyam and his wife, Katherine, helped the villagers when their relatives died. One evening in August 1666, Mompesson and his wife were walking in the fields. Katherine said she could smell something sweet. This was the first sign of the plague. A few days later Katherine died. Mompesson, himself, lived for another 44 years.

 2 Read the text and find three facts about each of these people.

- George Viccars
- William Mompesson
- Emmott Sydall
- Katherine Mompesson

 3 What do you think about the people of Eyam? Imagine something like this in your town. What would you do?

4 Here are some answers about George Viccars. What were the questions?

Example
What was George Viccars' job?
He was a tailor.

a .... ?
He was a tailor.

b .... ?
In the Derbyshire village of Eyam.

c .... ?
A parcel.

d .... ?
From London.

e .... ?
Cloth.

f .... ?
He hung it in front of the fire.

g .... ?
Because it was damp.

h .... ?
He was very ill.

i .... ?
A few days later.

j .... ?
Large purple rings.

5 Look at the dialogues. Then read the story again and answer these questions.

• Who said it?
• What were they doing when they said it?

Example
Katherine Mompesson said it.
She was walking in the fields with her husband.

a The flowers smell very sweet this evening. Aren't they beautiful?

b Are you there, my love? Can you hear me?

Yes, I'm here. I miss you so much. When will we meet again?

I don't know. The plague is still in the village.

c Put the clothes over there and take the money. But wash it in vinegar first. Quickly.

d Hmmm, it's a bit damp, but if I hang it here it'll be dry in the morning.

e Quickly. Leave everything. Are the horses ready? Come on, hurry up. If we stay here, we'll get the plague.

f Look at those spots. I can't do anything for him, Mrs Viccars. It's . . .

No, it can't be.

Yes, it is. It's the plague.

Oh no! Lord have mercy. No.

W O R D   W O R K

6 a Find all the words in the story connected with 'disease'.

b Find the missing words in the story and the dialogues.

somebody	something	somewhere
....	....	everywhere
anybody	....	anywhere
....	nothing	....

FOLLOW UP

7 Imagine you are William Mompesson. Tell his story. Begin like this:

It all began in September 1665. George Viccars, our local tailor, received . . .

This is a rhyme about the plague. Today children sing it.
What do you think the 'ring of roses' was?

Ring-a-ring o' roses
A pocket full of posies
Atishoo! Atishoo!
We all fall down.

LISTENING

The cat

1. • Point out the title *The cat*.
   • Students look at the pictures.
   • Say *For each picture, decide who you can see, where they are and what they are doing.*
   • Students look at the pictures for about two minutes.
   • Elicit ideas about questions **a–c** for each picture.

2. a • Say *These pictures make a complete story, but they're in the wrong order. What should the order be?*
   • Students decide on the correct order of the pictures.
   • In pairs, students compare their orders.

> **Note**
> This story describes an authentic British situation! Many people have cats as pets, and they do sometimes climb trees and are unable to get down. Occasionally their owners cannot get them down and the fire brigade has to come with their ladders to 'rescue' the cat.

   • Students give their ideas. Don't say whether they are right or wrong.
   b • Draw students' attention to the empty space.
   • In their pairs, students think about what picture should go in the space.
   • Elicit suggestions.

3. • Say *I'm now going to play a cassette of the story. Listen carefully and put a number by each picture to show where it comes in the story.*
   • Add *You may find a few **differences** between what you hear on the tape and what you see in the pictures. Don't worry about these **yet**!*
   a • Play the cassette.
   • Students listen to the dialogue and number the pictures.
   b • In their pairs, students compare orders. They also compare these with their previous orders.
   • Elicit order.

> **Answer key**
> The pictures should be numbered:
> 6 1 8 7 4 10 9 5 3 2

 The cat

Mother Hello, Mum. What are you doing in the garden?
Peter Hello, Gran.
Carol What's wrong, Gran?
Grandma It's Timmy. He's up in that tree and he won't come down.
Father Don't worry. We'll get him down. Have you got a ladder?
Grandma Yes, it's in the garage.
Father Come on, Peter. Up you go.
Peter Why me? Why can't Carol go up?
Carol I can't climb up there. I'm wearing my new dress.
Mother Come on, Peter. Be a hero. Your Dad will hold the ladder.
Peter Oh, why must I? It's only a cat.
Father It's your Grandma's cat. Now go on. But be careful.
Carol Oooh, be careful, Pete. Don't fall.
Mother Oh, he's got it. Come on down now.
Peter Ow. The blooming thing scratched my face. Oh no.
Carol Look out.
Mother He's falling. Hold the ladder.
Father I am holding the ladder.
Mother Oh Peter. Are you all right?
Peter I think so. No. My arm. I've hurt my arm. Where's that cat? I'll kill it.
Carol He ran under the car. Poor thing.
Father We must take Peter to the hospital. Come on. Get in the car.
Carol Stop. The cat's under the car.
Peter Aaaargh. My arm.
Father What?
Mother Look out.
Grandma There, there, Timmy. Were you frightened?

Voice over tannoy The Robinson family, please.

4. a • Say *You may already have noticed the mistakes in the pictures. Three of them don't fit with the cassette. Now, I'll play the cassette again. Find the three mistakes.*
   • Play the cassette. Students listen carefully for the three mistakes in the pictures.
   • Elicit mistakes.

> **Answer key**
> *In the pictures:*
> *The girl is wearing jeans, not a dress.*
> *When the boy climbs the ladder, his mother holds it, not his father.*
> *The cat bites the boy's finger. It doesn't scratch the boy's face.*

T60

b
  - In pairs, students discuss whether their original idea about the missing picture is correct.
  - Elicit ideas about the missing picture.
  - Continue until you get the correct answer.

> **Answer key**
> *Family at hospital*

  - Students draw the missing picture in the space.

The past continuous and the past simple

BUILD UP

 5
  - Students turn back to *Victoria Road* on page 54.
  - Students look at the picture of Kamala, Jackie and Terry in the shop.
  - Point out that Kamala is continuing to do something, whereas Jackie and Terry have just done something.

a
  - Students complete the gapped sentence with verbs in the correct forms.
  - Elicit answer.

> **Answer key**
> *While Kamala was putting some things on the shelves, Terry and Jackie came in.*

  - Ask students what the two different tenses in the sentence are.

> **Answer key**
> was putting: *past continuous*
> came: *past simple*

  - Point out *Notice the difference …* and read the five following lines aloud.

b
  - Students complete the rule.
  - Check answers.

> **Answer key**
> *We use the past continuous for a continuous activity. We use the past simple for a completed activity.*

c
  - Students use the rule to complete the two sentences. They should leave two lines between the sentences.
  - Check answers.

> **Answer key**
> *While Kamala's father was not (or **wasn't**) looking, Terry picked up some packets of cigarettes.*
> *As Terry was putting the cigarettes in his pocket, he saw Kamala.*

d
  - Students translate these two sentences into their first language.
  - They write the translations under the English sentences.
  - In pairs, students compare translations.
  - Students decide whether the tenses in the two languages are the same or different.
  - Elicit ideas and comment yourself.

e
  - Students complete the two sentences.
  - In pairs, they compare answers.
  - Check answers.

> **Answer key**
> *When Terry **saw** Kamala, he **went** bright red. He **put** the cigarettes back and then he and Jackie both **left** the shop.*

  - Ask *Why are all the verbs in the past simple?*
  - In pairs, students discuss the reasons.
  - Elicit answer.

> **Answer key**
> *All the activities are completed. None is still continuing when the other happens.*

FOLLOW UP

6
  - Students read the list of verbs and the gapped passage.
  - Say *You are now going to write 'The Cat' from Peter's point of view. Use the gapped passage and the verbs above it. Some verbs will be past simple and others will be past continuous.*
  - Students complete the story.
  - Check answers.

> **Answer key**
> was looking   was crying   was sitting
> fetched   was wearing   went   got
> was coming   scratched   fell   hurt
> ran   got   were driving   remembered
> was lying   grabbed   screamed   crashed

LISTENING

The cat

 Look at the pictures.

a Who is in each picture?

b Where are they?

c What are they doing?

 a **Put the pictures in order to make a story.**

b **What do you think the empty space shows?**

 Listen to the dialogue on the tape.

a Number the pictures in the correct order.

b Compare this order to your own ideas.

 Listen again.

a Find three mistakes in the pictures.

b Draw the picture for the last space.

The past continuous and the past simple

BUILD UP

 Look at the Victoria Road story.

a Complete this sentence.

While Kamala ....

some things on the shelves, Terry and

Jackie .... in.

- What are the two tenses used?
- Notice the difference.

Kamala was putting some things
a continuous activity
on the shelves.

Terry and Jackie came in.
a completed activity

b Complete this rule.

> We use the 'past continuous' for a ....
> activity.
> We use the 'past simple' for a .... activity.

c Now complete these sentences using the verbs in brackets in their correct form.

While Kamala's father .... , Terry

.... some packets of cigarettes.

(not look/pick up)

As Terry .... the cigarettes in his

pocket, he .... Kamala. (put/see)

d Translate the sentences into your language. Are the tenses the same or different?

e Complete these sentences.

When Terry .... Kamala, he .... bright

red. He .... the cigarettes back and then

he and Jackie both .... the shop.

Why are all the verbs in the past simple?

FOLLOW UP

 Use the following verbs to complete the story of the cat.

hurt   fetch   look   get   scream   run   crash
cry   wear   get   sit   remember   come   go
lie   fall   grab   scratch   drive

Last Saturday we visited Grandma. When we

arrived she was in the garden. She .... into a

tree and she .... Her cat .... in the tree.

Dad .... a ladder. Carol said she couldn't climb

the tree, because she .... her new dress. So I

.... up the ladder and I .... the cat. But, as

I .... down, the cat .... me. I

.... off the ladder and I .... my arm. The

cat .... under the car. We all .... into the

car. But as we .... away, Carol .... the cat.

It .... under the car. She .... my arm and I

.... Dad was so surprised that he .... the

car.

INTERACTION

- Students read the story.
- Ask *What's the word for* **scar** *in your (our) first language?*
- Elicit answer.

- Students read the example questions.
- Tell them to think of two or three more questions about people's scars. 'The Cat' will give them some ideas.
- Elicit some further questions.

> **Answer key**
> (possible questions)
> *Did you cry?*
> *Did it hurt?*
> *Did you go to hospital?*

- In pairs, students try to find out as much as possible about the other person's scar by asking as many questions as possible. They note down the answers.
- Repeat, with different pairs.

- One student reports to the class what he or she has found out about the other person's scar.
- Repeat with three or four more students.

FOLLOW UP

- In class or for homework, students write the story of one of their own scars.

> **Note**
> This story can be as short as the story in **1**, or a little longer. Stories of two paragraphs could be organized as follows:
> Paragraph 1: *How I got the scar*
> Paragraph 2: *What happened then*

PROJECT

Your life

- Students read newspaper headlines.
- Class brainstorms what each of the headlines refers to, e.g. *Who or what could be rescued? In what way could someone 'save the day'?*
- List these ideas on the board.
- Students choose one of the headlines and decide whether to write a story about: **a** an exciting rescue to do with their own life; or **b** an exciting rescue from the news.

a
- Students note down facts: *Who? Where were they? What were they doing? What happened?*
- Remind students that newspaper articles usually have several short paragraphs. Each paragraph contains a new point.

b
- Students write the story in their exercise books.
- Take in work and correct as before, i.e. for organization and clarity as well as grammar, punctuation and spelling.
- Students rewrite their newspaper story correctly.
- Students illustrate their stories with one or two pictures.
- Display the stories.
- After two or three days, students put their stories into their project file.

▶ **Pronunciation: page T112**

LEARNING DIARY

- Students turn to the first page of Unit 6.

A They draw faces on the symbols to indicate how well they know each thing.

B In class or for homework, they do the self-check exercises in the Workbook.

C In class, in pairs, students compare answers. Check answers.

Note
If students have got any answers wrong, try not to let them feel discouraged. However, students should realize *why* they are wrong. They should also know that they can learn from their mistakes. Encourage students to *ask* for further information or explanation when they feel they need it.

Refer students to the appropriate pages of a pedagogic grammar if they are still confused, or if they are interested in knowing more about past continuous and past simple verb forms.

D Through class discussion, elicit what students liked best in this unit, and why.

Note
This will give you useful feedback about what students like to learn and the way they prefer to learn it. However, *you* will have to decide if what they say is *useful* in terms of language learning!

CULTURE SPOT
Workbook page 53

- Divide the class into pairs or groups of three or four.
- Students look quickly at the text.
- Ask *What is the text about?*
- Students give their ideas.
- Ask *What do you already know about this topic?*
- Students give their ideas. Discuss these ideas.
- Say *Read the Culture Spot text. Note anything that you find interesting or unusual.*
- Ask comprehension questions about the text.
- Students give their answers. Explain any words that students need.
- Ask *Did you find anything interesting or unusual?*
- Students give their ideas.
- Read each comparison question in turn.
- Discuss each question. Encourage students to compare their situation to the one in the text.

INTERACTION

1 Read this story.

My scar

I've got a scar above my right eye. I got it when I was three years old. We lived on a farm then. One day I was riding on a tractor with my father, when I fell off. One of the wheels on the plough cut my forehead. I cried, of course. An ambulance took me to hospital and the doctors stitched it. I was lucky, because I almost lost my eye.

2 Everyone has at least one scar. Work in groups. Prepare questions to ask people about their scars.

Example
Where is it?
How old were you?
What were you doing?
What did you do when ... ?

Look at the story above for ideas.

3 Find two people in the class and ask them about their scars. Try to find out as much as possible.

4 Tell the group what you have found out.

FOLLOW UP

5 My scar. Write the story about one of your scars.

► Pronunciation: page 112

62

PROJECT

Your life

Look at these newspaper headlines.

Young Heroine to the Rescue

Young Hero Saves the Day

Write your own newspaper story about an exciting rescue. Write about:

- an incident from your own life.
  or
- a story from the news.

First write down the facts.

- Who?
- Where were they?
- What were they doing?
- What happened?

Now write the story.

Learning diary

Look at the list on the first page of this unit.

A How well do you know each thing? Complete the circles to make faces.

B Try the self-check in the Workbook.

C Compare your self-check answers with a partner's. Do you understand everything? If you don't understand something, look in a grammar book or ask your teacher.

D What did you like best in this unit? Why?

6

7 comparisons

comparing

Contents

Victoria Road: Sue fights back   64
Language work: Comparative
       and Superlative   66
Reading: 20th century fashion   68
Listening: A sound journey   70
Interaction: Shopping   71
Project: Modern fashions   72

Language work •• •• ••

Grammar

comparative and superlative - regular
short, shorter, shortest
wide, wider, widest

\- double consonant
slim, slimmer, slimmest

\- y ending
pretty, prettier, prettiest

\- irregular
good, better, best

\- more/most
expensive, more expensive, most expensive

singular and plural with clothes
I like this shirt.
I like these jeans.

a pair of
a pair of shorts
a pair of shoes, two pairs of shoes

Word work

clothes

•• •• •• Learning objectives

In this unit you will learn how to:

compare people and things

describe clothes

pay a bus fare

buy things in shops

ask about and give sizes of clothes

VICTORIA ROAD

Sue fights back

- Ask *What happened in the last part of 'Victoria Road'?*
- Elicit ideas.
- If students have forgotten, they turn back to page 54 to check.

Answer key
While Sue was in Spain, Terry tried to steal some cigarettes for Jackie from Kamala's parents' shop. Kamala saw him. She told Sue, who was very upset.

- Read the three questions aloud.
- Students look quickly at the story and the pictures for the answers. Stop them after about one minute.
- Elicit answers.

Answer key
Kamala and Sue are talking about Jackie and Terry. They're in the park. Kamala is showing Sue a magazine article.
Kamala and Sue are shopping for clothes for Sue. They are in a clothes shop.
Sue, Kamala, Jackie and Terry are at a disco. Jackie wants to leave the disco.
Terry borrows some money from Sue.

- Students say what's happening in the story.

Answer key
Sue and Kamala see Jackie and Terry together. Sue wants to get Terry away from Jackie. Kamala shows her an article about being more attractive. Sue goes out to buy some new clothes and makeup and she has a new hairstyle for a disco. At the disco Jackie is bored and wants to leave, but Terry hasn't got any money. He borrows some from Sue. Then he very tactlessly praises Jackie in front of Sue.

- Say *Now, I'm going to play the cassette. Listen carefully and follow in your books.*
- ▭ Play the cassette. Students listen and read.
- Rewind the cassette.

Notes
Doesn't it make you sick? Kamala means 'It's completely unfair *and* it upsets me'.

I don't know what he sees in her. Kamala means 'I don't know why he likes her'.

kidding means 'pretending'. *Who are you kidding?* means 'Why are you saying I'm as pretty as Jackie when obviously I'm not?'

I'll pay you back means 'I'll return the money you lent me'.

- You *borrow* something *from* someone. You *lend* something *to* someone.
- *Quid* is slang for 'pound' – British money.
- *Couple* is an informal way of saying 'two'. However, it is not very precise and often means 'a few'. This is what Terry means here.

- Read aloud the questions below the dialogue, in turn, and elicit ideas.

Note
There are obviously no right answers. Try to encourage as many students as possible to offer ideas.

Answer key

(possible answers)

What is Sue trying to do?

Sue is trying to make herself more attractive. She is hoping that Terry will then show an interest in her rather than Jackie.

What do you think of Terry?

Terry obviously sees Sue as a good friend, since he asks her to lend him money. He seems to do what Jackie wants – he himself doesn't want to go to another place since he doesn't have any more money. He seems completely unaware of Sue's feelings: he compliments her on her dress, then says 'Jackie's got a dress the same as that. She looks great in it'. It is certainly tactless to compliment one girl then immediately talk favourably about another girl.

How does Sue feel at the end of the story?

*At the end of the story, Sue may feel very upset: she's spent a lot of money on making herself look attractive – but Terry hasn't shown any more interest in her. In fact, he's borrowed money from her to spend on another girl. **And** he's told Sue that Jackie looks great in a dress which is the same as the one that Sue's just bought. Sue may of course finally realize that she's wasting her time. She may start thinking about something else or someone better than Terry.*

What will Sue do now?

She might tear up the dress or give it away.
She might leave the disco and go home and cry.
She might look for another boy at the disco and ask him to dance.
She might decide that boys are a waste of time and that she's happier using her word processor or spending time with Kamala.

- Students read questions **a–j**.
- Ask **a–j** in turn.
- Elicit answers (short or long forms).

Answer key

(possible answers)

a *They're talking about Jackie.*
b *She thinks Jackie's more attractive than she is.*
c *She thinks Jackie isn't as pretty as Sue.*
d *She lends Sue her magazine so that Sue can make herself more attractive.*
e *It gives advice about making the best of your appearance: your clothes, hair and makeup.*
f *It costs £30.*
g *She also buys perfume, makeup, shoes and tights.*
h *She thinks it's terrible ('the worst disco in the world').*
i *He needs it to get into another disco – he probably wants to pay for Jackie.*
j *He says that he likes it – and that Jackie's got a dress just like it!*

Note

Several of the questions can be answered in different ways, and the answers are not all obvious. This is an opportunity for class discussion. So don't race through the questions – take as long as you need and continue as long as the class is interested.

- Students close their books.
- Say *Now, I'm going to play the cassette of the story. Listen carefully. You should understand nearly all of it now.*
- ▬ Play the cassette.

Sue fights back

1 What do you remember? What happened in the last part of the story? Look back at page 54 and check your ideas.

2 Look at this episode. Who is in this part? Where are they? What are they doing?

> I don't know what he sees in that Jackie. You're just as good as her, Sue.

> Have a look at this article in this magazine.

TAKE
a good look
IN THE MIRROR
Can you be more attractive?
Do you wear the best clothes for your figure?
Do you look after your hair?
Do you need new makeup?

> Can I borrow it?

3 📼 Listen and follow in your books.

Kamala Doesn't it make you sick? I don't know what he sees in that Jackie. You're much better than her, Sue.

Sue Well, I'm not very nice to Terry. I tease him all the time. Anyway, Jackie is much prettier than me.

Kamala Oh no she's not, Sue. You're just as pretty as she is.

Sue Who are you kidding, Kamala? She's taller than me. In fact, she's the tallest girl in our class. She's slimmer than me and she's got nicer hair. In fact she's altogether better than me.

Kamala That's not true. She is tall but she's not as pretty as you. She hasn't got friendly eyes or your lovely smile. Anyway, have a look at this article in this magazine.

Sue Can I borrow it?

Sue That's it. We'll see who's the best. I'm going shopping.

At the shops

Kamala Isn't it funny? The shortest dresses are always the most expensive. Do you like those dresses over there?

Sue No, I want something more modern. Mmm, I like this. What do you think, Kam?

Kamala But it's £30, Sue. There must be something less expensive here.

Sue I want the best. And now I need some perfume, makeup, a pair of new shoes, a pair of black tights and a handbag . . . hmm maybe not, but I must go to the hairdresser's.

At the disco

Jackie This is the worst disco in the world, Terry. Let's go somewhere else. It can't be worse than this.

Terry (thinks) I haven't got any money.

Terry Oh, all right. Just a minute.

Kamala He's coming over, Sue. And Jackie doesn't look very happy.

Terry Hi, Sue. Can you lend me a couple of quid?

Sue Oh . . . er . . . Oh yes, of course. Here you are.

Terry Thanks, Sue. You're a real friend. I'll pay you back next week. Oh, I like your dress.

Sue Do you? It's new.

Terry Jackie's got a dress the same as that. She looks great in it. Thanks for the money. See you.

What do you think?

- What is Sue trying to do?
- What do you think of Terry?
- How does Sue feel at the end of the story?
- What will Sue do now?

4 Answer these questions.

a Who are Kamala and Sue talking about?

b What does Sue think about Jackie?

c What does Kamala think about Jackie?

d Why does Kamala lend her magazine to Sue?

e What advice does the magazine article give?

f How much does Sue's new dress cost?

g What else does Sue buy?

h What does Jackie think of the disco?

i Why does Terry borrow money from Sue?

j What does Terry say about Sue's new dress?

5 Close your book. Listen again.

> Isn't it funny. The shortest dresses are always the most expensive.

③

> This is the worst disco in the world, Terry. Let's go somewhere else. It can't be worse than this.

> I haven't got any money.

④

> Hi, Sue. Can you lend me a couple of quid?

> Oh... er... Oh yes, of course.

> Jackie's got a dress the same as that. She looks great in it.

⑤

65

Useful expressions

- Students read 'Useful expressions'.
- Write these two 'clues' on the board: *funny* has two meanings; *quid* is slang for a word you already know.
- Say *If you're not sure about the meaning of any of the phrases in the chart, go back to 'Victoria Road' and work it out.*
- In pairs, students discuss the meaning of each phrase. They translate it into their first language. They write the first language equivalents in the chart.
- Elicit and comment on answers. (See **Notes** after Exercise 3.)
- Students amend charts as necessary.

> **Note**
> Ask students whether they have two different words for *borrow* and *lend* in their first language. Refer students to the Workbook exercise (page 56) if you and/or they feel they need more examples and practice.

a
- Divide the class into groups of four.
- Say *Now, choose who will play each part. There's Kamala, Sue, Jackie and Terry.*
- Students choose parts.

b
- Students read the dialogue in their groups. Walk round, answer any questions, and correct any individual serious pronunciation errors.
- Select one or two groups to 'perform' their dialogues for the class.

FOLLOW UP

- Students turn back to the story.
- Say *You are now going to write sentences to compare Sue and Jackie.*
- Add *Some differences are fact, for example, 'Jackie is taller than Sue'. Other differences are a matter of opinion. 'Sue is friendlier than Jackie'.*
- Students write ten sentences giving the differences between Sue and Jackie.

LANGUAGE WORK

The comparative and superlative

BUILD UP

- Students look at the picture of Jackie, Sue and Kamala.
- Point out that they look different in several ways. For example, they are not the same height.
- Students look at the words *shortest*, *taller*, *shorter* and *tallest*.
- Students complete the four gapped sentences by filling each gap with one of the words.
- Check answers.

> **Answer key**
> *Sue is taller than Kamala. Jackie is the tallest.*
> *Sue is shorter than Jackie. Kamala is the shortest.*

- Students look at the note below the gapped sentences.
- Point out the two different forms: adjective + *-er*, and *the* + adjective + *-est*.
- Point out the terms *comparative* and *superlative*.
- Ask for the equivalents in the students' first language.
- Comment on these as necessary.

a
- Students look at the table.
- Point out the terms *comparative* and *superlative*.
- Say *Now, you're going to complete the table with words from 'Victoria Road'. Look back at the story to check spellings!*
- Students complete the table. While they are doing this, copy it onto the board.
- In pairs, students compare answers.
- Elicit answers. One student writes these in the table on the board.
- Students amend their tables as necessary.

> **Answer key**
> taller   tallest
> slimmer
> shortest
> nice   nicer
> prettier
> better   best
> worse   worst
> more modern
> expensive   most expensive
> more attractive

T66

b • Remind students that the comparatives and superlatives of some adjectives are formed with *more* and *most*.

• Ask *So when do we use **more** and **most**?*

• Add *It's something to do with the number of syllables in the adjective. Work it out for yourself.*

• Give students a minute to think about this.

• Elicit the rule.

Answer key
*When an adjective has two or more syllables, the comparative is formed by putting **more** before the adjective and the superlative is formed by putting **most** before the adjective.*

• Read out the exception, e.g. *happy, happier, happiest.*

• Students find an example in their table.

Answer key
pretty, prettier, prettiest

 • Put students into groups of three.

• Say *Now, you have two minutes only to do this next task. Think of as many adjectives as you can, in their positive, comparative and superlative forms, and add them to the table in 2a.*

• Students brainstorm adjectives and add these to the table.

• Time them carefully. Say *Stop* after two minutes.

• Check answers, as follows. Say *Has any group got an adjective beginning with A?*

• Elicit examples, with positive, comparative and superlative forms. Write them on the board.

• Repeat with B, and continue through the alphabet.

Note
This checking is necessary to make sure students' examples are correct. It can be done briskly.

SPOT THE DIFFERENCE

 • Say *Look at the two pictures. They look the same, but there are **eight** differences between them. Try and find them. You have one minute.*

• Students look at the pictures for one minute and find as many differences as they can.

• Say *Now for the answers. As we go through these, put a circle round the differences on the **second** picture.*

• Elicit the eight differences.

• Students circle the differences on the second picture. Make sure everyone is doing this!

Answer key
In the picture on the right:
The man has got shorter hair.
The scales show a heavier weight.
There are no grapes in front of the cash till.
The dog's tail is thinner.
The boy's shoes are darker.
The boy is taller.
The 'i' in difference is not capital.
The plums are more expensive.

 • Read aloud the instructions.

• Students each choose two friends or family members.

• Students write ten sentences in their exercise books. Each sentence must indicate a difference between the two friends/family members.

• Choose individual students at random to read out *one* of their sentences.

• Correct as necessary.

FOLLOW UP

 • In class or for homework, students write eight sentences. Each sentence must indicate one difference between the two pictures (Exercise 4).

• Take in the work and correct as necessary.

Useful expressions

6 **How do you say these expressions in your language?**

Doesn't it make you sick?

I don't know what he sees in her.

(just) as ... as ...

Who are you kidding?

That's not true.

Can I borrow ... ?

Isn't it funny?

Can you lend me a ... ?

a couple of quid

I'll pay you back next week.

7 a **Work in groups of four. Each person takes one of the parts.**

b **Read the dialogue.**

FOLLOW UP

8 **Look back at the story.
Compare Sue and Jackie. Write down five differences.**

Example
Sue has nicer eyes than Jackie.
Jackie is taller than Sue.

LANGUAGE WORK

The comparative and superlative

BUILD UP

1 **Look at the picture. Complete the sentences with these words.**

shortest   taller   shorter   tallest

Sue is .... than Kamala. Jackie is the

....

Sue is .... than Jackie. Kamala is the

....

tall**er**, short**er**: We call this the **comparative**.
tall**est**, short**est**: We call this the **superlative**.

66

2 **a** Complete this table with words from the Victoria Road story.

adjective	comparative	superlative
tall	....	....
slim	....	slimmest
short	shorter	....
....	....	nicest
pretty	....	prettiest
good	....	....
bad	....	....
modern	....	most modern
....	more expensive	....
attractive	....	most attractive

b When do we use 'more' and 'most'? Count the number of syllables.
Exception: For two syllable words ending in 'y', change 'y' to 'i' and add 'er' or 'est'.

3 Work in groups. Add as many words as possible to the table. See which group can add the most in two minutes.

4 Can you find eight differences between these two pictures?

Example
This fruit is more expensive.

5 Choose two of your friends or members of your family. Write down ten differences between them.

Example
John is nicer than Carl.
Carl has got darker hair.

FOLLOW UP

6 Write the answers to Exercise 4.

SPOT THE DIFFERENCE

SPOT THE DIFFERENCE

READING

20th century fashion

This reading section has a number of aims:

- Encouraging students to predict, from their own background knowledge. As a result, they will read the text to check their ideas.

- Reading for specific information.

- Using texts, pictures and background knowledge to work out vocabulary items.

 • Students look at the pictures of people wearing clothes from different periods of the twentieth century.

- Students look at the dates.

- Say *For each date there is one woman and one man.*

- Students try to match each date to two pictures.

- Say *Write each date twice, next to the two pictures you have chosen.*

- In pairs, students compare answers.

- Elicit answers but do not confirm these.

 • Students read *20th Century Fashion* and check their ideas from Exercise 1.

- Check answers.

Answer key

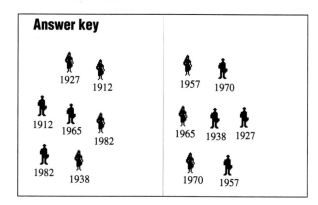

W O R D   W O R K

 a • Students read the text again and list the names of all the items of clothing. (These can be in the singular or plural form.) They can use the pictures to help them.

- In pairs, students compare lists.

- Elicit answers. Write these on the board. Students add to their own list.

Answer key

*suit(s)   dresses   corsets   coats   tie   hat
trousers   Oxford Bags   jackets   'drainpipes'
jumpers   blouses   skirts   socks   shoes
'winklepicker' shoes   mini-skirt   boots
maxi-skirts   jeans   shirts   T-shirts*

b • Students find an example of each item of clothing in the pictures and label it. (Walk round and check while students are doing this. Answer questions as required.)

CLOTHES (SINGULAR AND PLURAL)

 • Students look at the pictures.

- Read aloud the sentences.

a • Ask *What do you notice about the second sentence?*

- Elicit suggestions.

Answer key

Jeans refers to a single item of clothing, but it looks like a plural noun because it has -s on the end, and because we use these and they're when referring to them.

b • Read aloud the first sentence.

- Say *Jeans is one of the items of clothing that is always plural.*

- Elicit ideas about the reason for this – but do not comment on ideas yet!

- Students write *jeans* at the top of the right-hand column of the table.

- Say *Now, put the other words for clothes in the correct columns.*

- Students put the items of clothing in the correct columns. While they are doing this, copy the table onto the board.

- In pairs, students compare tables.

- Elicit answers. One student writes these in the table on the board.

Answer key

singular	always plural (no singular)
skirt	jeans
T-shirt	trousers
jumper	tights
shirt	knickers
bra	underpants
vest	shorts

- Ask *Why do you think the words in the right-hand column are always plural?*

- Elicit suggestions.

Answer key

They are all something to do with the legs (they're either worn on the legs or we put our legs through them). And, as we have two legs, these items of clothing also either have two legs, or two holes for our legs.

- Students close their books.
- Ask *Do you remember what 'Oxford Bags' were?*
- Elicit suggestions.

Answer key
trousers
very wide legs
fashionable in the 1920s

- Students open their books and read the description of Oxford Bags.
- Read the list of words aloud.
- Students write a description for each of the other words in their exercise books, using the text.
- Elicit three or four descriptions of each item. Comment on each. (There are many possible descriptions.)
- Give students a few minutes to change any of their descriptions.

Answer key
(possible answers)
'Teddy Boys' were teenage boys in the 1950s. They wore long jackets in very bright colours and very tight trousers called 'drainpipes'.
'Winklepickers' were shoes with long pointed toes. Men and women wore them in the 1950s. Women's winklepickers had high stiletto heels, too.
'Drainpipes' were very tight trousers. Teddy Boys wore them in the 1950s.
'Stilettos' were shoes with very high heels. Women wore them in the 1950s.
A 'mini-skirt' was a short skirt. Women wore them in the 1960s.
'Hippies' were young men and women in the late 1960s and early 1970s. They wore 'flower power' style clothes: loose maxi-dresses, jeans and brightly coloured shirts or T-shirts.
'Punks' were teenagers in the 1980s. They wore red, blue, purple and green hairstyles and brightly coloured makeup.

- Divide the class into groups of three or four.
- Each group discusses the different fashions. They try to agree which they like *most* and *least* – and *why*. (This should take about five minutes.)
- Each group reports its decisions to the class. Note these on the board.
- Identify the most and least popular fashions.
- Elicit reasons for the choices.

FOLLOW UP

- Students list what they like wearing: *for everyday* and *for parties* or *going out*. Students should describe the clothes (e.g. colour, style, shape).
- Students list what they are wearing now.

Note
The following Extra activity is suitable for students who do **not** wear a school uniform.

EXTRA ACTIVITY

- Each student writes his or her name on a small piece of paper.
- Collect papers.
- Redistribute the papers round the class. Any student who gets their own gives it back and takes another one.
- Say *Now, think about how to describe the clothes worn by the person whose name is on your paper. I'm going to give you a minute to think about this. Then I'm going to ask some people to describe what the person is wearing. You mustn't say the person's name! Everyone else then has to guess who you're describing.*
- Students think for a minute. (Tell them not to look too obviously at the person on the paper!)
- Ask for a volunteer to describe what the person on his/her paper is wearing.
- The student describes his/her person. Anyone who thinks they know who is being described calls out the person's name.
- The first student to give the right answer stands up and describes what the person on *his/her* piece of paper is wearing.
- Continue for five to ten minutes – or for as long as the class is interested.

READING

1 Look at the pictures. Match these dates to the correct pictures.

1912 1938 1965
1927 1957 1970
1982

2 Read the text and check your ideas.

20th century fashion

■ *Before the First World War* fashions did not change very quickly. Men wore dark suits. They had short hair and moustaches were popular. Women wore long dresses and they had long hair. Under their dresses they wore stiff corsets. These gave women a very narrow waist, but they were very uncomfortable.

■ *In the Roaring Twenties* dresses and hair became much shorter. People saw women's knees for the first time! Corsets disappeared. A straight figure with no waist or bust was fashionable. For men, trousers with very wide legs became fashionable. They were called Oxford bags.

■ *In the 1930s and 40s* hair, dresses and coats became longer again. Men's fashion didn't change very much. Men wore a suit, a tie and usually a hat, too. Moustaches were less popular.

■ *In the 1950s* people were richer and teenagers spent a lot of money on clothes. For men this was the age of the teddy boy. Teddy boys wore long jackets in very bright colours – pink, orange or yellow – and very tight trousers called 'drainpipes'. For women jumpers and blouses with wide skirts and short socks were the fashion. Both men and women wore 'winklepicker' shoes with long pointed toes. The women's shoes had high stiletto heels.

■ *The 1960s* saw a revolution in clothes. Everything changed. This was the time of the mini-skirt and long boots. For the first time in the twentieth century men had long hair – the famous Beatle haircut.

■ *In the late 1960s* and the early 70s the hippy 'flower power' style was in. Women wore loose maxi-dresses. Men wore jeans and brightly coloured shirts or T-shirts. Clothes were very colourful. Very long hair was fashionable for men and women, and beards became more common (but only for men).

■ *The 80s* brought teenagers with punk hairstyles in red, blue, purple and green, and brightly coloured makeup.

Where will we go from here?

3
a Make a list of all the names of clothes in the text.

b Label one example of each item on the pictures.

Clothes (singular and plural)

4 Look:

I like **this** dress, but **it's** too small.

I like **these** jeans, but **they're** too tight.

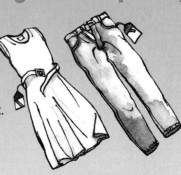

a What do you notice about **jeans**? Compare the two sentences carefully.

b Some names of clothes are always plural. Add the names of these clothes to the correct column.

skirt	tights	bra	vest
trousers	jumper	knickers	shorts
t-shirt	shirt	underpants	

singular	always plural (no singular)

5 Describe these.

Example
Oxford Bags were trousers with very wide legs. They were fashionable in the 1920s.

Oxford Bags	drainpipes	hippies
Teddy Boys	stilettos	punks
winklepickers	a mini-skirt	

6 What do you think of these fashions? Which do you like or dislike? Why?

FOLLOW UP

7 What do you like wearing:

- every day?
- for parties or going out?

What are you wearing now? Describe your own clothes.

LISTENING

A sound journey

1
- Read the instructions aloud.
- Students look at the pictures.
- Students read the place names.
- Students match the pictures and the place names. They label each picture with the correct name.
- In pairs, students compare answers.
- Check answers.

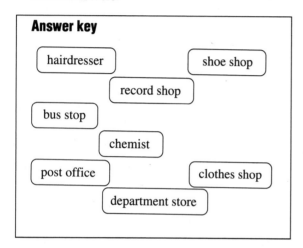

Answer key

- hairdresser
- shoe shop
- record shop
- bus stop
- chemist
- post office
- clothes shop
- department store

2 a
- Say *I'm now going to play a cassette about Jackie and Terry. You will hear several conversations. Each conversation has a number. After each conversation, put its number by the picture it is about.*
- Play the cassette.
- Students number the pictures.
- Check answers.
- Rewind the cassette.

Answer key
1 *bus stop*   2 *department store (and shoe department)*   3 *record shop*   4 *post office*
5 *clothes shop*   6 *Millers*

b
- Ask *Which places didn't they visit?*
- Elicit answers.

Answer key
chemist's
hairdresser's

 A sound journey
Bus sounds
Conductor Fares, please.
Terry Two to the Square, please.
Conductor Ninety pence.
Terry Thank you.
Conductor Thank you. Any more fares, please?

Bus stopping, walking sounds
Assistant 1 Shoes are on the third floor. The escalator's over there.
Jackie Can I try on a pair of these, please?
Assistant 2 What size do you take?
Jackie Size five.
Assistant 2 Here you are.
Terry They're nice, Jackie.
Jackie No, I don't like them. Can I try on those over there . . .

Loud music
Terry Have you got 'Brothers in Arms' by Dire Straits?
Assistant What?
Terry 'Brothers in Arms'.
Assistant Dire Straits?
Terry Yes.
Assistant No, sorry.

Post office
Jackie Two first class stamps and three second class, please.
Assistant Eighty-five pence, please.
Jackie Thank you.
Assistant That's fifteen pence change.

Loud music in boutique
Assistant Here you are. Do you want to try them on?
Jackie I think they're too tight, Terry. You need a bigger size. What size are they?
Terry Thirty.
Jackie You're getting fat.
Terry I'm sure I take a size thirty, you know.
Jackie Have you got these jeans in a size thirty-two?
Assistant I think so. Let me have a look. Yes, here you are.

Bus sounds
Terry We've missed it and there isn't another one for twenty minutes. And my feet are killing me.
Jackie Come on. I haven't got my shoes yet. Let's go and have a look in Millers.
Terry Oh no. (Groans) . . .

Note
first class/second class stamps First class post is more expensive, but letters posted first class should arrive the next day. Second class takes two or three days. These only apply to internal mail, not international.

3
- Tell students you are going to play the cassette again, pausing often.
- Say *Listen carefully for **what happened** in each place – and be ready to tell the class.*
- Play the cassette, pausing it after each part. At each pause, ask *What happened?* and elicit the answer.
- Rewind the cassette.

4
- Students read questions **a–e**.
- Students note down the short answers in their exercise books.
- In pairs, students compare answers.
- Say *Now, I'll play the cassette again. Check your answers.*
- Play the cassette. Students check their answers and amend as necessary.
- Elicit answers.

A PAIR OF

5 **a**
- Read the examples aloud.
- Call out the names of kinds of clothes. Students say *a pair of* where necessary.
  Example
  You: *skirt.*
  Student: *A skirt.*
  You: *Jeans.*
  Student: *A pair of jeans.*

b
- Students look at the pictures on pages 68 and 69 again.
- Students read the list of clothing items.
- Individually, students count how many pairs of each item they can find in the pictures.
- For each, they note down the number of pairs.
- In pairs, students compare numbers. They try to resolve any differences.

- For each item, ask *How many pairs of . . . are there?*
- Elicit answers.

A GAME

 6
- Students read Exercise 6.
- Check comprehension.
- Say *I'll start.* Read A's sentence aloud.
- Say *Who'll be B?* Pick one student. He or she reads B's sentence aloud.
- Say *C?* and repeat as above.
- Say *Next?* and ask another student to continue.
- Continue with two or three more students, until everyone has got the idea.
- Say *This time, you have to listen even more carefully – and watch me.*
- Start the game again, but ask a student to start. After each *For my holidays . . .* point to the student who will continue.

Note

Keep the game going. If a student makes a mistake give him or her a chance to correct it – or say it correctly yourself (if you can!).

Ways of continuing the game

a If your class is 20 or less, put students in a circle. Choose one student to start. The person next to him or her continues, and so on – going round the circle clockwise. A student who makes a mistake is *dead*. Continue (each time starting with the person next to the person who *died*) until there is only one person left. This person is the winner.

b Divide students into groups of between five and ten. Groups play the game simultaneously. Insist on students speaking quietly, and walk round the class to check.

FOLLOW UP

 7
- Read instructions aloud.
- Students look at their answers to Exercises 1–4.
- Students describe the shopping trip.
- Get one or two students to read their descriptions. All students compare answers.

continued on T71a

LISTENING

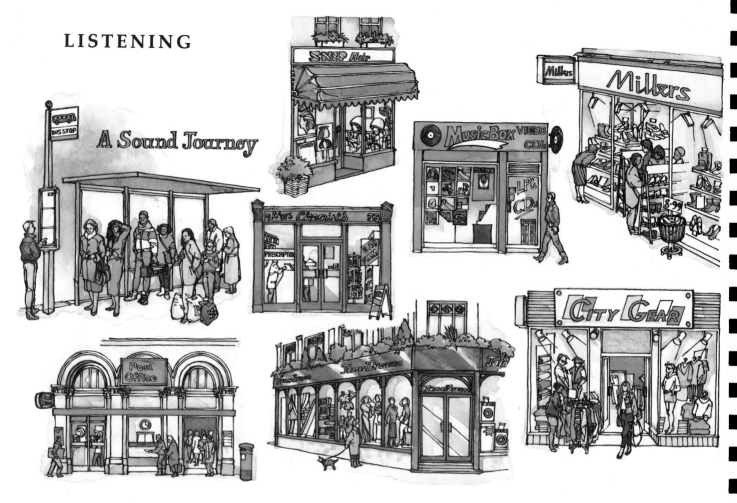

A Sound Journey

Last Saturday Terry and Jackie went shopping in town.

1 ▼ First look at these pictures. Match the names to the places.

shoe shop
department store
record shop

post office
chemist's
hairdresser's

bus stop
clothes shop

2 ▼ a 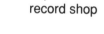 Now listen. Number the pictures in the correct order to match the conversations.

b Which places didn't they visit?

3 ▼ Listen again. What happened in each place?

4 ▼ Answer these questions.

a What was the bus fare into town?

b What size shoes does Jackie take?

c What record did Terry want to buy?

d If a first class stamp costs 20p, how much is a second class stamp?

e What kind of shop is Miller's?

A pair of . . .

5 ▼ a Look.

a pair of jeans   two pairs of jeans

b Look at the pictures on page 68. How many of each of the following can you find?

trousers   jeans   shoes   skirts   hats   boots

6 ▼ A game. For my holidays . . .

A 'For my holidays I packed a shirt.'

B 'For my holidays I packed a shirt and two pairs of trousers.'

C 'For my holidays I packed a shirt, two pairs of trousers and three dresses.'
    etc.

FOLLOW UP

7 ▼ Describe the shopping trip. Say:

* where they went.
* what they wanted.
* what happened.

Start like this.

First they took the bus. They got off at the Square and then they went to . . .

INTERACTION

Shopping

 Put this dialogue in the correct order.

Yes. Have you got these trainers in a size 9, please?
They're £13.40.
Thank you very much. £15.00 – that's £1.60
  change. Goodbye.
Let me see. Yes, here you are. Do you want to try
  them on?
That's £13.40, please.
Goodbye.
Here you are.
Yes, please.
Can I help you?
Are they comfortable?
Fine. I'll take them.
Yes, they fit very well. How much are they?

2 **Role play your dialogue with a partner.**

Sizes

3 British and Continental sizes are not the
same. Look at these tables.

waist, chest, bust		shirts	
British	**Continental**	**British**	**Continental**
28	71	13	34
30	76	14	36
32	81	15	38
34	86	15-1/2	39/40
36	91	16	41
38	97	16-1/2	42
40	102	17	43
42	107		

shoes			
British	**Continental**	**British**	**Continental**
3	36	8	42
4	37	8$\frac{1}{2}$	42/43
5	38	9	43
5$\frac{1}{2}$	39	9$\frac{1}{2}$	44
6	39/40	10	44/45
6$\frac{1}{2}$	40	10$\frac{1}{2}$	45
7	40/41	11	46
7$\frac{1}{2}$	41		

a Write down your measurements in British
and Continental sizes.

b Ask people in your class.

Example
What size shoes do you take?

4 **Make new shopping dialogues for these
items. Use your own sizes.**

£36.50
£5.95
£18.40
£12.99

FOLLOW UP

5 **Write one of your dialogues from Exercise 4.**

continued from T71

INTERACTION

Shopping

- Say *This is a dialogue about someone going shopping. Number it so that it makes sense.*

- Students number the different utterances.

- In pairs, students compare answers.

- Ask one pair to read their dialogue.

- Discuss any difficult points, e.g. *What is the difference between the assistant's two mentions of £13.40?*

> **Answer key**
> *Can I help you?*
> *Yes. Have you got these trainers in a size 9, please?*
> *Let me see. Yes, here you are. Do you want to try them on?*
> *Yes, please.*
> *Are they comfortable?*
> *Yes, they fit very well. How much are they?*
> *They're £13.40.*
> *Fine. I'll take them.*
> *That's £13.40, please.*
> *Here you are.*
> *Thank you very much. £15.00–that's £1.60 change.*
> *Goodbye.*
> *Goodbye.*

- In pairs, students read the dialogue. (They should read it twice, each time taking different roles.)

- Walk round the class, answering questions and listening for and correcting any serious errors of pronunciation (including stress, rhythm and intonation).

- Correct any common, serious errors of pronunciation.

- Choose one or two pairs to 'perform' their dialogue for the class.

Sizes

- Draw students' attention to the two different tables.

- Check understanding of what the tables represent.

a • Students make a note of their measurements in British *and* Continental sizes.

b • Read the example.

- Ask one student. Student answers.

- Get another student to ask a question. A third student answers.

- In pairs, students ask each other about sizes.

> **Note**
> British sizes are based on inches, so a size 15 collar means 15 inches. Nowadays most clothes in Britain carry both British and Continental measurements.

- Students look at their dialogue for Exercise 1 again.

- In pairs, students look at the items in the picture.

- One student is a customer, one is an assistant. Students make dialogues for buying one of the items in the picture.

- Students reverse roles and make the dialogue for another item.

- Get a few pairs to 'perform' their dialogues in front of the class.

FOLLOW UP

- In class or for homework, students write out one of their dialogues.

PROJECT

Your life

- Students turn back to page 68.

- They look again at the pictures showing the history of twentieth century fashion and reread the article.

- Say *Now, it's your turn. You're going to write a magazine article about* **modern** *fashions – what people wear in the 1990s.*

- Ask *What sort of vocabulary can you use?*

- Elicit words to describe some modern fashions. Write these on the board.

- Say *I want you to write your article in three paragraphs – I'll put these on the board.*

- Write on the board:
  Paragraph 1 *Fashionable things for men and women*
  Paragraph 2 *What these modern fashions look like*
  Paragraph 3 *What is unfashionable?*

- Students write a rough draft of their descriptions.

- Correct descriptions, as necessary.

- Students write their descriptions neatly.

- Students arrange their descriptions with illustrations to make their project.

- Display projects.

▶ **Pronunciation: page T112**

LEARNING DIARY

- Students look at the list on the first page of Unit 7.

A Students complete the face next to each item to show how well they know it.

B In class or for homework, students do the self-check exercises in the Workbook.

C In pairs, students compare answers.

Check answers.

Explain any items or exercises which several students had problems with.

Refer students who want to know more to the relevant page of a pedagogic grammar.

Encourage any student who is still confused to come and talk to you.

D Students make a note of what they liked best about this unit.

Find out what were the most popular things.

List these on the board.

Try and find out why these were the most popular, and why other things were less popular. What does this tell you about the way your learners learn best?

CULTURE SPOT
Workbook page 63

- Divide the class into pairs or groups of three or four.

- Students look quickly at the text.

- Ask *What is the text about?*

- Students give their ideas.

- Ask *What do you already know about this topic?*

- Students give their ideas. Discuss these ideas.

- Say *Read the Culture Spot text. Note anything that you find interesting or unusual.*

- Ask comprehension questions about the text.

- Students give their answers. Explain any words that students need.

- Ask *Did you find anything interesting or unusual?*

- Students give their ideas.

- Read each comparison question in turn.

- Discuss each question. Encourage students to compare their situation to the one in the text.

U N I T   8   Revision

LISTENING

 • Students look at the pictures.

a • In pairs, students discuss what is happening in each picture.

b • Say *Now, in your pairs number the pictures to make a story.*

  • Students decide on the story and number the pictures.

 • Pairs compare stories.

- Choose volunteers to tell their pair's story to the class.

 • Say *Now, I'm going to play a cassette of a news broadcast about the pictures. It might be the same as your story, or it might be different. Listen carefully, and put numbers next to the pictures to show the order in which* **this** *story happened.*

- Add *You may find some mistakes in the pictures. Do not worry about these yet.*

- • Play the cassette. Students listen and number the pictures.
- • In pairs, students compare answers.
- • Elicit answers.
- • Rewind the cassette.

▣ Radio 5 News

Two prisoners escaped from Garfield prison this afternoon by helicopter. Our reporter, Julia Summers, is at the prison now.

At about one o'clock today, a man called Mr Lake went to Stansted airport, more than 100 miles from Garfield. He hired a helicopter. The helicopter took off, but as it was flying towards Birmingham, Mr Lake took out a gun. He told the pilot, Mr Peter Evans, to fly north to Garfield.

At exactly 3.15, the helicopter landed on the prison sports field. The prisoners were playing football at the time. When the helicopter landed, Webster and Dean ran to the helicopter. They climbed in and the helicopter took off. The helicopter was in the prison for less than thirty seconds.

The helicopter then flew towards the village of Dingley, where a black Ford car was waiting for them. The three men tied the pilot to the helicopter. They ran to the car and drove away.

This is Julia Summers for Radio 5 News at Garfield prison.

Police inspector Gordon Gregson described the men. Both men are thirty-seven. Dean is tall and slim with short black hair, brown eyes and a beard. Webster is shorter and fatter. He has got fair hair and blue eyes and he wears glasses. The men were wearing prison clothes when they escaped, but they changed their clothes in the helicopter. When they left the helicopter, Webster was wearing brown trousers, a green jumper and a brown coat. Dean was wearing a light blue jumper, black trousers and a dark blue jacket. Lake was wearing a dark grey suit, a white shirt and a red tie. The men have got guns and they are very dangerous. If you see them, telephone the police immediately. Remember. Don't be a hero. Phone the police.

Now the rest of the news ...

▼**4** **a** • Say *There are **four** mistakes in the pictures. Listen carefully, and put a cross on each mistake in the picture it is in.*
  • Play the cassette again. Students listen and indicate mistakes with a cross.

- • In pairs, students compare answers.
- • Elicit the mistakes in the pictures.

b • Students look at the two columns.
  • Say *Match each person with the correct description. To do this, draw a line between them.*
  • Check answers.

- • Say *Now, look at the pictures again and find these six people.*
- • Ask *Which picture or pictures is Peter Evans in?*
- • Elicit answer.
- • Say *How do you know?*
- • Elicit answer.
- • Continue, as above, with the other five people.

▼**5** • Students complete the description.
- • In pairs, students compare answers.
- • ▣ Play the cassette again, from *Police Inspector, Gordon Gregson* to *very dangerous.*
- • Students check their answers.
- • Elicit answers. Check spelling of the 'clothing'.

continued on T74

PROJECT

Your life

Look at the history of 20th century fashion. Write a magazine article about modern fashions.

- What is fashionable for men and women?
- What is unfashionable?

Describe modern fashions. Illustrate your description with magazine pictures or photographs.

Learning diary

Look at the list on the first page of this unit.

7

A How well do you know each thing? Complete the circles to make faces.

B Try the self-check in the Workbook.

C Compare your self-check answers with a partner's. Do you understand everything? If you don't understand something, look in a grammar book or ask your teacher.

D What did you like best in this unit? Why?

▶ Pronunciation: page 112

8 revision

LISTENING

1 Work in pairs. Look at these pictures.

a What is happening in each?

b Put them in order to make a story.

2 Compare your order to another pair's.

3 📼 Listen and number the pictures in the correct order.

4 Listen again.

a Find four mistakes in the pictures.

b Match these people to the descriptions.

people	descriptions
Peter Evans	reporter
John Webster	prisoner
Gordon Gregson	prisoner
Julia Summers	helicopter pilot
Sydney Dean	hired the helicopter
Mr Lake	police inspector

Find the people in the pictures.

5 Complete this description of the two prisoners. Use the pictures to help you.

Police inspector, ... , described

the men. .... men are 37. Dean is .... and slim

with .... black hair, brown .... and

a .... Webster is shorter and ....

He has got fair .... and .... eyes and he wears

.... The men .... prison

clothes when they escaped, but they changed their

.... in the helicopter. When they left the

helicopter, Webster ....

.... brown .... , a green

.... and a .... coat. Dean was wearing a

.... blue jumper, ... trousers and a ....

blue .... Lake was wearing a dark grey

......., a .... shirt and a red ..... . The men have

got .... and they are very dangerous.

FOLLOW UP

6 Webster and Dean are planning the escape. What will they say? Start like this:

We'll escape on 12 June at 10 o'clock. X will go to . . . . He'll hire a helicopter.

continued from T73

FOLLOW UP

- Read the instructions and the example aloud.
- Students write down what Webster and Dean say. They use the future simple.

Answer key
(possible answers)
We'll escape on 12 June at three o'clock. Lake will go to Stansted airport.
He'll hire a helicopter.
He'll tell the pilot to fly north to Garfield.
He'll land on the sports field.
When he lands, we'll run to the helicopter and climb in.
The other prisoners will hold on to the officers.
The helicopter will take off again straight away.
We'll change our clothes in the helicopter.
We'll fly to Dingley. A black Ford will wait for us there.
We'll tie the pilot to the helicopter.
We'll drive away in the Ford.

INTERVIEWS

- Say *I'm going to play the cassette of the news broadcast again. Listen to it carefully. While you listen, look at the pictures.*

- ▣ Play the cassette. Students listen and look at the pictures.

a
- Say *Now you're going to do part of an interview, Julia Summers is interviewing Peter Evans.*

- Say, *Now, who's Julia Summers?*

- Elicit answer.

Answer key
The reporter

- Say *And who's Peter Evans?*
- Elicit answer.

Answer key
The helicopter pilot

- Say *Read each of Peter Evans' answers carefully and decide what question Julia Summers asked to get this answer. Write her question on the line above the answer.*

- Students complete the interview.

- Elicit Julia Summers' questions. Try and get as many different questions for each of Peter Evans' answers as possible.

Note
There are several possible questions Julia Summers could have asked for each of Peter Evans answers.

Answer key
(possible questions)
What happened first?
Where did he want to go?
What was Mr Lake wearing?
What did you do when you took off?
When did you land in the prison?
And where did you land?

---

b
- In their exercise books, students write the rest of the interview between Julia Summers and Peter Evans.

- Students give their ideas.

Answer key
(possible interview)
JS *What were they doing?*
PE *They were playing football.*
JS *What did they do when you landed?*
PE *They ran to the helicopter and climbed in.*
JS *How long were you on the ground?*
PE *Less than 30 seconds.*
JS *Where did you go then?*
PE *I took them towards the village of Dingley.*
JS *Did they do anything while they were in the helicopter?*
PE *The prisoners changed their clothes.*
JS *What happened when you landed?*
PE *They tied me to the helicopter and ran to the nearest road. A Ford car was waiting for them. They got in and the car drove away.*
JS *How did you get free?*
PE *I shouted for help. A farmer was passing and he untied me. Then I called the police.*
JS *Thank you very much, Mr Evans.*

---

c • In pairs, students role play their interviews. Walk round, answer questions and correct any serious pronunciation errors (including stress, rhythm and intonation).

• Select one or two good interviews to be role played for the whole class.

FOLLOW UP

 • Students use the pictures on page 73 and their interviews to tell Peter Evans' story.

Answer key
(possible story)
At about one o'clock today a man came to Stansted airport. He hired a helicopter. He wanted to fly to Birmingham. I agreed. As we were flying towards Birmingham, the man took out a gun and told me to fly to Garfield prison. The helicopter landed on the prison sports field, where the prisoners were playing football. Two men ran to the helicopter and climbed in. The other prisoners were holding on to the officers. I flew the two prisoners and the man who hired the helicopter towards the village of Dingley. On the way, the prisoners changed their clothes. When they landed at Dingley, a Ford car was waiting. They tied me to the helicopter and ran towards the car. The car drove away. I shouted for help. A farmer was passing and untied me. Then I called the police.

WRITING

 a • Revise the story of the jailbreak.

b • Put students into groups of three or four.

• Students look at the two pictures: the prisoners back in jail, and the prisoners on the beach.

• Each group decides:
whether the prisoners escaped *or* were recaptured;
and
if they escaped, how? *or*, if they were recaptured, how?
Give students three or four minutes to do this.

c • Students write a news item about the end of the escape story. This should be about two paragraphs long. The first paragraph of the news items should continue by saying *either* how Webster and Dean were recaptured, *or* how they escaped. The second paragraph should describe their lives now: back in prison, or enjoying their freedom somewhere.

• Comment and correct as appropriate.

• Students write a second draft of their news items correctly.

• Display the news items. Give all students an opportunity to read them.

VOCABULARY

 • In pairs, students complete the dialogue.

• Get one pair to read dialogue **a** and another pair to read dialogue **b**. Other pairs check their own dialogues.

• Pairs role play their completed dialogues.

Answer key
a *please Single will time train past what get (catch) you'll that at won't in*
b *help pair size take you want them they they're Have size these better much They're are you change*

---

continued on T75a

INTERVIEWS

  Look at the pictures and listen to the news broadcast again.

  Julia Summers is interviewing Peter Evans.

a Match the questions to Mr Evans' answers.

Julia Summers' questions
Where did he want to go?
What did you do when you took off?
What happened first?
And where did you land?
What was Mr Lake wearing?
When did you land in the prison?

Julia Summers ....

Peter Evans At about one o'clock today a man called Mr Lake came to Stansted airport and hired a helicopter.

Julia Summers ....

Peter Evans He said he wanted to fly to Birmingham.

Julia Summers ....

Peter Evans A dark grey suit, a white shirt and a red tie.

Julia Summers ....

Peter Evans As we were flying towards Birmingham, Mr Lake took out a gun and told me to fly to Garfield.

Julia Summers ....

Peter Evans At exactly 3.15.

Julia Summers ....

Peter Evans On the prison sports field.

b Complete the interview with Peter Evans. Ask more questions.

c Role play your interview.

FOLLOW UP

3 **Tell Peter Evans' story.**

WRITING

 a Look at the story of the jailbreak again.

b Work in groups of three or four. Decide on an ending for the story.

- Did the police recapture the convicts or did they escape completely?
- How did they do it?

c Write a news item about the ending.

VOCABULARY

1 Complete these dialogues.

a **Passenger** Birmingham, ...

Ticket clerk .... or return?

Passenger Return, please.

Ticket clerk That .... be £17, please.

Passenger What .... is the next .... ?

Ticket clerk Half .... nine.

Passenger And .... time is the train back?

Ticket clerk If you .... the 9.45 from Birmingham, ... get back at 11 o'clock.

Passenger Is .... the last train?

Ticket clerk No, there's a train .... midnight, but you .... get back till two o'clock .... the morning.

Passenger Thank you.

b **Assistant** Can I .... you?

Customer Yes. I'd like a .... of jeans, please.

Assistant Sure. What .... do you ....?

Customer 32.

Assistant Here .... are. Do you .... to try .... on?

Customer Yes, please.

Assistant Are .... all right?

Customer No, ... too big. .... you got them in a smaller ....?

Assistant Yes. Try ....

Customer Oh, yes. These are .... I'll take them. How .... are they?

Assistant .... £23.60.

Customer Here you ....

Assistant Thank .... That's £1.40 ....

2 Find the odd one out. Look at these lists. In each list there is an odd word.

a hat   jeans   T-shirt   socks   dress

b leg   tail   wing   arm   beak

c Asia   India   Europe   Africa   America

d summer   winter   equator   autumn   spring

e airport   luggage   station   shop   bus stop

f sun   pole   earth   moon   star

g prettiest   tallest   better   worst   shortest

h doctor   tailor   vicar   dentist   tractor

i most   south   east   north   west

j pink   purple   orange   yellow   narrow

3 Work with a partner. Do the quiz.

> ### QUIZ What can you remember?
>
> **a** What was the name of the vicar of Eyam?
>
> **b** What is another name for the Arctic?
>
> **c** Which ocean is to the west of Africa?
>
> **d** What were 'winklepickers'?
>
> **e** What was Terry stealing from Kamala's parents' shop?
>
> **f** What did Peter hurt, when he fell off the ladder?
>
> **g** What is size 42 for shoes in British sizes?

4 Make you own quiz.

a Work in groups of four.

b Write five questions about things in units 5–8.

c Exchange your quiz with another group. Answer their quiz.

FOLLOW UP

5 Write the answers to the quiz in Exercise 3 in full.

continued from T75

 2

- In pairs, students look at the lists.
- Make sure students understand 'odd one out'.
- Do the first example with the whole class.
- Students do **b–j**.
- Students give answers and reasons.

Answer key

(Note that other possibilities may be correct.)

a dress: *all the others are unisex; only women and girls wear dresses*
b arm: *not part of a bird*
c India: *not a continent*
d equator: *not a season*
e luggage: *not a place*
f pole: *part of the earth; others are planets or stars*
g better: *not a superlative*
h tractor: *not a job*
i most: *not a point of the compass*
j narrow: *not a colour*

 3

- Students read the quiz.
- In pairs, students answer as many of questions **a–g** as they can. (They can use short answers.)
- When they have finished, say *Look back through Units 5, 6 and 7. Check your answers, and also find the answers to the questions you couldn't do.*
- Students look back at Units 5, 6 and 7.
- Elicit answers to **a–g**. Students correct/amend as necessary.

Answer key

(See Exercise 5.)

---

 4 a

- Put students into groups of four. (If the numbers do not work out, include some groups of three.)

b
- Each group elects a secretary.
- They work out a quiz of five questions about things in Units 5, 6 and 7.
- The secretary writes the quiz on a piece of paper.

c
- Put groups into 'pairs of groups'. Groups exchange quizzes.
- Each group tries to answer the other group's quiz questions. The secretary writes the answers on the quiz paper. After five minutes say *Stop*.
- Groups give back the quiz papers to the quiz-writers.
- Quiz-writers give a mark out of five, and return the quiz papers.
- Ask *How many groups got all five questions right?*
- Groups raise their hands if they got all five questions right.
- Repeat with *four questions right* and *three questions right*, etc.

FOLLOW UP

 5

- Say *Last of all, write the answers to the quiz questions a–g in full sentences in your exercise books.* (This can be done in class or as homework.)

Answer key

a *The name of the Vicar of Eyam was William Mompesson.*
b *Another name for the Arctic is the North Pole.*
c *The ocean to the west of Africa is the Atlantic Ocean.*
d *'Winklepickers' were shoes with long pointed toes worn in the 1950s.*
e *Terry was stealing some packets of cigarettes from Kamala's parents' shop.*
f *Peter hurt his arm when he fell off the ladder.*
g *Size 42 in continental sizes is size 8 or 8½ in British sizes.*

GAME

- Students look at the game.

- Discuss the aim and rules of the game. Make sure everyone understands.

- Divide the class into groups of four or five.

- Give each group a dice, if you have them. Alternatively students can make their own dice from a hexagonal pencil or ballpoint pen. They scratch numbers 1–6 on each face of the pencil. They then roll the pencil to get numbers.

- Students play the game, using paper counters. Go round and help with any problems.

> **Note**
> Students should speak English. They miss a turn if they don't.

▶ **Pronunciation: page T113**

Can you escape from the evil Professor X?

START

Road block. You must throw a 4 or a 6 to go on.

You dig a tunnel. Go forward 2.

Guards find your tunnel. Miss a turn.

You find a road through the forest. Go to number 42.

The guards are searching the village. You mustn't go out. Miss a turn.

The plane crashes into the sea. You swim back to the island. Go back to number 47.

There is no fuel in the plane. Go back to 62.

You stop for a rest. Miss a turn.

The guard is asleep. You steal his keys. Go forward 4.

You find a map of the island. Double your next throw.

Someone recognizes you from a WANTED poster. Escape to number 23.

It's Professor X's birthday. All the guards are at the party. Go forward 4.

You can't cross the river until it's dark. Miss a turn.

The guards catch you. Go back to the start.

You steal the guards' lorry. Have an extra turn.

The weather is foggy. You can't take off. Miss a turn.

You find a boat. Go to number 21.

It's a dark night. Nobody can see you. Add 2 to your next throw.

Dangerous marshes. Go back 5.

There are too many guards at the airfield. Miss a turn.

REWARD WANTED 10,000

GUARD ROOM

AIRFIELD

FINISH

▶ Pronunciation: page 112

76

9 visitors

the present perfect

Contents

Victoria Road: Jackie's cousin arrives   78
Language work: The present perfect tense   80
Reading: A visit to London   82
Listening: Strange visitors   84
Interaction: Contacts with English   85
Project: Important events in your life   86

Language work 😊 😐 ☹️

Grammar

the present perfect tense - statements
I've met Jackie's friends.
She has gone to the airport.

- negatives
I haven't seen her today.
He hasn't been to London yet.

- questions
Where have you been?
Has Greg telephoned his parents?

the present perfect and the past simple
We've been on patrol for six hours now.
We were on patrol for six hours yesterday.

Word work

places in a city

😊 😐 ☹️ Learning objectives

In this unit you will learn how to:

introduce people

talk about past events that affect the present

ask about and say what you have done

talk about your contacts with the English speaking world

talk about recent events in your life

VICTORIA ROAD

Jackie's cousin arrives

 • Ask *What happened in 'Victoria Road' in Unit 7?*
• Elicit answers.

Answer key
Kamala reassured Sue that she was as good-looking as Jackie.
Sue decided to buy some new clothes.
She went shopping with Kamala and bought a dress.
Jackie, Terry, Kamala and Sue went to a disco and Sue wore her new dress.
Terry said he liked it. He also said, 'Jackie's got a dress the same as that. She looks great in it.' Sue was upset.

 • Read the questions aloud.
• Students look quickly at the dialogue and the pictures to find the answers.

Answer key
The new character is Jackie's cousin, Greg.
He's from America. or He's from the States.
*Terry is surprised and upset to discover Jackie has an interesting **male** cousin visiting her. He's jealous! (He may also be upset that Jackie hasn't told him about Greg.)*

 • Say *Now I'm going to play the cassette. Listen and follow in your books.*
• Play the cassette. Students listen and read.
• Rewind the cassette.

• Draw students' attention to the questions under the story and the picture of Terry and his cowboy hat.
• Ask the first question.
• Elicit as many answers as possible. (Short answers are fine.)
• Repeat with the second question.

Answer key
Terry is surprised. He didn't know Jackie had an American cousin. He is even more surprised to learn the cousin is male. He feels jealous of Greg. He thinks Greg must be an interesting person, as he (Terry) thinks America is interesting. This gives Terry another reason to be jealous! When he meets Greg, he does not know what to do. He definitely does not want to spend time in Greg's company.

*There are two possible reasons why Terry has thrown his hat in the bin. First, he may suddenly feel it is childish to own a cowboy hat, especially now he has met a 'real' American. Second, he may not want anything to do with American things any more. Of course, **both** reasons may be true.*

 • Ask question **a**.
• Elicit a short answer.
• Continue until a student gives the correct answer.
• Repeat with **b–k**.

Answer key
a *Jackie*
b *yesterday*
c *to the airport*
d *to meet her cousin from America or Her cousin from America is arriving today.*
e *at about eight o'clock*
f *He met Jackie and her mum while he was doing his paper round.*
g *that the cousin will be a girl*
h *last summer*
i *She's seen the cowboy hat (from America) on Terry's wall.*
j *The cousin is a boy.*
k *He has thrown it in the bin.*

• Say *Now, close your books. I'm going to play the cassette again. Listen carefully. You should understand everything.*
• ▪ Play the cassette. Students listen carefully.

T78

Notes

just is used with the present perfect tense when something has happened *very* recently.

You must introduce me is a request: the speaker (in this case Terry) really *wants* to meet the person in question (in this case, Jackie's American cousin).

The States is a short way of saying 'The United States of America'.

Pleased to meet you (with *I'm* omitted) is a polite way of addressing someone when you have just been introduced.

Good Lord is an expression of surprise. It is very mild, not swearing.

Is that the time? This is another way of saying 'I didn't know it was so late'. It is usually used as a reason (or excuse) to leave.

See you around is a way of saying 'I'll see you again', without making a definite arrangement. Terry doesn't want to have anything to do with Greg. But he is also confused and upset. This could explain his behaviour.

• Mention Vince's *paper round*. He delivers newspapers to houses to earn money. Many young British teenagers (boys and girls) do this before they go to school in the morning.

• Like Sue, Terry has his own bedroom, where he can put what he wants on the walls. Many young people in Britain have their own rooms and decorate them as they like.

Useful expressions

• Students read the chart.

• Say *Think about each expression, and write down how we (you) say this in our (your) language. Don't just translate word for word. Write down how we express each idea **as a whole**. If you are unclear about the meaning of any of the expressions, look back at the story and work it out.*

• Students write down each expression in their own language in the chart.

• In pairs, students compare answers.

• Check answers. Discuss and explain as necessary.

EXTRA ACTIVITY

• For homework, students learn the English expressions in the chart.

• In the next class, choose three or four of the expressions in the students' own language.

• Call these out and elicit the English equivalents.

 a • Put students into groups of three.

• Students decide parts, using the instructions in **7a**.

b • Students read the dialogue. While they are doing this, walk round, answer any questions, and correct serious errors of pronunciation (including stress, rhythm and intonation).

• Repeat, with each student taking a different role.

• Choose one group to 'perform' the dialogue. Rest of class listens carefully.

FOLLOW UP

 • Students write out the answers to Exercise 4 in full sentences in their exercise books.

• In pairs, students compare answers.

• Check answers.

Answer key

a *Terry was looking for Jackie.*
b *Sue saw her yesterday.*
c *She has gone to the airport.*
d *She's gone to the airport to meet her cousin from America.*
or
Her cousin from America is arriving today.
e *She went at about eight o'clock.*
f *Vince met Jackie and her mum while he was doing his paper round.*
g *Terry expects that the cousin is a girl.*
h *Terry's dad went to America last summer.*
i *Jackie knows Terry's dad has been to America because she's seen the cowboy hat (from America) on Terry's bedroom wall.*
j *Terry is surprised that the cousin is a boy.*
k *He's thrown his hat in the bin.*

Jackie's cousin arrives

1 What do you remember? What happened in the last part of the story? Look back at page 64 and check your ideas.

2 Look at this episode. Who is the new character? Where is he from? What is wrong with Terry?

> Have you seen Jackie this morning?

> No. I saw her in town yesterday, but I haven't seen her today.

①

> Her cousin from America is arriving today.

> I didn't know she had an American cousin.

②

> I've never met anyone from America. What's her name?

> *His* name is Greg.

④

3 🖭 Listen and follow in your books.

Terry Have you seen Jackie this morning?

Sue No. I saw her in town yesterday, but I haven't seen her today.

Vince She's gone to the airport.

Terry What has she gone there for?

Vince Her cousin from America is arriving today.

Terry I didn't know she had an American cousin. When did she go?

Vince She went with her mum at about 8 o'clock. I met them when I was doing my paper round.

   Later

Terry Hi, Jackie. Has your cousin arrived?

Jackie Yes, but the plane was late. So we've only just got back.

Terry My dad's been to America, you know. He was there last summer.

Jackie I know. I've seen the cowboy hat on your bedroom wall.

Terry Oh yes. You must introduce me. I've never met anyone from America. What's her name?

Jackie *His* name is Greg. He's brought me lots of things from the States. You'll like him, Terry. Oh, here he is now.

Jackie Greg, this is Terry.

Greg Hi, Terry. Pleased to meet you. I've heard all about you from Jackie.

Terry Hello. Good Lord. Is that the time? I must go. See you around.

   Later

Vince Terry. What have you done with your cowboy hat?

What do you think?

- How does Terry feel about Greg?
- Why has he thrown the hat in the bin?

My dad's been to America, you know. He was there last summer.

I know. I've seen the cowboy hat on your bedroom wall.

3

Greg, this is Terry.

Hi, Terry. Pleased to meet you.

5

Useful expressions

6 How do you say these expressions in your language?

Have you seen ... ?

We've only just got back.

you know

You must introduce me.

the States

Here he is.

Pleased to meet you.

Good Lord!

Is that the time?

I must go.

See you around.

Terry. What have you done with your cowboy hat?

6

4 Answer these questions.

a Who was Terry looking for?

b When did Sue see her?

c Where has she gone?

d Why has she gone there?

e When did she go?

f How does Vince know?

g What does Terry expect about Jackie's cousin?

h When did Terry's dad go to America?

i How does Jackie know?

j What is Terry surprised about?

k What has Terry done with his hat?

5 Close your book. Listen again.

7 a Work in groups of three. One person is Terry, one is Sue and Jackie and one is Greg and Vince.

b Read the dialogue.

FOLLOW UP

8 Write the answers to Exercise 4 in full.

79

LANGUAGE WORK

The present perfect tense

BUILD UP

- Read sentences in **1** aloud.
- Students turn back to *Victoria Road*.
- Students find and list more examples of the present perfect tense.
- In pairs, students compare lists.
- Check examples.

> **Answer key**
> *What has she gone there for?*
> *Has your cousin arrived?*
> *So we've only just got back.*
> *My dad's been to America …*
> *I've seen the cowboy hat on your bedroom wall.*
> *I've never met anyone from America.*
> *He's brought me lots of things from the States.*
> *I've heard all about you from Jackie.*
> *What have you done with your cowboy hat?*

- Get students to read the rule and the examples aloud.

- Tell students they are now going to form the present perfect tense.
- Students look at the chart.
- Get students to identify the two parts (*have/has* and the past participle) in the examples they found in Exercise 1.

a
- Students complete the table with the correct forms of *have*. While they are doing this, copy the table onto the board.
- Choose one student to complete the table on the blackboard.
- Students correct their own tables as necessary.

> **Answer key**
> *have not*
> *has*
> *'s*
> *hasn't*

- Students make six sentences using the table.

b
- Students look at the participles in the table.
- Point out that all the participles are 'regular'.
- Ask *So how do we make the regular past participle?*
- Elicit ideas.

> **Answer key**
> *To make the regular past participle, we add -ed to the verb (or -d if it ends in an 'e') – just like a regular past tense form.*

- Students copy the above rule into their books.

c
- Remind students that many verbs have *irregular* past participles.
- Read the example aloud.
- Draw students' attention to the list of verbs.
- Students find and list irregular past participles.

> **Note**
> Some of the words are in the questions after the story and in Exercise 4.

- In pairs, students compare lists.
- Check answers.

> **Answer key**
> | | |
> |---|---|
> | met | brought |
> | heard | done |
> | had | thrown (occurs in |
> | got | *What do you think* question) |

d
- Students read the gapped rule and the five items above the box.
- Students complete the rule by writing two of the five items in the gaps.
- Check answers.

> **Answer key**
> *To make the present perfect, we use **the verb 'to have'** plus **the past participle**.*

3 • Read the instructions aloud.

• Students read the list of things Greg wants to do.

• Check comprehension of vocabulary and ideas. Use the pictures to explain.

• Explain the ticks.

• Read aloud the two examples.

• Students read through the list again. They decide whether Greg has or hasn't done each thing.

• Elicit sentences saying what Greg has and hasn't done. (Students should use contracted forms in their answers if possible.)

> **Answer key**
> *He hasn't sent postcards to his friends.*
> *He's had a rest.*
> *He hasn't got presents for his family.*
> *He hasn't travelled on the London Underground.*
> *He hasn't spent a day at Covent Garden.*
> *He's met Jackie's friends.*
> *He's watched a cricket match.*
> *He's changed some money.*
> *He's taken a lot of photographs.*
> *He's unpacked his suitcase.*
> *He hasn't seen Buckingham Palace.*
> *He hasn't bought any new clothes.*

• In class or for homework, students write out the sentences about what Greg has and hasn't done.

The present perfect tense: questions

BUILD UP

4 • Remind students that they have been practising *statements* which use the present perfect tense. They will now practise questions.

a • Students read the gapped sentences.

• Students complete the sentences *using the appropriate present perfect forms*. They look back at the story if necessary.

• In pairs, students compare answers.

• Check answers.

> **Answer key**
> *Have you seen Jackie this morning?*
> *Has your cousin arrived?*

• Point out that the subject of the first sentence is *you*, which is preceded by *have*. The subject of the second sentence is *your cousin*, which is preceded by *has*.

b • Students arrange each group of words to make a statement *and* a question.

• Check answers.

> **Answer key**
>
> | statement | question |
> |---|---|
> | *You have been to the States.* | *Have you been to the States?* |
> | *She has gone to the airport.* | *Has she gone to the airport?* |

c • Tell students to complete the rule. They should use the chart in **b** to help them.

• In pairs, students compare answers.

• Check answers.

> **Answer key**
> *have   has   subject*

5 • Students look back to Exercise 3.

• Say to one (good!) student *You are Greg. Okay? Have you got presents for your family?*

• Student replies *No, I haven't.* (If the student cannot answer, repeat with another student.)

• Put students into pairs. One person is A and the other is B (i.e. Greg).

• One pair 'performs' the example for the class.

• All pairs ask and answer about what Greg has and hasn't done. A asks and B (Greg) answers.

• Students change roles and repeat.

> **Answer key**
> *Have you sent …?   No, I haven't.*
> *Have you had …?   Yes, I have.*
> *Have you got …?   No, I haven't.*
> *Have you travelled …?   No, I haven't.*
> *Have you spent …?   No, I haven't.*
> *Have you met …?   Yes, I have.*
> *Have you watched …?   Yes, I have.*
> *Have you changed …?   Yes, I have.*
> *Have you taken …?   Yes, I have.*
> *Have you unpacked …?   Yes, I have.*
> *Have you seen …?   No, I haven't.*
> *Have you bought …?   No, I haven't.*

FOLLOW UP

6 • Ask *Now, what has everyone here done this week?*

• Elicit answers round the class – one answer from each student if possible. Students should use contracted forms, i.e. *I've …* rather than *I have …*

• Students list ten things they have done this week. They should write full sentences but use contracted forms and should pay special attention to the past participle. Encourage them to ask you if they are not sure about any irregular forms.

• In pairs, students compare lists.

LANGUAGE WORK

The present perfect tense

BUILD UP

1 Look at these sentences.

Have you **seen** Jackie this morning?
I **haven't seen** her today.
She**'s gone** to the airport.

We call this the **present perfect** tense.
Find more examples in the Victoria Road
story.

> The present perfect shows an
> activity in the past which tells us
> something about the present.

Example
I haven't seen her today.
= I don't know where she is now.
She has gone to the airport.
= She is at the airport now.
He has thrown his hat in the dustbin.
= The hat is in the dustbin now.

2 How do we make the present perfect?

- The present perfect has two parts.

He	has	arrived
	the verb 'to have'	a past participle

a Complete this table with the correct parts of the verb 'to have'.

I	have	arrived.
You	've	recorded many hits.
We	....	painted the hall.
They	haven't	collected some souvenirs.
		practised on the computer.
He	....	received a letter.
She	....	worked here for ten years.
It	has not	appeared on TV.

b All the verbs in this table have regular past participles. How do we make the regular past participle?

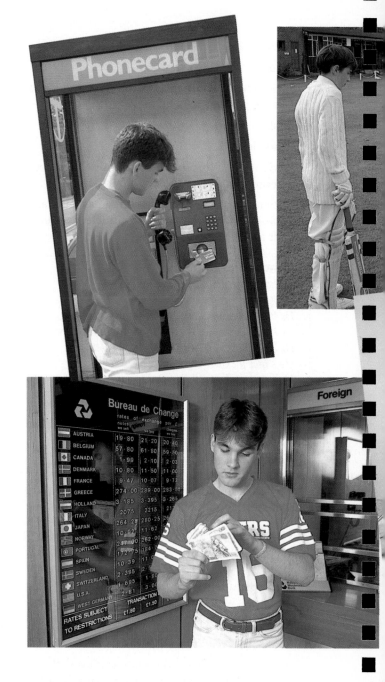

c A lot of verbs have irregular past participles.

Example
*I haven't **seen** Jackie today.*

- Find the past participles of these verbs in the story.

  meet hear have get bring do throw

d Complete the rule with two of these.

the verb 'to be'   the infinitive
the verb 'to have'   the past participle
· the past tense

> To make the present perfect we use ....
> .... plus ....
> ....

The present perfect tense: questions

4 **a** **Complete these sentences from the story.**

.... you .... Jackie this

morning? (see)

.... your cousin .... ? (arrive)

b **Arrange these words to make a statement and a question.**

	statement	question
you to have the States been		
the gone airport has she to		

c **Complete this rule.**

> To make questions in the present perfect we
> put .... or .... in front of the ....

3 Greg has been in England for three days. Here are the things he wants to do while he is in England. Look at the list and say what Greg has and hasn't done.

Example
He hasn't visited the Tower of London.
He has telephoned his parents.

- ☐ visit the Tower of London
- ☑ telephone his parents
- ☐ send postcards to his friends
- ☑ have a rest
- ☐ get presents for his family
- ☐ travel on the London Underground
- ☐ spend a day at Covent Garden
- ☑ meet Jackie's friends
- ☑ watch a cricket match
- ☑ change some money
- ☑ take a lot of photographs
- ☑ unpack his suitcase
- ☐ see Buckingham Palace
- ☐ buy some new clothes

5 Work in pairs. Look at the list in Exercise 3. Ask Greg questions.

Example
A *'Have you visited the Tower of London?'*
B *'No, I haven't.'*
A *'Have you telephoned your parents?'*
B *'Yes, I have.'*

FOLLOW UP

6 What have you done this week? Write ten things.

READING

A visit to London

This activity encourages students to tackle a text that is probably too difficult for them. They are looking for specific information and don't need to read the whole text. (Discourage dictionary use!) However, it is necessary for them to *think* carefully, since the answers are not given *directly*.

- Students read the instructions in **1**.
- Draw students' attention to *Greg and Jackie …*
- Read aloud *Greg and Jackie … of the stars.*
- Check understanding. Ask *What's a brontosaurus?*, *Who's the British Prime Minister?*, *Who's Michael Jackson?* and elicit answers for each.
- Tell them to read 'Things to see in London'. Say *While you are reading, list the places Jackie and Greg have visited, using the four clues in* **1**.
- Students read 'Things to see in London' and list the places Jackie and Greg have visited.
- In pairs, students compare answers.
- Check answers.

> **Answer key**
> *The Tower of London (where the Crown jewels are)*
> *The Natural History Museum (where there are dinosaur skeletons, e.g. brontosaurus)*
> *Madame Tussauds, Marylebone Road (where there are waxworks of pop stars, e.g. Michael Jackson, and Prime Ministers)*
> *The Royal Observatory, Greenwich (where there are displays about astronomy, e.g. stars)*

> **Note**
> In Exercise 1 (and 3, opposite), students have to use their imagination and common sense and be prepared to work the answers out. You may wish to use **1** and **3a** as examples of how the answer can be *inferred*.

- Students look at the pictures of places and things in London.
- They match each picture with one of the places mentioned in 'Things to see in London'.
- In pairs, students compare answers.
- Check answers.

> **Answer key**
> (left to right)
> *The Houses of Parliament*
> *The Tower of London*
> *Hyde Park*
> *Downing Street*
> *The Royal Observatory, Greenwich*
> *The Natural History Museum*
> *Madame Tussauds*

- Students read questions **a–f**.
- In their exercise books, students write short answers to the questions, using 'Things to see in London'.
- In pairs, students compare answers.
- Check answers.

> **Answer key**
> **a** *a lake*
> **b** *another name for the Houses of Parliament*
> **c** *10 Downing St*
> **d** *Kensington*
> **e** *The Royal Observatory, Greenwich*
> **f** *Two places: Hyde Park, The Natural History Museum*
> *Four places: The Tower of London, The Natural History Museum, The Royal Observatory, Madame Tussauds*

W O R D W O R K

- Students read examples of place names.
- Students look again at 'Things to see in London'.
- They list all the names of places they can find in it.
- In pairs, students compare lists.
- Elicit answers and list these on the board. Add your own. (Students are unlikely to have *all* the words listed below.)
- Check understanding of words.

> **Answer key**
> *street home palace building bridge clock tower park forest restaurant bar lake prison place of execution zoo Royal Mint observatory museum gift shop cafeteria book shop hill video theatre shop souvenir shop bridge road chamber*

EXTRA ACTIVITY
(Next class)

- Ask students how many of these places they can remember.
- Elicit as many answers as possible. (Students keep their exercise books closed!)
- Students open their books and look for the words they did *not* remember.

 • Put students into pairs.

a • In pairs, they decide on two things they have done or seen on an imaginary day out in London (one minute).
- Read aloud the example.
- Students write down the two things they have done or seen on a piece of paper.
- While students are writing, walk round the class and check that they are doing this correctly.

Note
They should *not* write down where they have *been*.

b • Put each pair with another pair.
- Pairs exchange papers.
- Students read what is written on the piece of paper they have received.
- Draw students' attention to the example. Say *If someone has written 'We have seen Big Ben', this must mean they have been to the Houses of Parliament. So you would write 'You have been to the Houses of Parliament'.*
- Each pair writes, on the 'new' piece of paper, a sentence giving the places (or place) where the other pair has been.
- Students return papers.
- Each pair confirms whether the places identified are correct.
- Ask one or two pairs to say what was written on their 'new' paper and how they decided where the other pair had been.

FOLLOW UP

 • Students read questions **a–e** and look for the answers in the text.
- In class or for homework, students answer the questions in full sentences in their exercise books.

Answer key
a *You can see butterflies at the Natural History Museum.*
b *The Tower of London is nine hundred years old.*
c *The Royal Observatory, Greenwich, opens at half past ten in the morning.*
d *You can see the Prime Minister at 10 Downing Street or the Houses of Parliament and at Madame Tussauds, Marylebone Road.*
e *The Tower of London is not open on Sunday mornings.*

READING

A VISIT TO LONDON

1 Greg and Jackie have been to London for the day. They have done these things.

- They have seen the Queen's crown.
- They have had lunch with a brontosaurus.
- Greg has taken photographs of Jackie with the Prime Minister and Michael Jackson.
- They have looked at photographs of the stars.

Look at this list of things to do in London. Which places have Greg and Jackie visited? How do you know?
Remember: You don't have to understand every word.

Things to see in London

Hyde Park
London's largest and most fashionable park. It was once a royal hunting forest. Restaurants and bars at each end of the lake. Swim or hire a boat on the Serpentine.

Downing Street
Number 10 Downing Street has been the home of the British Prime Minister since 1735.

The Houses of Parliament
Its official name is the Palace of Westminster. Most of the building was built in 1840 after a fire in 1834 destroyed the old palace. At the north end of the building by Westminster Bridge is the famous clock tower, Big Ben. In fact Big Ben is really the name of the bell in the tower not the clock.

The Tower of London
London's oldest building. Since it was built by William the Conqueror in the 11th century, this castle has been a royal palace, a prison, a place of execution, a zoo, the Royal Mint and an observatory. Today it's a museum and houses the Crown Jewels. Gift shop.
Open Monday–Saturday
* 9.30–5.45*
Sundays 2–5.45

The Natural History Museum
Situated in Kensington. One of London's greatest museums. A huge collection of animals and plants, including a quarter of a million butterflies, a blue whale and the famous dinosaur skeletons. Cafeteria, gift shop and book shop.
Open daily 10–5.45

Madame Tussauds, Marylebone Road
This famous waxworks has models of famous people from pop stars to prime ministers. Displays of battles and Chamber of Horrors. Gift shop.
Open every day 10–5.30, except Christmas Day

The Royal Observatory, Greenwich
10 miles outside London on a hill above the River Thames. The Observatory contains telescopes and displays about astronomy, including Halley's Comet and Black Holes. The international meridian line runs through the Observatory. Video theatre and souvenir shop. Picnic in Greenwich Park. Take a river boat to Greenwich from Westminster Bridge.
Open 10.30 am to 5.30 pm
Closed 25–28 December

2 Match the pictures to the places.

3 Find the answers to these questions.

a What is the Serpentine?

b What is the Palace of Westminster?

c What is the Prime Minister's address?

d Where is the Natural History Museum?

e Where can you stand with one foot in the western hemisphere and one foot in the eastern hemisphere?

f At how many places can you:
* buy something to eat?
* buy souvenirs?

| W | O | R | D | | W | O | R | K |

4 Find all the names of places in the texts.

Example
museum   palace   zoo

5 Work in pairs. Make your own day out. You can visit two places.

a Write down two things that you have done or seen on your day out.

Example
We have seen Big Ben.

b Give your things to another pair. They must say where you have been.

Example
You have been to the Houses of Parliament.

FOLLOW UP

6 Answer these questions.

a Where can you see butterflies?

b Which building is nine hundred years old?

c Which places open at half past ten in the morning?

d Find two places where you can see the Prime Minister.

e Which place is not open on Sunday mornings?

LISTENING

Strange visitors

- Students read the introduction to the dialogue.
- Point out that McLintock and Owen are listening to the radio.
- Students read the dialogue silently.
- Check understanding. Explain the following items, if necessary:
  DJ   on patrol   Constable   Sergeant   base   search   mine

Notes
- *Wales* is a very mountainous part of Britain. Very few people live in the mountains, apart from some sheep farmers.
- *Constable* is the rank of an ordinary policeman or policewoman.

The present perfect and past tenses

BUILD UP
- Say *You have been practising the present perfect tense. This is used to refer to the past, but so is the past simple tense. So how are they different? Exercise 2 will help answer this.*

a
- Read the instruction and two questions aloud, from *Look at … to … second sentences.*
- Students look at the sentences.
- One student reads out the first pair of sentences. Another reads out the second pair of sentences.

b
- Read aloud the two questions.
- Tell students to look at the time phrases as well as the verb forms.
- Elicit suggestions.

Answer key
The first two sentences refer to actions which started in the past and are still going on. They are about present as well as past time.

The second two sentences refer to actions which happened in the past and are now finished. They are about past time only.

- Check comprehension. Explain as necessary, drawing attention to the features of the sentences which indicate the *time* they refer to, i.e. *now, yesterday.*

c
- Students look at the diagram.
- Point out that the circles on the left and right overlap with the circle in the middle. They do not overlap with each other.

- Point out the word *present* in the right hand circle and the words *present perfect* and *past* to the left of the circles.
- Ask what these are all names of.
- Elicit the answer *verb tenses.*

d
- Students complete the diagram by putting one of the verb tenses beside the diagram into each empty circle.

Answer key
(left to right)
past   present perfect   present

- Point out how this shows that the present perfect is about the present *and* the past. Add that it often refers to events which began in the past but which continued and are still continuing.
- Give other examples of the 'duration' use of the present perfect tense, e.g.
  I've lived in Madrid for two years.

Note
Before they do this exercise, remind students that if the present perfect verb form is negative, i.e. *haven't/hasn't* + past participle, the past simple tense verb form will be *didn't* + infinitive.

- Students read the list of things that have happened to the policemen tonight.
- Say *Now, if yesterday was the same as today, what happened yesterday?*
- Read the example aloud.
- Students write answers to *What happened yesterday?*
- In pairs, students compare answers.
- Check answers.

Answer key
We were on patrol for six hours yesterday.
We didn't see anything.
The thieves didn't come.
We didn't have any luck.
We searched the hills.
We talked to all the farmers.
The weather was very cold.
We listened to the radio.

- Ask *What was the last thing that McLintock said?*
- Elicit the answer.

Answer key
I've just seen a light by the old mine.

- Tell students they will now hear the continuation of the story on cassette.

- Say *Listen carefully for what happened.*

- Play the cassette. Students listen carefully.

- Rewind the cassette.

- Elicit suggestions about what happened.

- Play the cassette again. Students listen and check their own and others' suggestions.

- Rewind the cassette.

Strange visitors

DJ It's 3.30 am on Thursday September 23rd and you're listening to the *Late Late Show* on Radio Wales.

Owen We've been on patrol for six hours tonight. We haven't seen anything.

McLintock We were on patrol for six hours yesterday. We didn't see anything then. Call Sergeant Jones.

Owen OK. Car CX7 to base. Car CX7 to base. We've had no luck, Sarge. The thieves haven't come. Can we come in now?

Sergeant Base to CX7. Have you seen anything?

Owen Nothing but sheep. We've searched the hills and we've talked to all the farmers.

Sergeant All right. Come back to the station.

Owen Mmm. We're on our way back to a nice cup of tea at the station now. I don't know why …

McLintock Wait a minute, Taff. What's that over there? I've just seen a light by the old mine.

Owen I can't see anything. Perhaps it was an aeroplane. No, you're right. I saw it that time. Let's take a look.

McLintock That's strange.

Owen What's wrong?

McLintock The engine's stopped.

Owen Look. That light. It's getting closer. It's moving very fast.

McLintock Car CX7 to base. Car CX7 to base. Now the radio's gone dead.

Owen It's getting closer. It's coming straight towards us.

McLintock Oh no. Help! Help! It's … (Later) What's happened? Where has it gone? It was in front of us and now it's gone.

Owen Look. It's landed behind us. What is it?

McLintock I don't know, but it's disappeared now.

Owen Scottie? We're not in the same place.

McLintock What do you mean? No, you're right. We were by the road to the old mine. That's two miles from here.

Owen Come on. Let's get back to the station. No one will believe this …

(Later) Hello, Sarge. You won't believe this, but we've seen a UFO. It was …

Sergeant Where have you been?

Owen It was. Been? What do you mean. Where have we been? We've just come back from patrol.

Sergeant Where have you been since September 23rd?

McLintock Oh come on, Sarge. Is this a joke? It's September 23rd today. Look at the calendar …

Sergeant The calendar says March 19th, McLintock. You and your patrol car disappeared on September 23rd last year. We have searched every inch of this county for you. And now you walk in here as if nothing has happened. I'll ask you again, Owen and McLintock. Where have you been for the last seven months?

▼**5** • Students read the list of things that happened.

- Say *Put the events in the correct order by numbering them 1, 2, 3, and so on. If something happened more than once, it will have **two** numbers.*

- Play the cassette. Students number the events.

- Rewind the cassette.

- In pairs, students compare answers.

- Play the cassette again. Students check answers.

- Elicit answers.

> ### Answer key
> | | |
> |---|---|
> | look for thieves | radio goes dead |
> | call base | light gets closer |
> | start the car | light disappears |
> | return to station | see light behind them |
> | see a light | light disappears |
> | car engine stops | return to the station |
> | light gets closer | look at the calendar |
> | call base | |

▼**6** • Divide the class into groups of three.

- Students note down ideas about what actually happened to the two policemen (one minute).

- Students compare ideas.

- Elicit ideas. Write notes on the board.

- In their groups of three, students list what has happened at home while the policeman have been away. (They should use their memories *and* their imagination.)

- Elicit ideas, making sure that students use the present perfect tense correctly.

FOLLOW UP

▼**7** • Students read the beginning of this piece of writing. Point out the use of the past simple and past continuous tenses.

- In class or for homework, students write the story of McLintock and Owen using the events in Exercise 5. These should now be in the right order!

Strange visitors

1 Read this.

One night in September 1983 Constable David
(Scottie) McLintock and Constable Peter Owen
were on patrol in the mountains of North Wales.
Some thieves were stealing sheep from the local
farms. The two policemen were looking for the
thieves.

DJ It's 3.30 am on Thursday 23 September and
you're listening to the *Late Late Show* on Radio
Wales …

Owen We've been on patrol for six hours now.
We haven't seen anything.

McLintock We were on patrol for six hours
yesterday. We didn't see anything then. Call
Sergeant Jones.

Owen OK. Car CX7 to base. Car CX7 to base.
We've had no luck, Sarge. The thieves
haven't come. Can we come in now?

Sergeant Base to CX7. Have you seen
anything?

Owen Nothing but sheep. We've searched the
hills and we've talked to all the farmers.

Sergeant All right. Come back to the station.

Owen Mmm. We're on our way back to a nice
cup of tea at the station now. I don't know
why …

McLintock Wait a minute, Taff. What's that
over there? I've just seen a light by the old
mine.

2 a Look at these sentences.
What tense is used in the first two sentences?
What tense is used in the second two sentences?

> We'**ve been** on patrol for six hours **tonight**. We **haven't seen** anything.
> We **were** on patrol for six hours **yesterday**. We **didn't see** anything **then**.

b Why are they different? What time are they about?

c Complete this diagram with the names of the tenses.

present
present perfect
past.

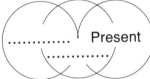

········· Present
·········

3 Look at what has happened to the policemen tonight. What happened yesterday?

Example
We've been on patrol for six hours tonight.
We were on patrol for six hours yesterday.

We've been on patrol for six hours tonight.
We haven't seen anything.
The thieves haven't come.
We've had no luck.
We've searched the hills.
We've talked to all the farmers.
The weather has been very cold.
We've listened to the radio.

4 What was the light by the old mine? Listen and find out what happened.

5 Put these in the correct order.

return to the station	look at the calendar
car engine stops	light disappears
look for thieves	call base
see light behind them	radio goes dead
see a light	light gets closer
start the car	

6 What do you think?

- What has happened to the two men?
- What has happened at home while the two men have been away?

FOLLOW UP

7 Use the cues from Exercise 5. Tell the story of McLintock and Owen. Begin like this.

Constables McLintock and Owen were on patrol.
They were looking for thieves. At half past three they
decided to return to the station. But as they were
driving past . . .

INTERACTION

Contact with English

How much contact have you had with English? You have certainly listened to records in English and seen films in English. But have you ever spoken to someone in English outside your classroom – a tourist perhaps? Have you ever visited an English-speaking country or read an English magazine?

1 Conduct a class survey on contacts with English. Find out:

- what kind of contact people have had.
- what they did.

2 First decide what kind of contact you will ask about.

3 Make a questionnaire like this.

> **QUESTIONNAIRE**
>
> **1 a** Have you ever watched an English language TV programme? YES ☐ NO ☐
>
> **b** If YES, what did you watch?
>
> _____
>
> **2 a** Have you ever... _____

4 Go round the class and ask your questions.

5 Report your findings to the class.

6 Make a graph like this.

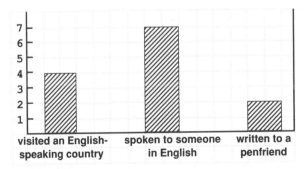

FOLLOW UP

7 Write about your graph.

Example
In our class six people have spoken to a tourist in English.

INTERACTION

Contact with English

- Choose a student to read the introduction aloud (from *How much contact* to *English magazine*).

- Quickly elicit: who has spoken to an English-speaking tourist; who has visited an English-speaking country; and who has read an English magazine. (Students raise their hands.)

- Read this instruction aloud. Elicit further examples of contact students might have had, e.g. visiting a friend in Britain, being asked the way by a tourist.

- Elicit what they *did*, e.g. went shopping with the friend, explained the way to the tourist.

- Give examples yourself, if necessary.

- Elicit further kinds of contact people may have had.

Answer key
(possible answers)
- *Meet English-speaking exchange students at school*
- *Attend a concert performed by a British, American or Australian band*
- *Listen to a radio station in English*

- Students decide on two *sorts* of contact they will ask about.

- They think of two questions beginning *Have you ever ...?*

- Students look at the questionnaire.

- Point out that it has not been completed as it only shows two questions.

- Say *I want you to design a questionnaire which has as many questions as you can think of. Each question must ask if someone has had a certain sort of contact with English.*

- Students design questionnaires.

Note
Students will need to *elongate* the *Yes* and *No* boxes. This will allow them to indicate the number of people who answered each question. The box below could also be enlarged vertically to allow for the recording of several different answers.

- Students walk round the class, ask their questions of as many people as possible, and record their answers on the questionnaire. (Allow about fifteen minutes for this.)

- Students in turn report what they have found to the class. (Before they start, check the tense they will use, i.e. the present perfect.)

Note
Students may need an example of the language needed to do this, e.g.
*Twelve people have watched an English language TV programme. Most people watched **Eastenders**, **Top of the Pops** and **Hill Street Blues**. Two people have written letters to people in America ...*

- Students look at the graph.

- Say *The vertical axis shows **how many people** have done something and the horizontal axis shows **what** they have done.*

- Students draw a graph in their exercise books to show the answers to their questions. Walk round and check that students have got the right idea.

- In pairs, students compare graphs.

FOLLOW UP

- Students write a few sentences about what their graph shows.

Note
The structure of the paragraph could be as below:
Our graph shows that people in our class have had these contacts with English:
Six people have ...
One person has ...
Encourage students to give numbers. They can also give examples, e.g. of TV programmes people have watched, and of things that do not actually appear on the graph.

PROJECT

Your life

This project can be done individually or in groups.

- Students look at the pictures.
- Say *These show events in this girl's life in the last year. What has she done?*
- Students give their ideas. Introduce any new vocabulary students need to express their answers.

Answer key
(possible answers)
She's been a bridesmaid.
Someone in her family has got married.
She's been to a wedding.

She's been the captain of a basketball team.
Her team has won a championship.

She's had a birthday party.

Her family has moved house.

They've knocked down some buildings near the town hall.

- Read the instructions aloud.
- Students note some things that have happened in their lives in the last year. Encourage them to write about other family members, too.
- Ask for ideas.
- Ask follow up questions *When did you ...?, Did you ...?, Where did you ...?,* etc.
- Students write a rough draft of what has happened in their life in the last year. They should write as much detail as possible.
- Correct students' drafts. Pay particular attention to the correct use of the present perfect and past tenses.
- Students do a neat draft of their year's diary.
- Students find pictures and photographs to illustrate their year.
- Students arrange their diary and illustrations to make a project. Students should also give their project a title.

▶ **Pronunciation: page T113**

LEARNING DIARY

- Students look back at the list on the first page of Unit 9.

A Students circle draw faces on the symbols to indicate how well they know each item.

B In class or for homework, students do the self-check exercises in the Workbook.

C In pairs, students compare answers.

Check answers.

Do not ask for numbers of correct answers, but try and get a feel for which exercises caused problems. Go over these again carefully. Refer interested students and students with problems to the appropriate section of a pedagogic grammar book.

Remind students that the Workbook exercises are not 'tests'. They are one way they can find out about the progress they are making, and the items they need more practice with.

D Students make a chart with two columns.

They head the one on the left *What I Liked Best,* and the one on the right *Why.*

They list what they liked best, and why. Walk round while they are doing this.

In pairs, students compare charts.

Different pairs compare charts.

From what you have seen while walking round, tell the class what you *think* they liked. Try to get possible reasons. This will give you insights into the activities the students liked as well as the language items they found easy and difficult.

CULTURE SPOT
Workbook page 76

- Divide the class into pairs or groups of three or four.
- Students look quickly at the text.
- Ask *What is the text about?*
- Students give their ideas
- Ask *What do you already know about this topic?*
- Students give their ideas. Discuss these ideas.
- Say *Read the Culture Spot text. Note anything that you find interesting or unusual.*
- Ask comprehension questions about the text.
- Students give their answers. Explain any words that students need.
- Ask *Did you find anything interesting or unusual?*
- Students give their ideas.
- Read each comparison question in turn.
- Discuss each question. Encourage students to compare their situation to the one in the text.

PROJECT

Your life

What has happened in your life in the last year?

- What has happened in your family?
- Have there been any changes at school?
- Have there been any important events in your town?

Write down:

- what has happened.
- when and where it happened.
- how you feel about it.

Learning diary

Look at the list on the first page of this unit.

9

A How well do you know each thing? Complete the circles to make faces.

B Try the self-check in the Workbook.

C Compare your self-check answers with a partner's. Do you understand everything? If you don't understand something, look in a grammar book or ask your teacher.

D What did you like best in this unit? Why?

▶ **Pronunciation: page 113**

Contents

Victoria Road: Jackie's surprise   88
Language work: some / any   90
countable / uncountable   91
a bit / a few / a lot of   91
how much? / how many?   91
Reading: Pizza Palace   92
Listening: Boston burgers   94
Interaction: In a cafe   95
Project: Your own menu   96

10 food

quantity

Language work ☺ ☺ ☹

Grammar

some / any
I've already lent you some money.
Have you got any money?
I haven't got any money.

countable / uncountable
an apple / some apples
some bread / some bread

a bit / a few / a lot of
a bit of meat / a few onions
a lot of meat / a lot of onions

how much? / how many?
How much cheese do you want?
How many eggs do you want?

a bottle of . . etc.
a bottle of lemonade
two bottles of lemonade

Word work

food

☺ ☺ ☹ Learning objectives

In this unit you will learn how to:

express quantities

describe what a meal consists of

read a menu

order a meal in a cafe

understand and give a recipe

VICTORIA ROAD

Jackie's surprise

- Ask *What happened to the people in 'Victoria Road' in Unit 9?*
- Students give answers.
- Refer back to page 78 to check.

> **Answer key**
> *Jackie's American cousin, Greg, arrived. Terry was surprised and upset to find out that the cousin was a boy.*

- Read the questions.
- Students look at the picture story and find the answers to the questions.
- Students give their answers.
- Ask *How do you know?* Students justify their answers with examples from the picture story.

> **Answer key**
> *Casey, Terry, Sue, Jackie, Greg are in the story. They're in the street and then in the Fat Cat cafe. They are eating, drinking and talking. A waitress is also in the cafe. Jackie is telling the others that she is going to America.*

- Say *Now look at the dialogue and listen.*
- ◼️ Play the cassette. Students listen and read.
- Rewind the cassette.

> **Notes**
>
> **I'm broke.** This means 'I haven't got any money.' It is very informal.
>
> **I've got to** This means 'I must' or 'I have to.' It is common in British English but not in American English.
>
> **I wish Jackie were here.** Jackie is not there – but Casey would like it very much if she were there.
>
> **Buffalo Bill** Buffalo Bill was a hero of the American wild west. Terry is being rude about Greg!
>
> **Can I help you?** This is often used by waitresses, waiters and shop assistants to ask customers what they want.
>
> **Could we have ...?** This is a polite way of ordering in a cafe or restaurant.
>
> **How many cups of tea did you want?** *Did* here is less direct and more polite than *do*. The waitress is being very polite because she forgot exactly what Greg had ordered.
>
> **French fries – I mean chips** *French fries* is American English and *chips* is British English. Greg uses the American expression then changes to the British one.
>
> **Americans have got big mouths.** Terry is being rude again. He means Americans 'talk a lot' or 'boast' – another meaning of 'having a big mouth'.
>
> **Haven't you heard?** is short for 'Haven't you heard that ...?' In this case, it means 'Haven't you heard that I'm going to live in America for a year?'
>
> Cafes and snack bars in Britain usually serve coke, tea, milk (and coffee), and food such as sandwiches, burgers and chips. They do not usually serve alcohol.

- Read the 'What do you think?' questions.
- Elicit ideas about each question.

Answer key

*Terry doesn't like Greg. He calls him 'Buffalo Bill'
and is rude about Americans. He is obviously
jealous of him. Terry probably feels even worse
now! Jackie is going away for a year – and she
didn't even tell him.*

*Greg probably feels proud because he will be able to
show Jackie things like real American hamburgers.*

*Jackie obviously feels very pleased, because she's
getting an opportunity that the others aren't.*

*Sue probably has conflicting emotions.
She may be pleased that her rival, Jackie, is going,
but she may also feel a bit sorry for Terry.*

 • Students answer the questions.

• Check answers.

Answer key

a *Casey, Terry and Sue are deciding what to do.*
b *They haven't got any money.*
c *She bought some birthday presents yesterday.*
d *He's got to (or He must) buy a lot of things for
   his bike.*
e *Greg is with Jackie.*
f *He calls him 'Buffalo Bill'. He wants to be rude
   about the fact that Greg is American.*
g *She offers to pay.*
h *They order two glasses of coke, two cups of tea
   and a glass of milk.*
i *He thinks they are not real cheeseburgers.*
j *An American cheeseburger is made with the best
   steak, at least two slices of cheese, a lot of onions
   and a lot of salad.*
k *She will find out about American hamburgers in
   September.*
l *She's going to live in America with Greg's
   family for a year.*

 • Students close their books.

• Say *Now listen carefully*.

• ▭ Play the cassette.

Jackie's surprise

1 What do you remember? What happened in the last part of the story? Look back at page 78 and check your ideas.

2 Look at this episode. Who is in it? Where are they? What are they doing?

> I'm bored and I'm broke. Have you got any money, Sue?

> I've already lent you some money this month, Terry.

①

> Come on, you lot. We're going to the Fat Cat. Are you coming? We'll pay.

②

3 📼 Listen and follow in your books.

Casey What shall we do?

Terry I'm bored and I'm broke. Have you got any money, Sue?

Sue I've already lent you some money this month, Terry. And I bought some birthday presents yesterday. So I haven't got any money now.

Terry How much money have you got, Case?

Casey I've got a bit, but I've got to buy a lot of things for my bike. I wish Jackie was here. She's always got a lot of money.

Sue Here she is now with Greg.

Terry Oh no, not Buffalo Bill. Is he still here?

Jackie Come on, you lot. We're going to the Fat Cat. Are you coming? We'll pay.

In the cafe

Waitress Can I help you?

Greg Yes please. Could we have two glasses of Coke, two cups of tea and I'll have a glass of milk.

Waitress I'm sorry. How many cups of tea did you want?

Sue Two.

Waitress Do you want anything to eat?

Greg Yes, can we have two sandwiches – one ham, one chicken, one cheeseburger with a plate of french fries – I mean chips. And two hamburgers.

Terry Have you got any packets of crisps?

Waitress No, I'm sorry, we haven't.

Terry That's okay. Thanks.

Later

Greg You can't get real cheeseburgers in England, you know. Now, in an American hamburger we only use the best steak and it doesn't have just a few onions, a bit of salad and one slice of cheese. It has at least two slices of cheese, a lot of onions and a lot of salad, too – tomatoes, lettuce, cucumber and . . .

Sue Mmm. It must be very big.

Terry Well, Americans have got big mouths, haven't they?

Jackie Don't be childish, Terry.

Greg Anyway, Jackie. You'll see for yourself in September.

Terry Why? What's happening in September?

3

4

5

Jackie Oh, haven't you heard? I'm going to live in the States for a year with Greg's family. Isn't it wonderful?

What do you think?
● What does Terry think about Greg? How do you know?
● How does each of them feel at the end?

4 Answer these questions.

a What are Casey, Terry and Sue doing?
b Why can't they go to the cafe?
c Why hasn't Sue got any money?
d What must Casey do?
e Who is with Jackie?
f What does Terry call Greg? Why?
g What does Jackie offer to do?
h What do they order to drink?
i Why doesn't Greg like British cheeseburgers?
j What is a real American cheeseburger like?
k When will Jackie find out about American hamburgers?
l What is Jackie going to do?

5 Close your book. Listen again.

6

Useful expressions

- Students look at the 'Useful expressions'.
- Students write the mother-tongue equivalent of each item next to that item. If students are not sure, say *Go back to the story and work it out from the situation.*
- While they are doing this, copy the chart on to the blackboard.
- In pairs, students compare charts.
- Elicit and discuss answers. Write the expressions in your blackboard chart.
- Students correct and amend their own charts.

- Divide class into groups of four.
- Students choose their roles.
- Students read the dialogue in their groups. Walk round the class. Note any serious errors in pronunciation.
- Correct serious pronunciation errors (if any).
- Choose one group to read their dialogue aloud to the class.
- If time, students change roles and read the dialogue again.

FOLLOW UP

- In class or for homework, students write the answers to the questions in Exercise 4 in full.
- Check answers.

> **Answer key**
> See **Answer key** for Exercise 4.

CULTURE SPOT

- Ask *What phrase did Greg use and then correct?*

> **Answer key**
> *french fries*

- Read the 'Culture spot' box. Say *There are other examples, too.*
- Students read the examples. Check understanding of words.

> **Notes**
> *Gas* and *pants* both also exist in British English, but with different meanings from their American English meanings. A *gas*, in British English, is something that is neither solid nor liquid, e.g. *oxygen*. *Gas* is used for cooking and heating. *Pants* means underwear: knickers (for females) and underpants (for males). In American English *gas* means *petrol* and *pants* means *trousers*.

- Students look at the list of British English words.
- In pairs, students use their dictionaries to find the American English words for these.
- Students write the American English word next to the British English equivalent.

> **Answer key**
>
> | flat | apartment |
> |------|-----------|
> | cinema | the movies |
> | lift | elevator |
> | shop | store |
> | film | movie |
> | colour | color |
> | motorway | freeway |
> | programme | program |

LANGUAGE WORK

Some/any

BUILD UP

a
- Students turn back to *Victoria Road*.
- They complete the three gapped sentences.
- Check answers.

> **Answer key**
> *any   any   some*

b
- Read the questions.
- Students complete the rule. While they are doing this, copy the 'rule box' on to the blackboard.
- In pairs, students compare rules.
- Ask one student to complete the 'rule box' on the blackboard.
- Students correct their rules as necessary.

> **Answer key**
> *any   some*

- Say *This rule works nearly every time. But you will find some exceptions, for example in interrogative sentences that are used to offer something.*
  Example
  Would you like some tea?

- Students complete sentences **a–j** with *some* or *any*.
- In pairs, students compare answers.
- Check answers.

T90

Answer key

a	*some, any*	f	*any*
b	*any*	g	*some*
c	*any*	h	*any*
d	*any, some*	i	*any*
e	*any*	j	*Some*

Note

The *some/any* rule also applies in compounds like *somewhere/anywhere* and *something/anything*.

Countable/uncountable

 a • Read the statements and examples.

- Elicit ideas about the countable/uncountable distinction in the students' mother tongue.

b • Read the lists of examples of uncountable things.

c • In pairs, students identify the uncountable things and add these to the appropriate list in **b**.

- Check answers.

Answer key

These things are uncountable:

bread (food)	*water (drinks)*
wood (materials)	*orange juice (drinks)*
meat (food)	*soap powder (other*
shampoo (other things)	*things)*

Note

Countable and uncountable nouns

- Abstract nouns are often uncountable, e.g. *discipline, advice, peace.*

- Several nouns have both countable and uncountable uses. If students ask about this, explain that:
  - a countable noun refers to separate things, e.g. *two pizzas* (= two whole pizzas)
  - an uncountable noun refers to an amount of a certain thing, e.g. *some pizza* (= a piece of pizza).

- It is common in informal speech to make some 'drinks' words countable, e.g. *two coffees, three teas*. But this means 'two cups of coffee', 'three cups of tea'.

- Some uncountable words can have a plural, e.g. *some cheeses, some shampoos*. But here it means different kinds of cheese or shampoo.

 a • Students turn back to *Victoria Road*.

- They write down the phrases from the story containing the expressions.

- Check answers.

Answer key

a bit of salad
a few onions
a lot of onions
How much money have you got, Case?
How many cups of tea did you want?

b • Read the question.

- Elicit answers.

Answer key

A lot of, *a few* and *How many* with countable nouns.

A bit of, *How much* and *a lot of* with uncountable nouns.

- Students add C (countable) or UC (uncountable) next to the phrases they have written in **4a**.

 • Read the dialogues in the boxes.

- Divide class into pairs.

- They turn back to Exercise **3c**.

- In pairs, students make their own dialogues like those in the boxes, using the words in **3c**.

- If time, each pair performs one dialogue for the class.

Answer key

... some cheese. How much ...? ... a bit.
... some tomatoes. How many ...? ... a few.
... some shampoo. How much ...? ... a bit.
... some orange juice. How much ...? ... a bit.
... some bread. How much ...? ... a bit.
... some pencils. How many ...? ... a few.
... some wood. How much ...? ... a bit.
... some water. How much ...? ... a bit.
... some meat. How much ...? ... a bit.
... some soap powder. How much ...? ... a bit.
... some apples. How many ...? ... a few.

FOLLOW UP

 • Read the list of food words.

- Check understanding of the words.

- Read the examples.

- For homework, students look in the fridge or a cupboard at home and write a statement for each food item, like the example statements.

Useful expressions

6 How do you say these expressions in your language?

I'm broke.

How much … ?

I've got to … (= I must)

I wish Jackie was here.

Come on, you lot.

Are you coming to the cafe?

We'll pay.

Can I help you?

Could we have … ?

How many … ?

Don't be childish.

You'll see for yourself.

Haven't you heard?

7 a Work in groups of four. One person is Terry, one is Greg, one is Sue and Jackie and one is the waitress and Casey.

b Read the dialogue.

FOLLOW UP

8 Write the answers to the questions in Exercise 4 in full.

Culture spot: Some words are different in British and American English.

Here are some examples.

American	British
french fries	chips
drug store	crisps
chips	chemist
pants	trousers
automobile	car
truck	lorry
gas	petrol

Use a dictionary. Find the American words for these.

flat   cinema   lift   shop   film
colour   motorway   programme

LANGUAGE WORK

Some/any

BUILD UP

1 a Complete these sentences with 'some' or 'any'.

Have you got .... money?

I haven't got .... money.

I bought .... birthday presents yesterday.

b What is the rule? When do you use 'some' and when do you use 'any'? Complete the rule.

> We use .... in questions and negative statements.
>
> We use .... in positive statements.

2 Write 'some' or 'any'.

a I need .... new shoes, but I haven't got .... money.

b Have you got .... brothers or sisters?

c Is there .... food in the fridge?

d We didn't get .... Maths homework yesterday, but we got .... Geography homework.

e There isn't ....one at home.

f I haven't got ....thing to do.

g I've got ....thing in my eye.

h Are there .... shops in your street?

i I didn't see ....one at the club.

j ....one has stolen my purse.

90

Countable/uncountable

3 a Read this.

Some nouns are countable. They have a singular and a plural.

a person   some people
a sandwich   some sandwiches
a cup   some cups

Some nouns are uncountable. They have no plural.

some cheese   some cheese

some money   some money

b These things are usually uncountable

kinds of drinks: milk, tea, coffee ....
....

kinds of food, which you eat only part of at a time: cheese, lettuce, cucumber, fish ....
....

materials: paper, plastic, iron, leather ....
....

some other things: music, money, information, news ....
....

c Do you think these things are countable or uncountable? If they are uncountable, add them to the lists in 3b.

tomatoes   shampoo   stamps   orange juice

bread   pencils   wood

water   meat   soap powder   apples

91

4 a Look at the Victoria Road story again. Find the phrases with these expressions in.

a bit of ....

a few ....

a lot of ....

How much . . . ? ....

How many . . . ? ....

b Which expressions do we use with countable nouns and which with uncountable nouns?

5 Work in pairs. Use the words in Exercise 3a and c to make dialogues like this:

> **A** 'I need some money.'
>
> **B** 'How much do you need?'
>
> **A** 'Just a bit.' (or 'Just a little.')

> **A** 'I need some stamps.'
>
> **B** 'How many do you need?'
>
> **A** 'Just a few.'

FOLLOW UP

6 When you get home, look in your fridge or cupboard. Which of these are in it? How much is there?

Example
There aren't any onions in our fridge.
There is a lot of milk.
There isn't any tea in our cupboard.
There are a lot of potatoes in our cupboard.

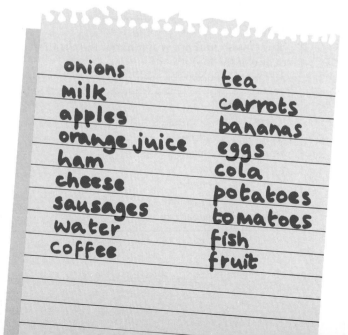

onions   tea
milk   carrots
apples   bananas
orange juice   eggs
ham   cola
cheese   potatoes
sausages   tomatoes
water   fish
coffee   fruit

READING

This is a 'reading for information' activity. Students do not need to understand or read the whole text. They only have to find the information they are asked for.

1
- Draw students' attention to the menu.
- Read the questions.
- Students look quickly at the menu and find the answers.
- In pairs, students compare answers.
- Check answers.

Answer key
a *Pizza Palace*
b *Mainly pizzas, but also soup, bread, jacket potatoes, salad, desserts and drinks*
c *chips, hamburgers, chocolate cake, sandwiches, pancakes*
d *The taste of the sea (if she eats fish)*
  Vegetarian delight
  Traditional

2
- Students look at the pictures.
- Ask *Which of these foods are not in any of the pizzas?*
- Students read the pizza menu to find which are not included.
- Elicit answers.

Answer key

green olives	*carrots*
cucumber	*beans*
apples	

3
- Say *This is one order that was given to the chef.*
- Students look at the menu and list the ingredients the chef will need.
- Check answers.

Note
Students should not worry about the *quantity* of any of the ingredients.

Answer key

potato	*sardines*
butter	*cheese*
bread	*tomato*
garlic	*ham*
tuna	*chicken*
mussels	*pineapple*
anchovies	*sweetcorn*

4
- Students read the three orders.
- Divide the class into pairs.
- In pairs, students write down each order.
- They work out how much each order will cost.
- Students give details of each order. Refer to the menu.
- List these on the board.
- Ask for the total cost of each order.
- Write this on the board.
- If there is disagreement, do the arithmetic with the class to find the total cost of each order.

Answer key
a

Home-made tomato soup	*70p*
Salad	*£1.35*
The big one	*£3.55*
Traditional	*£2.60*
Fruit salad and ice cream	*£1.65*
Ice cream with chocolate sauce	*75p*
Coffee	*49p*
Hot chocolate	*40p*
Large ice cold drink	*75p*
Standard ice cold drink	
(or pure orange juice)	*60p*
	£12.84

(If students have calculated the two bills separately, the cheapest possible meal comes to £5.05 and the most expensive to £7.79.)

b

Some like it hot	*£3.30*
Extra mushrooms	*25p*
Extra black olives	*25p*
Lemon cheesecake	*£1.35*
	£5.15

5
- Say *Now, you're going to decide what you would order in Pizza Palace.*
- Students write down their own meal. They put the price next to each item, as in Exercise 4.
- Find out the following:
  Who had garlic bread?
  Who chose 'The Taste of the Sea'?
  Who had extra salami? Extra sweetcorn?
  Who didn't have a dessert?
  Who didn't have a hot drink?
  What was the most popular pizza?
  Who had the most extras?
  Whose meal cost the most?
  Whose meal cost the least?
  etc.

WORD WORK

6 **a** • Students write the headings 'Countable words' and 'Uncountable words' in their exercise books.

• They find ten countable and ten uncountable words from the menu and list them under the headings.

• Walk round and check.

• In pairs, students compare lists.

Answer key

Countable words	Uncountable words
potato	soup
tomato	bread
onion	butter
pepper	ham
bean	lettuce
pizza	sausage
olive	fish
mushroom	cheese
mussel	water
anchovy	chicken
sardine	pineapple
chilli	sweetcorn
bottle	tuna
glass	fruit salad
	ice cream
	apple pie
	cheesecake
	coffee
	tea
	hot chocolate
	cola
	lemonade
	mineral water
	apple juice
	beer
	wine

---

b • Divide the class into pairs.

• In pairs, students write down names of foods which are similar to names in their language.

• Elicit these and list on the board.

• Comment on any names which seem similar but which are actually different.

• Students list the names of food they do not know.

• They look these words up in the dictionary and write down the mother-tongue equivalents.

• Walk round the class. Give help where necessary.

7 • In class or for homework, students design their own pizza. They use the same style as in the menu. The pizza must have a name and a list of ingredients.

• Collect and display. Students look at each other's pizzas.

FOLLOW UP

8 • Read the instructions.

• Divide the class into pairs.

• Student A points to each pizza name and asks *What's this one?* in his/her own language. Student B translates the English name into their own language.

• Change roles and repeat. **or** Students make a written translation of the list for homework.

READING

1 Look quickly at this menu and find the answers to these questions.

a What is the name of the restaurant?

b What kind of food does it sell?

c Which of these can't you buy at this restaurant?

soup   tea   bread   chips   mineral water

hamburgers   chocolate cake   ice cream

fruit juice   sandwiches   pancakes

d Kamala doesn't eat meat. Which pizzas can she eat?

Pizza Palace

STARTERS

Home–made tomato soup	70p
Garlic bread	80p
Jacket potato with butter	75p

Salad

Make your own salad from our salad bar: cucumber, tomatoes, onions, lettuce, peppers, sweetcorn, beans   £1.35

PIZZAS

The big one

A traditional pizza with ham, salami sausage, black olives, green peppers and sliced mushrooms   £3.55

The taste of the sea

If you like fish, you'll love this pizza. It has tuna, mussels, anchovies and sardines on a traditional cheese and tomato base   £3.40

Some like it hot

You get a free glass of water with our special hot pizza: beef, hot chillies, red and green peppers, onions and tomatoes   £3.30

Vegetarian delight

A healthy alternative with green peppers, mushrooms and onions on a cheese and tomato pizza   £3.15

Hawaiian style

An exotic pizza from the South Seas: ham, chicken, pineapple and sweetcorn   £3.10

Traditional

Cheese and tomato   £2.60

All our pizzas are available with traditional or wholemeal base.

Why not add some delicious extra toppings to your pizza? Or make a pizza to your own recipe.

Extras

Cheese, mushrooms, black olives, green peppers, sweetcorn, pineapple, chicken, onions, salami, tuna, mussels   25p each

DESSERTS

Fruit salad and ice cream	£1.65
Lemon cheesecake	£1.35
Traditional apple pie and cream	£1.25
Ice cream with chocolate sauce	75p

BEVERAGES

Coffee	49p per cup
Tea	45p per pot
Hot chocolate	40p per cup

ICE COLD DRINKS

	Large	Standard
Cola	75p	60p
Diet cola	75p	60p
Lemonade	75p	60p
Mineral water	65 per bottle	
Apple juice	70p	
Orange juice	60p	

ALCOHOLIC DRINKS

Beer	95p per bottle
Red wine	99p per glass
White wine	99p per glass

Important note

We can only serve alcoholic drinks with meals.
We cannot serve alcoholic drinks to customers under 18 years of age.
Families: See our special Children's Menu.
There is no service charge included in your bill.
During busy periods we serve only meals.
All prices include VAT.
Take-away service:
All our pizzas are available to take away at a 10% discount on menu prices.

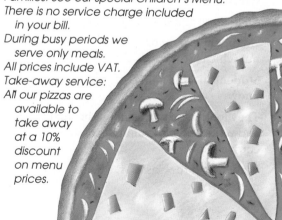

2 Which of the following is not in any of the pizzas?

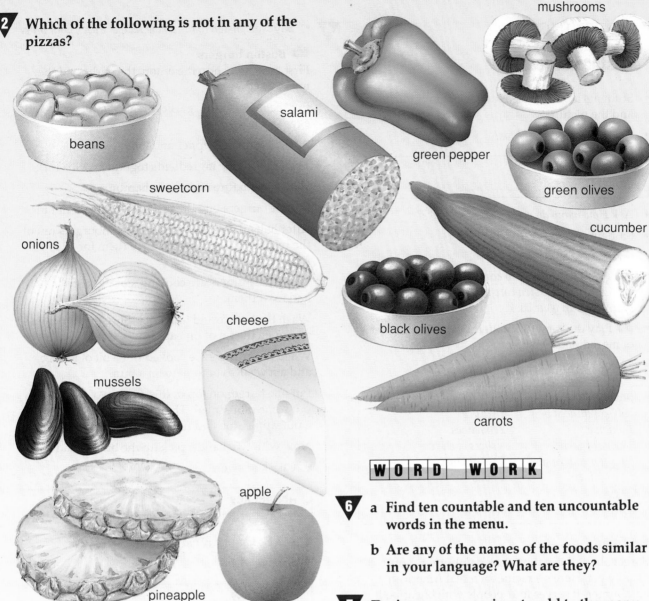

beans

salami

mushrooms

green pepper

green olives

cucumber

sweetcorn

onions

cheese

black olives

carrots

mussels

apple

pineapple

3 Look at this order. Make a list of all the ingredients the chef will need.

1 × jacket potato   1 × Taste of the Sea
1 × garlic bread   1 × Hawaiian style

4 Write down the orders. What will each person pay?

  a Two customers, aged 14, had a starter, a pizza, a dessert, a cold drink and a hot drink each. One had the cheapest possible meal, the other had the most expensive meal possible.

  b One customer, aged 20, had a pizza with extra mushrooms and black olives. He had the second most expensive dessert. He didn't buy a drink, because he got a free one.

5 Choose your own meal. How much will it cost?

W O R D   W O R K

6 **a** Find ten countable and ten uncountable words in the menu.

  b Are any of the names of the foods similar in your language? What are they?

7 Design your own pizza to add to the menu. Give it a name and say what it contains.

FOLLOW UP

8 **a** Look through the list of pizzas. Find any words that you do not know. Use a dictionary to find out what they mean.

  b You are with a friend in England. Your friend does not speak English. Translate the list of pizzas for him/her.

What is worse than finding a worm in your apple? Finding half a worm in your apple.

LISTENING

Boston burgers

 • Students look at the gapped list of ingredients and the pictures.

• Ask *What is the recipe for?*

> **Answer key**
> *Boston burgers*

• Ask *How many do you think it will make?*

• Students suggest answers.

 • Say *Now you're going to hear the ingredients for Boston burgers. Listen carefully and list the ingredients in your book.*

• ▄▄ Play the cassette. Students complete the list of ingredients.

• Check answers.

> **Answer key**
> 750 g of minced beef   1 lettuce
> 1 onion   2 tomatoes
> 1 clove of garlic   4 slices of cheese
> 50 g of breadcrumbs   1 tin of pineapple rings
> 50 g of nuts   4 buns
> 2 eggs
> a little salt, pepper and lemon juice

▄▄ **Boston burgers**
Forget about those thin weak hamburgers you usually get. Here's a recipe for a real American hamburger. It serves four people with big appetites (and big mouths).

For this recipe you will need:
750 g of minced beef
1 onion
1 clove of garlic
50 g of breadcrumbs
50 g of nuts
2 eggs
a little salt, pepper and lemon juice
1 lettuce
2 tomatoes
4 slices of cheese
1 tin of pineapple rings
and 4 buns

 • Students look at the pictures.

a • For each, ask *What is happening here?*

• Students suggest answers, using the present continuous.

b • Students number pictures 1–12 to show correct order.

• Students give their ideas.

 • Say *Now, listen to the whole recipe. Check your order.*

▄▄ **Boston burgers**
First, peel and chop the onion, the garlic and the nuts.

Put the meat, onion, garlic, breadcrumbs, nuts and eggs in a bowl.

Add a little salt, pepper and lemon juice.

Then mix all the ingredients together with a fork.

With the mixture make four hamburgers.

Put the burgers into the refrigerator for 30 minutes.

After half an hour, take the cold hamburgers out of the refrigerator and grill (or fry) them for 10 to 15 minutes each side.

While the burgers are cooking, cut the buns in half and toast them.

Wash the lettuce and tomatoes. Slice the tomatoes and open the tin of pineapple.

When the burgers are cooked put a bit of lettuce and a few slices of tomato on a bun.

Put one burger on top of this. On top of the burger put some more salad. Then put on a slice of cheese, a pineapple ring and finally the top of the bun.

Now with two hands, pick up the burger and eat.

• Check answer.

> **Answer key**
> (As per order in the tapescript above.)

• Ask *So how many burgers will this recipe make?*

• Elicit answer.

> **Answer key**
> *four*

 a • Ask *What do you think about the Boston burger? Is it good for you?*

• Elicit ideas.

> **Notes**
> It contains protein: meat, nuts, eggs and cheese.
>
> Grilling food is better for you than frying it.
>
> The garlic, tomato, lettuce and pineapple contain important vitamins.
>
> So it seems it is good for you.
>
> However:
> minced beef can be very fatty;
> too much red meat may be bad for you.

b • Ask question b.

• Students give their ideas.

⬛W⬛O⬛R⬛D⬛ ⬛W⬛O⬛R⬛K⬛

6
- Read aloud *a glass of milk* and *two glasses of milk*.
- Say *We call a glass a container, because it contains something. Look at the list of other containers.*
- One student reads the list (*bottle*, etc.) aloud.
- Students look at the pictures. They match the names to the correct pictures.
- Read the examples. Write these on the blackboard.
- Students call out the names of the other containers in the unit and what is inside them.
- Add these to the list on the blackboard.

Answer key
a cup of tea
a bottle of tomato ketchup
two bottles of water
a box of soap powder
a bottle of shampoo
a box of orange juice
two bowls of olives
a bowl of beans
a packet of breadcrumbs

FOLLOW UP

7
- In class or for homework, students write the recipe for Boston burgers. They write one sentence for each picture.

INTERACTION

In a cafe

1
- Students read the dialogue.
- They number each sentence to show the correct order.
- In pairs, students compare answers.
- Check answers.
- In pairs, students read the dialogue. One is the waiter or waitress and the other is the customer.
- If time, students change roles.

Answer key
1 *Yes, please?*
2 *Could I have chicken and chips, please?*
3 *Do you want anything to drink?*
4 *I'll have a glass of milk, please.*
5 *Chicken and chips and a glass of milk. Anything else?*
6 *No, thanks. Oh, er, yes. I'll have a tomato salad.*
7 *One tomato salad. Is that it?*
8 *Yes.*
9 *Thank you.*

2
- Students read the waitress's note book.
- They write a dialogue for both orders. Walk round and check this.
- In pairs, students read their dialogues.
- Choose three pairs to read one dialogue each.

Answer key
(possible dialogues)
Table 10
Waitress *Yes, please?*
Customer *Could I have two Big One pizzas, please.*
Waitress *Do you want anything to drink?*
Customer *We'll have two cups of tea, please.*
Waitress *Two Big Ones and two pots of tea. Anything else?*
Customer *Yes – I'll have a fruit salad and ice cream, please.*
Waitress *Fruit salad and ice cream. Is that it?*
Customer *Yes.*
Waitress *Thank you.*

Table 5
Waitress *Yes, please?*
Customer *Could I have a Traditional pizza, please?*
Waitress *Do you want anything to drink?*
Customer *I'll have a glass of lemonade, please.*
Waitress *A Traditional pizza and a lemonade. Anything else?*
Customer *Oh er yes – I'll have soup, please.*
Waitress *One soup. Is that it?*
Customer *Yes.*
Waitress *Thank you.*

3
- Students reread the Pizza Palace menu and decide what they would like to order.
- Divide the class into pairs. One student is the customer and one is the waiter or waitress.
- Pairs role play ordering their meals from the menu.
- Students reverse roles and repeat.

FOLLOW UP

4
- In class or for homework, students write dialogues for their orders in Exercise 3.

LISTENING

1 Look at the ingredients.

a What is the recipe for?
b How many do you think it will make?

2  Listen to the ingredients for the recipe. Complete the list of ingredients.

Boston burgers

Serves .... *people*

Ingredients:

750 g minced beef

1 ....

1 clove garlic

50 g breadcrumbs

.... nuts

2 ....

a little .... ,

.... and

lemon ....

1 ....

2 ....

....
cheese

1 tin ....
rings

.... buns

3 Look at the pictures.

a What is happening in each picture?
b Put them in the correct order.

4  Listen to the whole recipe. Check your order.

5 What do you think about the Boston burger?

a Is it good for you?
b Should people eat so much when other people are dying of starvation?

A bottle of etc

6 **Look.**

a glass of milk   two glass**es** of milk

These are containers.

bottle   packet   glass   cup   tin

Look at all the pictures in this unit.
What can you see in containers?

Example
two glasses of cola
a tin of pineapple

FOLLOW UP

7 Using the pictures, write the recipe for
Boston burgers.

INTERACTION

In a cafe

1 **Look at this dialogue. Put it in the correct order.**

Do you want anything to drink?

Yes, please?

Could I have chicken and chips, please?

One tomato salad. Is that it?

Thank you.

No, thanks. Oh, er, yes. I'll have a tomato salad.

Yes.

Chicken and chips and a glass of milk. Anything else?

I'll have a glass of milk, please.

2 **Look at the menu on page 92.**
Here is the waitress's note book. Make the
dialogues for the orders.

Pizza Palace Order

Table 10 2 x the big one
         1 x fruit salad and icecream
         2 x pot tea

Table 5 1 x traditional pizza
         1 x standard lemonade
         1 x soup

3 You are in the Pizza Palace. Order something
from the menu.

FOLLOW UP

4 Write a dialogue for your order at the Pizza Palace.

PROJECT

Your life

This project can be done individually but it will work best in groups.

- Say *Now, let's forget about pizzas and hamburgers. What's your favourite food?*
- Go round the class asking students to name their favourite food.
- Discuss the picture.
- Say *Imagine you have a speciality restaurant which serves this food. You're going to make a menu in English for your restaurant.*

a
- Divide the class into groups of three or four.
- Students think of and list the kinds of food and drink their speciality restaurant will serve.

b
- Students name each dish their restaurant will serve.
- They list and describe each dish.
- They give each dish a price, and mention any extra charges, e.g. for extra portions of something, or if the dish is cooked in a special way.

c
- They decide on a name for the restaurant.
- In class or for homework, students write out the menu for their restaurant. The restaurant's name should be at the top of the menu.

d
- Divide class into groups of three.
- Each group chooses which group's restaurant to eat in first.
- The chosen group puts its menu on the 'table'.
- Groups role play ordering, using the menu. Walk round.
- Students change roles (and menus). Walk round the class.
- Choose two or three groups to role play ordering.
- As follow up, students write out a dialogue and stick it in their project file.

▶ **Pronunciation: page T113**

LEARNING DIARY

- Students turn back to the list of items on the first page of Unit 10.

A Students draw faces on the symbols next to each item to indicate how well they know it.

B In class or for homework, students complete the self-check exercises in the Workbook.

C In pairs, students compare answers.

Elicit answers. Students correct as necessary. Identify 'common problem exercises' or 'common problem language items'.

Spend a few minutes explaining these.

Refer students who still do not fully understand (or who are particularly interested) to the relevant page of a pedagogic grammar.

D Ask what students liked best in this unit, and why. (See procedure in Unit 1.)

CULTURE SPOT
Workbook page 84

- Divide the class into pairs or groups of three or four.
- Students look quickly at the text.
- Ask *What is the text about?*
- Students give their ideas.
- Ask *What do you already know about this topic?*
- Students give their ideas. Discuss these ideas.
- Say *Read the Culture Spot text. Note anything that you find interesting or unusual.*
- Ask comprehension questions about the text.
- Students give their answers. Explain any words that students need.
- Ask *Did you find anything interesting or unusual?*
- Students give their ideas.
- Read each comparison question in turn.
- Discuss each question. Encourage students to compare their situation to the one in the text.

PROJECT

Your life

Open your own restaurant to serve your favourite food. Make a menu in English for your own restaurant.

a Decide which kinds of food and drink you will serve in your restaurant.

b Write them down and describe them. Give them prices and write down any special charges.

c Give your restaurant a name.

d Serve some customers in your restaurant.

BETTY'S CHIP SHOP
MENU
CHIPS — 40P
FISH AND CHIPS £1·40 CHIP PIE £1·50
CHICKEN AND CHIPS £1·50 SANDWICH 50P
APPLE PIE AND CHIPS £1·20 CHIP SUNDAE £2
CHOC CHIP ICE CREAM 95P MORE CHIPS 30P
CHIP SOUP — 75P CHIP SURPRISE £3

Learning diary

Look at the list on the first page of this unit.

10

A How well do you know each thing? Complete the circles to make faces.

B Try the self-check in the Workbook.

C Compare your self-check answers with a partner's. Do you understand everything? If you don't understand something, look in a grammar book or ask your teacher.

D What did you like best in this unit? Why?

11 communication

the passive

Contents

Victoria Road: Terry in trouble 98
Language work: The passive voice 100
Reading: Why weren't we warned 102
Listening: The Top 40 104
Interaction: Buying a record 105
Project: Forms of communication 106

Language work 😊 😐 ☹️

Grammar

the passive - present
The film is taken out of the camera.
The photographs are printed.

- past
The roof was ripped off.
Two people were killed by the storm.

- future
The power lines will be repaired.
Some of the information won't be used.

- present perfect
I've been invited to a party.
The tree has been blown down.

passive and active
The shop's computer records the information.
The information is recorded by the shop's computer.

Word work

the weather

destruction

😊 😐 ☹️ Learning objectives

In this unit you will learn how to:

describe a process

produce a flow chart

talk about the weather

talk about natural disasters

buy a record in a shop

VICTORIA ROAD

Terry in trouble

- Ask *What happened to the people in 'Victoria Road' in Unit 10?*
- Students give answers.
- Refer back to page 88 to check.

Answer key

Terry, Sue, Casey, Jackie and Greg went to the Fat Cat cafe. While they were there Jackie said she was going to live in America, with Greg's family, for a year. Terry was upset.

- Read the questions.
- Students look at the picture story and find the answers to the questions.
- Students give their answers.
- Ask *How do you know?*
- Students justify their answers with examples from the picture story.

Answer key

In this episode, there is Terry's teacher, Terry, his father (Mr Moore) and Sue.
At the beginning of the story, Terry's teacher is getting angry with him because he does not work hard enough. She is going to send a letter to his parents.
Terry's father is angry with Terry. He won't allow him to go to the party. Sue decides not to go to the party either. She helps Terry with his Computer Studies homework instead.

- Say *Now look at the full dialogue and listen.*
- ▪️ Play the cassette.
- Read the *What do you think?* questions.
- Elicit ideas.

Answer key

Terry is lazy and doesn't try hard at school. He has also been spending a lot of time thinking about Jackie.
He likes Jackie but thinks he has lost her.
He likes Sue too. (Remember what he was doing before Jackie arrived?) He may like her even more now. He is probably starting to appreciate Sue's qualities. (She helps him with his homework.)
Terry may stop thinking about Jackie and start thinking about Sue again. Sue may continue to like Terry. But she may change her mind about him.

Notes

It's no laughing matter. This means 'It's not funny. It's very serious.'

The week before last This means 'the week before last week', i.e. two weeks ago.

What's wrong with you? Terry's teacher means 'Why is your school work so bad?'

You're grounded. Terry's father means 'You have to stay at home.'

And that's that. Terry's father means that what he says is definite. Nothing Terry says will change his mind!

Is that clear? This means 'Do you understand?'

I've had enough of your laziness. Terry's father means that Terry must stop being lazy.

young man When 'young man' is used to address someone like this, it usually means the 'young man' is being criticized.

er ... Sue is hesitating. She doesn't want to tell Terry that she is not at the party because he can't go.

Would you like a hand ... ? This means 'Would you like some help?'

I'm stuck. Terry means 'I can't go any further' or 'I don't know what to do next.'

Many schools in Britain now teach 'Computer Studies' or similar subjects.

4 • Ask questions **a–o** in turn.
- Students answer the questions.

Answer key
a *Terry is talking to his teacher.*
b *They are talking about History and Geography.*
c *The History question was 'Who discovered Australia?'*
d *Terry's answer was 'Columbus'.*
e *He laughed.*
f *He copied his homework from Casey.*
g *It was stolen.*
h *He was warned.*
i *His father was angry because of the letter. He was angry that Terry was lazy and doing badly at school.*
j *He was invited to a party.*
k *He was grounded. He could not watch TV until his homework was done properly.*
l *His pocket money will be stopped.*
m *Sue decided not to go because Terry couldn't go.*
n *He was doing his Computer Studies homework.*
o *He thinks she's a nice girl.*

 5 • Students close their books.
- Say *Now listen carefully.*
- 📼 Play the cassette.

Terry in trouble

1 What do you remember? What happened in the last part of the story? Look back at page 88 and check your ideas.

2 Look at this episode. Who is in this episode? What is happening at the beginning of the story? What happens?

3 📻 Listen and follow in your books.

Teacher Wrong, wrong, wrong. Terry, this is terrible. Macbeth wasn't written by Queen Elizabeth. It was written by Shakespeare. Australia wasn't discovered by Columbus. And look at this in your Geography test. Question: 'Where is coffee found?' Answer: 'In supermarkets.' It's no laughing matter, Terry. You've got exams next month.

Terry Yes, Miss.

Teacher Last week your homework was copied from Casey's. The week before last you said your bag was stolen and now this. What's wrong with you?

Terry Nothing, Miss.

Teacher Now you were warned last week, Terry. This time a letter will be sent to your parents.

Later

Terry But, Dad. I've been invited to a party.

Mr Moore And I said 'No'. You're grounded, and there'll be no TV until that homework is done properly. And that's that. And your pocket money will be stopped if I get any more letters from school like this. Is that clear? I've had enough of your laziness, young man!

Terry Oh, hi, Sue. Weren't you invited to the party?

What do you think?

- What is wrong with Terry?
- What does he feel about Jackie?
- What does he feel about Sue?
- What will happen now?

4 **Answer these questions.**

a Who is Terry talking to at school?

b What subjects are they talking about?

c What was the History question?

d What was Terry's answer?

e What did Terry do when the teacher read his Geography answer?

f What was wrong with Terry's homework last week?

g What happened to his bag?

h What happened to Terry last week?

i Why was Terry's father angry?

j Why did Terry want to go out?

k How was Terry punished?

l What will happen if Terry gets into trouble again?

m Why wasn't Sue at the party?

n What homework was Terry doing?

o What does Terry's father think about Sue?

5 **Close your book. Listen again.**

Sue Yes, but I didn't want to go, if you . . . er . . ., I mean . . . I was told you couldn't go.

Terry Did you see Jackie?

Sue Yes, she was telling everyone about her trip to America.

Terry Yes, she goes next week.

Sue Look. Would you like a hand with your Computer Studies homework?

Terry Yes, please. I'm stuck.

Sue Look, this is very simple. You see, the information is sent by the small computers. It is received by the main computer. It is checked and processed by the main computer. Then the results are stored on the hard disk.

Later

Terry Goodnight, Sue and thanks a lot.

Mr Moore She's a nice girl, Susan.

Useful expressions

6
- Students look at the 'Useful expressions'.
- Students write the mother-tongue equivalent of each item next to that item. If they are not sure, say *Go back to the story, and work it out from the situation.*
- While they are doing this, copy the chart on to the blackboard.
- In pairs, students compare charts.
- Elicit and discuss answers. Write the expressions in your blackboard chart.
- Students correct and amend their own charts.

7 a
- Divide the class into groups of four.
  - Each student in a group takes one part: Terry, his teacher, his father and Sue.

b
- Students read the dialogue in their groups. Walk round the class. Note any serious pronunciation errors.
  - Correct serious pronunciation errors.
  - Choose one group to read their dialogue aloud to the class.
  - If time, students change roles and read the dialogue again.

FOLLOW UP

8
- Students read the gapped letter from Terry's teacher to his parents.
- Students complete the letter, using the dialogue.
- In pairs, students compare letters.
- Check answers.

> **Answer key**
> *Terry   terrible   questions   was   Geography*
> *found   copied   said   stolen   what   him*
> *exams   was   write*

LANGUAGE WORK

The passive voice

BUILD UP

1 a
- Read the two sentences.
- Say *These verbs are in the 'passive voice'.*
- Write the sentences on the blackboard.
- Underline the verb forms, i.e.
  Your bag <u>was stolen</u>.
  The information *<u>is checked</u>* by the computer.
- Ask *Do we (you) have a passive voice in our (your) language?*
- Elicit ideas.

b
- Students turn back to *Victoria Road*.
- Say *Now, look for more sentences like this in 'Victoria Road'. Underline the passive verbs – like I have done with the examples on the blackboard.*
- Add *Some of these verbs are positive, some are negative, some are questions, some are statements, some are about the past, some are about the present and some are about the future.*
- Students underline the passive verbs in those sentences which contain the passive voice.
- Check answers.

> **Note**
> In some examples the passive is split by a pronoun, e.g. **Weren't** *you* **invited?**, or the auxiliary is missing, e.g. *It* **is checked** *and* **processed**.

> **Answer key**
> *Macbeth **wasn't written** by Queen Elizabeth.*
> *It **was written** by Shakespeare.*
> *Australia **wasn't discovered** by Columbus.*
> *Where **is** coffee **found**?*
> *Last week your homework **was copied** from Casey's.*
> *The week before last you said your bag **was stolen** ...*
> *Now you **were warned** last week. ...*
> *This time a letter **will be sent** to your parents.*
> *I've **been invited** to a party.*
> *You're **grounded.***
> *... there'll be no TV until that homework **is done** properly.*
> *And your pocket money **will be stopped**. ...*
> **Weren't** *you* **invited** *to the party?*
> *I **was told** you couldn't go.*
> *The information **is sent** by the small computers.*
> *It **is received** by the main computer.*
> *It **is checked** and **processed** by the main computer.*
> *Then the results **are stored** on the hard disk.*

a • Read the two sentences.

• Ask *Do these two sentences mean the same thing?*

• Elicit ideas.

Answer key
Yes

Note
The *emphasis* is different, i.e. in the first sentence it is on the computers and in the second it is on the information. However, students should not worry about this, since the basic meaning of the sentences is the same.

b • Briefly revise *subject*, *verb*, *object* and *agent*.

• Read the example and write it on the board.

• Point out that the subject is *Terry*, the verb is *was grounded* and the agent is *his father*. The agent is introduced by *by*.

• Students find the subject, verb, and agent in the sentence *The information is sent by the small computers*.

• Students give answers.

Answer key
subject: *the information*
verb: *is sent*
agent: *the small computers*

• Choose some more examples from the list made by the students in Exercise 1b. Ask students to find the subject, verb and agent (if any).

c • Students complete the gapped sentences with the correct forms of *receive*, *check* or *send*.

• While they are doing this, copy the gapped sentences on to the blackboard.

• Ask one student to complete the sentences on the blackboard.

• Students correct their sentences.

Answer key
receives
received
processes, checks
is checked and processed by the main computer
stores
The results are stored on the hard disk.

Developing a film

 • Students look at the pictures.

• They read the list of verbs.

• They complete the gapped sentences with the correct forms of the verbs.

• In pairs, students compare answers.

• Check answers.

Answer key

1	*are taken*	**7**	*is removed*
2	*is removed*	**8**	*is developed*
3	*is taken*	**9**	*is printed*
4	*is put*	**10**	*are checked*
5	*are written*	**11**	*are sent*
6	*are sent*	**12**	*are collected*

FOLLOW UP

 • Read the example.

• Students read the list of words.

• Check understanding of words.

• In class or for homework, students write sentences saying who or what does each stage in the film developing process.

• Check answers.

Answer key
1 *Photographs are taken by the customer.*
2 *The film is removed from the camera by the customer.*
3 *The film is taken to the shop by the customer.*
4 *The film is put in an envelope by the shop assistant.*
5 *The customer's name and address are written on the envelope by the shop assistant.*
6 *All the films are sent to the laboratory by the shop assistant.*
7 *The film is removed from the cassette by the laboratory assistant.*
8 *The film is developed by the developing machine.*
9 *The film is printed by the printer.*
10 *The photographs are checked by the laboratory assistant.*
11 *The photographs are sent back to the shop by the laboratory assistant.*
12 *The photographs are collected by the customer.*

Useful expressions

6 How do you say these expressions in your language?

This is terrible.

It's no laughing matter.

the week before last

What's wrong with you?

You were warned.

I've been invited to a party.

You're grounded.

And that's that.

Is that clear?

I've had enough of your laziness.

Would you like a hand?

I'm stuck.

7 a Work in groups of four. Each person takes one of the parts.

b Read the dialogue.

FOLLOW UP

8 Complete the teacher's letter to Terry's parents.

Hartfield Secondary School
West Hill, Hartfield, Bucks

Mr and Mrs Moore
20 Victoria Road
Hartfield HA9 4BJ

Dear Mr and Mrs Moore,

I'm writing to you about _____. His work has been _____ recently. Here is an example of his answers to some History _____:

Australia _____ discovered by Columbus.

And here is an example from his _____ test. Question: 'Where is coffee _____?' Answer: 'In supermarkets.'

Last week his homework was _____ from Casey Royston's. The week before that he _____ his bag was _____.

I don't know _____ is wrong with _____, but it is now very serious. He has got _____ next month. He _____ warned last week. This time I had to _____ to you. Please make an appointment to see me as soon as possible.

Yours sincerely

Mrs K. Jones

Mrs K. Jones

LANGUAGE WORK

The passive voice

BUILD UP

1 a Look at these two sentences.

Your bag **was stolen**.
The information **is checked** by the computer.

We call this the **passive voice**.

b Find more sentences like this in the story. Underline the passive verbs.

2 a Look at these pairs of sentences. Do they mean the same?

The small computers send the information.
active

The information is sent by the small computers.
passive

b In the sentences above, find the:

subject, verb, object, and agent

   Example
Terry   was grounded by his father
subject   verb   agent

c Complete the sentences with the correct form of these verbs.

receive   check   process   store

active The main computer .... the information.

passive The information is .... by the main computer.

active The main computer .... and .... the information.

passive The information ....
.... by ....

active The hard disk .... the results.

passive ....

> I've been invited to a party, but I can't go.

> Why not?

> The invitation says eight to twelve and I'm fourteen.

DEVELOPING A FILM

3 The pictures show the process for developing a film. Use these verbs to describe the process.

take   remove   put   develop   send   collect
print   check   write

1 Photographs ....

2 The film .... from the camera.

3 The film .... to the shop.

4 The film .... in an envelope.

5 The customer's name and address ....
.... on the envelope.

6 All the films .... to the
laboratory.

7 The film .... from the
cassette.

8 The film ....

9 The film ....

10 The photographs ....

11 The photographs .... back to
the shop.

12 The photographs ....

FOLLOW UP

4 Look at the sentences in 3. Say who (or what) each stage of work is done by. Use these words.

customer   shop assistant   laboratory assistant
developing machine   printer

   Example
Photographs are taken by the customer.

101

READING

Why weren't we warned?

Students read this text in two stages:

a They scan the text to establish the context.

b They find and classify the information in a chart.

- Say *Look at the text and picture quickly* (10 seconds).
- Ask *Where is it from?* and *What is it about?*
- Students give answers.

> **Answer key**
> **a** *a newspaper*
> **b** *a storm*

- Read questions **a–c**.
- Students read the text quickly and find the answers (2 minutes).
- Say *Stop now*.
- Students give answers.

> **Answer key**
> **a** *The headline is about storms in Britain. No one had been warned about them.*
> **b** *It's about South-East England.*
> **c** *The storms happened last night.*

- Students read the headings in the chart.
- Ask for an example for each heading.
- Copy the chart onto the blackboard.
- Write an example for each part of the chart.
- Students read the text carefully.
- They complete the chart with other information.
- Walk round and check charts.
- Students say what they have written in their charts.
- Write information correctly in blackboard chart.
- Students correct and amend own charts.

> **Answer key**
> **Injuries to people**
> *Two firemen were killed*
> *A woman in a Windsor hotel was killed when a chimney fell through a roof*
> *Twenty people were killed altogether*
> *Four firemen were injured*
> *Two people in Kent were taken to hospital with broken legs*
>
> **Damage to property**
> *Hundreds of houses were wrecked by winds*
> *Roofs and chimneys were ripped off*
> *Windows were smashed*
> *Thousands of trees were blown down*
> *Many rare trees and plants were destroyed at Kew Gardens*
> *Many power lines were brought down so many houses were without electricity*
> *Thousands of people were left without telephones.*
> *Many cars were crushed*
>
> **Transport problems**
> *Roads and railway lines were blocked by trees*
> *Dover harbour was closed*
> *Hundreds of small boats were smashed*
> *A ferry (Hengist) was thrown on to the beach*

W O R D   W O R K

- Students write two headings: *Destruction* and *The weather*.
- They read the text again.
- They list all the words connected with these under the correct heading.
- While they are doing this, write the headings on the blackboard.
- Walk round the class.
- Students give their words connected with *Destruction*.
- List these under *Destruction* on the board.
- Repeat with *The weather* words.

> **Answer key**
> (possible lists)
> **Destruction**
> *hit   killed   hurricane-force   injured   fell   on   wrecked   ripped off   smashed   blown   down   destroyed   brought down   broken   blocked   crushed*
>
> **The weather**
> *storms   records   hurricane-force   winds   blown   huge waves   warning   Meteorological Office   weather forecast   direction   strong winds   rain   flooded*

5 a • Read the questions.
- Tell students they will have to read the text *and* think carefully about the answers.
- Students read the text again and look for answers to the questions.
- In pairs, students compare answers.
- Students give their answers.

> **Note**
> There are no clear answers here. What is considered *serious*, *expensive* and *embarrassing* will be different for different students. So encourage expression of different ideas and use this as a discussion or fluency activity.

b • Read the questions.
- Elicit responses from different students.

Tenses in the passive

BUILD UP

6 a • Say *Think back to when you underlined the passive verbs in 'Victoria Road'. These were in different tenses.*
- Say *We are now going to look more carefully at the formation of the different tenses in the passive voice.*
- Read the instructions.
- Students read the list of tenses and examples.
- Students write four headings in their books: *Past*, *Present Perfect*, *Present*, and *Future*.
- They write the example given under its heading.
- They read the newspaper story on page 102 again and list other examples of passive verbs under their headings.
- Walk round and check.
- In pairs, students compare lists.
- While they are doing this, write the four headings on the blackboard.
- Students call out passive verbs to go under each heading in turn.
- Write these on the blackboard.
- Students correct and amend their lists.

> **Answer key**
> **Past**
> *was hit   were started   were killed   were injured   were wrecked   were ripped off   were smashed   was killed   were blown down   were brought down   were rescued   were taken   were blocked   were crushed   was closed   was thrown   weren't (we) warned   wasn't expected*
>
> **Present perfect**
> *have been closed   have been destroyed   have been followed*
>
> **Present**
> *is recorded   are flooded*
>
> **Future**
> *will not be repaired   won't be repaired*

b • Ask *So, which part of the verb changes according to the tense of the passive?*

> **Answer key**
> *The auxiliary or **to be**.*

7 • Say *The statements below were all made by people who experienced the storm. Read them and write a statement about who said each one.*
- Students read the example and **a–h**.
- Students say who said each of **a–h**. (The example provided is one of these.)

> **Answer key**
> (possible answers)
> a *Someone in the South or West*
> b *An MP*
> c *Someone from Kew Gardens*
> d *Someone from the Meteorological Office*
> e *Someone from the Electricity Board*
> f *A Dorset fireman*
> g *Someone in the hotel in Windsor*
> h *One of the Electricity Board workmen*

8 • Read the question and the example.
- Divide the class into groups of three and each group chooses a secretary.
- Group thinks of things that have been done. The secretary writes these down (5 minutes).
- In turn, secretaries call out *one* thing.
- List these on the blackboard.
- Add one or two yourself.

FOLLOW UP

9 • Students write the answers to Exercise 7.

READING

1 **Look at the text.**

 a Where is it from?

 b What is it about?

2 **Read the text quickly.**

 a What is the headline about?

 b Which part of Britain is it about?

 c When did it happen?

WHY WEREN'T WE WARNED?

Last night South-East England was hit by the worst storms since records were started. Twenty people were killed by the hurricane-force winds. In Dorset two firemen were killed and four were injured, when a tree fell on their fire engine.

Hundreds of houses were wrecked by winds of up to 110 mph. Roofs and chimneys were ripped off and windows were smashed. A woman was killed in a hotel in Windsor when a chimney fell through the roof.

Thousands of trees were blown down. At Kew Botanical Gardens in London many rare trees and plants – some of them over two hundred years old – have been destroyed. Many houses are without electricity now, because power lines were brought down. Thousands of people are without telephones, too. Many lines won't be repaired until next week. Two people were rescued when their car was found by Electricity Board workmen in Kent. They were taken to hospital with broken legs.

Roads and railway lines were blocked by trees and many cars were crushed. In London and the south of England schools, offices and shops have been closed today, because people cannot get to work. Dover Harbour was closed. Hundreds of small boats were smashed by huge waves, and the ferry, *Hengist*, was thrown onto the beach.

This morning angry MPs are asking: 'Why weren't we warned?' No warning was given by the Meteorological Office. The late night weather forecast is recorded early in the evening. At that time the storm wasn't expected to hit England. But about midnight it changed direction and moved north.

The strong winds have been followed by heavy rain and many parts of the south and west are flooded.

3 Now read the text more carefully and put the information into a chart like this.

Injuries to people
Damage to property
Transport problems

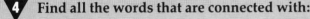

W O R D   W O R K

4 Find all the words that are connected with:
- destruction.
- the weather.

5 a **What do you think? What was:**
- the most serious result of the storm?
- the most expensive result?
- the most embarrassing result?

b **Have you ever been in a storm like this? What was it like?**

6 a **Look at the newspaper story on page 102. Find examples of passive verbs in the following tenses.**

	Example
past	*was hit*
present perfect	*have been closed*
present	*is recorded*
future	*will not be repaired*

b **Which part of the verb changes?**

7 **Who said it? Look at these statements. Who do you think said them?**

Example
This was said by someone in the South or West.

a There's water everywhere downstairs. We can't sit on the roof, because we haven't got one now. That was blown off by the wind.

b What do we pay these people for? That's what I want to know.

c They take hundreds of years to grow and then they're destroyed in seconds. It's terrible, terrible. And some of them are almost extinct now.

d We were taken by surprise. We expected it to hit France not us.

e I'm sorry, but we won't be able to repair it today. We're doing everything we can, but there are thousands of people in the same situation.

f We were going to rescue some people in a top floor flat, when the tree hit us.

g It was the lady in room 23. Oh dear. How terrible. The poor woman.

h Quick. There are people in here. Call an ambulance.

8 **What do you think has been done since the storm?**

Example
Trees have been removed from the railway lines.

FOLLOW UP

9 Write the answers to Exercise 7.

LISTENING

The Top 40

- Students read the passage.
- Ask questions **a–e.**
- Students give their answers.

> **Answer key**
> **a** *The Top 40*
> **b** *Radio 1*
> **c** *5 pm on Sundays*
> **d** *Gallup Chart Services*
> **e** *How the chart is produced*

- Students look at the flow diagram.
- Say *Some of the stages are missing.*
- Ask *What do you think the missing stages are?*
- Say *You can't work them out exactly, but you can get an idea of what they are.*
- In pairs, students work out the missing stages. (They should not write on the flow diagram.)
- Elicit suggestions for each missing stage.

- Say *Now, I'll play the cassette. You'll hear what the missing stages are. Write them in the diagram.*
- ▦ Play the cassette.
- Students complete the diagram.
- Rewind the cassette.
- Check answers.

> **Answer key**
> *Records are released.*
> *Copies of the record are sent to shops.*
> *The code numbers are recorded in the shop's computer.*
> *The information is sorted out.*
> *The programme is written by the producer and the disc jockey.*

▦ **The Top 40**

Every Sunday afternoon at five o'clock, the new singles chart is released on Radio 1's Top 40 programme. Radios in Britain and Europe are switched on to hear the latest news about pop music. The Top 40 is broadcast live on Radio 1 and it is Europe's most popular programme. The chart is produced by Gallup Chart Services. How is it done?

There are 4300 record shops in the UK. Information isn't collected from all of them. It is collected from 500 sample shops. Each of these shops has a computer.

Every week about 500 records are recorded and released in Britain. Each record is given a code number. Then copies of the record are sent to shops all over the country.

When a copy of the record is bought in one of the sample shops, its code number is recorded in the shop's computer.

Four times a week the information in each of the computers is sent by telephone to a main computer at Gallup Chart Services.

At the end of the week all the information is sorted out. About 20 per cent of all the information isn't used, because the code numbers are wrong.

The Top 40 is produced and is sent to the radio station. Then the programme is written by the producer and the disc jockey.

On Sunday afternoon the programme is presented by the DJ, Bruno Brookes.

Because each record has a code number, the computer can produce a lot of different charts. For example, charts for singles and albums are produced, or for records, cassettes and compact discs.

About 100,000 sales are needed for a number 1 record in the British charts.

- Students read questions **a–f.**
- ▦ Play the cassette.
- Students write down answers.
- Rewind the cassette.
- In pairs, students compare answers.

> **Answer key**
> **a** 4300
> **b** *about 500*
> **c** *four times a week*
> **d** *20%; the code numbers are wrong*
> **e** *singles, albums, records, cassettes, compact discs*
> **f** *100,000*

W O R D W O R K

a
- Students write the headings *Pop music* and *Computers* in their books.
- Write the headings on the blackboard.
- Elicit one example for each heading. Write these on the board.
- Students list words.

T104

b
- Say *Now, I'll play the cassette again. Listen carefully for more words connected with pop music and computers. Add these to your list.*
- Play the cassette.
- Students add more words to their lists.
- Students give their words in each list.
- Write these on the blackboard.
- Students amend their own lists.

> **Answer key**
> (possible lists)
> **Pop music**
> *singles   chart   released   Radio 1   Top 40
> broadcast   record   recorded   radio station
> programme   producer   disc jockey   DJ
> albums   cassettes   compact discs   sales
> number 1*
>
> **Computers**
> *Gallup Chart Services   information   collected
> sample   code number   recorded   main computer*

- Read the questions.
- Students give their ideas.

FOLLOW UP

- Students read the gapped text.
- In class or for homework, they fill in the gaps. They must use the passive voice.
- Check the completed text.

> **Answer key**
> *are released   is given   are sent   are bought
> are recorded   is sent   is sorted   is produced
> is sent   is written   is broadcast*

INTERACTION

 a
- Say *Tell me some names of records.*
- Students give names.
- Write these on the blackboard. Stop when you have 15 names.
- Ask for suggestions for a code system.
- Students give ideas.
- Give each record on the board a code number.

b
- In pairs, students copy the record list and code numbers.
- Each pair chooses their two favourite records on the list, and ticks them. (If they cannot agree, each student chooses their own favourite.)

- One person from each pair is the customer and the other is the assistant.
- Students read through Exercise 2.
- Arrange the class so that the 'assistants' are standing behind desks and 'customers' come to the front. The assistants keep the record lists.
- Customers go to different 'shops'. Assistants greet customers. Customers ask for the two records they ticked. Assistants and customers use the example dialogue.
- Assistants 'serve' each customer. They then make ticks on their list of records to show which records have been 'bought' (5 minutes).
- Students change roles. Assistants give their lists to their partners.
- Repeat activity.

- Students return to their seats.
- In their pairs, they add up the number of each record sold.
- They write the number of each record sold next to the record.

> **Note**
> They should add up *both* sets of ticks on the list.

- One person from each pair in turn says how many copies of each record they sold.
- Write numbers on the blackboard, next to each record.
- Add up the *total* number of each record sold (i.e. by all the 'assistants').
- Ask *So what record is number 1?*
- Students give the answer.
- Write *1* next to the record on the board.
- Repeat with numbers 2 to 10.

FOLLOW UP

> **Answer key**
> (possible answer)
> *First a list of 15 records was made. Each record was given a code number. The list of records and code numbers were copied down. Our two favourite records on the list were chosen and ticked.
> The customers each bought two records from the assistants. After each sale, the two records were ticked on the list.
> The information was collected. It was sorted. A top 10 was made.*

LISTENING

THE TOP 40

1 **Read the short passage below and answer these questions.**

   a What programme is it about?

   b On which radio station is it broadcast?

   c When is it broadcast?

   d Who is the Top 40 produced by?

   e What do you think the Listening text is about?

Every Sunday afternoon at five o'clock the new singles chart is released on Radio 1's Top 40 programme. Radios in Britain and Europe are switched on to hear the latest news about pop music. The Top 40 is broadcast live on Radio 1 and it is Europe's most popular programme. The chart is produced by Gallup Chart Services. How is it done?

2 **This diagram shows how the Top 40 programme is made. Some of the stages are missing. What do you think the missing stages are?**

3 📼 **Listen and complete the diagram.**

4 **Listen again and find the answers to these questions.**

   a How many record shops are there in Britain?

   b How many records are released each week in Britain?

   c How often is information sent to the central computer?

   d How much information isn't used? Why not?

   e Examples of different charts are given. What are they?

   f How many record sales are needed to make a number 1?

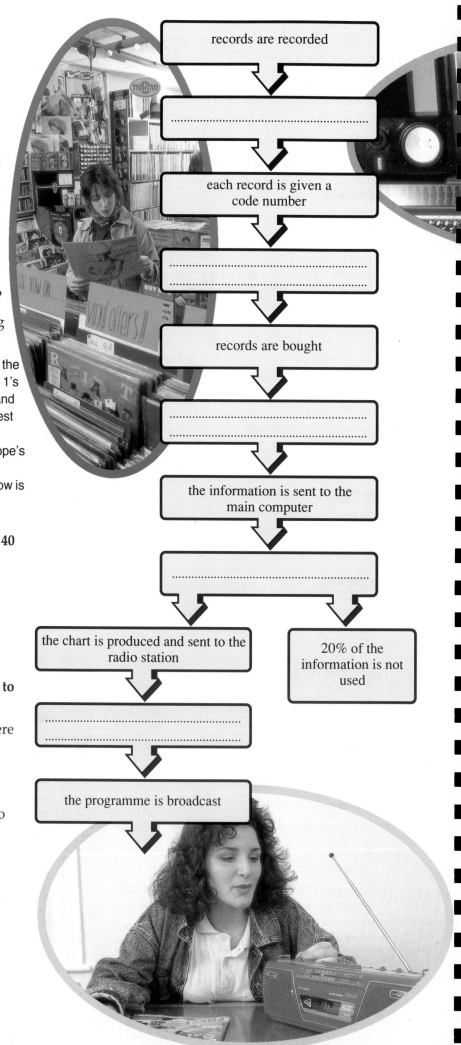

records are recorded

↓

....

↓

each record is given a code number

↓

....
....

↓

records are bought

↓

....
....

↓

the information is sent to the main computer

↓

....

↓↓

the chart is produced and sent to the radio station   20% of the information is not used

↓

....
....

↓

the programme is broadcast

WORD WORK

5 **a** Write down all the words you heard that are connected with:

- pop music.
- computers.

b Listen again. Can you add any more words to your list?

6 Do you think the system is secure? You are a dishonest record producer. Can you make sure that your record gets to number one?

FOLLOW UP

7 Complete this text with the correct form of the verbs in brackets.

First records are recorded. They

.... (release) and each record

.... (give) a code number. Then

copies of the records .... (send)

to shops. When records ....

(buy), their code numbers ....

(record) in the shop's computer. Then this

information .... (send) to the

central computer. The information ....

(sort) and the Top 40 chart ....

(produce). Then the chart ....

.... (send) to the radio station and the programme

.... (write) by the producer and

the D.J. Finally the programme ....

(broadcast) on Sunday afternoon.

INTERACTION

1 Make your own Top 10 programme.

a Make a class list of up to fifteen records on the blackboard. Give each record a code number.

b Work in pairs. Make a copy of the record list and code numbers.

c Choose your own two favourite records from the list.

2 One partner from each pair works as an assistant in a record shop. The other partner is a customer.

Customer
You have five minutes. You must go to as many shops as possible and buy your two records. You must ask for them in English. If you don't use English, your purchase will be rejected.

Assistant
When customers ask for records, make a tick on your list of records. If they don't ask in English, or if the record is not on the list, write nothing.

Example dialogue

Assistant *'Good morning. Can I help you?'*

Customer *'Have you got "Do they know it's Christmas?" by Band Aid, please?'*

or

Customer *'I'd like a copy of ...'*

Assistant *'Yes, here you are. That's £4.50.'*

Customer *'Thank you.'*

After five minutes, change roles. Shop assistants give their lists to their partners.

3 Work in pairs. Add up the number of each record sold.

4 Report your group numbers to the class and make the Top 10. What is number 1?

FOLLOW UP

5 Describe how your Top 10 was made. Start like this.

First a list of 15 records was made. Each record was given a code number. ....

PROJECT

Your life

This project can be done individually, in pairs, or in groups of three.

Find out what is in the library that is relevant; and what visits can be arranged for groups of students, e.g. to a local newspaper office, a local TV station, or the telephone exchange.

If visits are carried out, students will also need preparation beforehand, e.g. deciding what questions to ask. They will also need to do some follow-up work, e.g. writing up what they have seen and heard.

In all the above, do not forget that one of the 'products' of this project is a flow chart of the process. This will guide the students' reading, questions and observations.

- Read the first two questions.

- Elicit examples of forms of communication. Use the pictures as examples.

- List these on the blackboard. Add some yourself, if necessary.

- Next to each, write down in note form what students know about them.

- Students choose a form of communication.

- Check students' choices. The form of communication must be important to the student's life.

- Students go to the school library to try and find out more about how their form of communication works.

- Arrange out-of-school visits, as above, if possible.

- Students draw a flow chart for the process.

- Give help where necessary, e.g. when a stage in the process is unclear.

- Students write a description of what happens at each stage.

- Correct the work. Make sure that the passive verb forms are all correct. Suggest improvements in paragraphing, if necessary.

- Students rewrite their work (flow chart and description) correctly.

- Display flow charts. Students look at each other's work.

EXTRA ACTIVITY

- In pairs, students list all the different forms of communication mentioned in Unit 11.

- Students give their answers. List these on the blackboard.

- Students add to their lists.

▶ **Pronunciation: page T113a**

LEARNING DIARY

- Students turn back to the list of items on the first page of Unit 11.

A Students draw faces on the symbols next to each item to indicate how well they know it.

B In class or for homework, students complete the self-check exercises in the Workbook.

C In pairs, students compare answers.

Elicit answers. Students correct as necessary. Identify 'common problem exercises' or 'common problem items'.

Spend a few minutes explaining these.

Refer students who still do not understand (or who are particularly interested) to the relevant page of a pedagogic grammar.

D Ask what students liked best in this unit, and why. (See the procedure in Unit 1.)

CULTURE SPOT
Workbook page 93

- Divide the class into pairs or groups of three or four.

- Students look quickly at the text.

- Ask *What is the text about?*

- Students give their ideas.

- Ask *What do you already know about this topic?*

- Students give their ideas. Discuss these ideas.

- Say *Read the Culture Spot text. Note anything that you find interesting or unusual.*

- Ask comprehension questions about the text.

- Students give their answers. Explain any words that students need.

- Ask *Did you find anything interesting or unusual?*

- Students give their ideas.

- Read each comparison question in turn.

- Discuss each question. Encourage students to compare their situation to the one in the text.

The Florida Galleons

1 a • Say *Look at the picture. What three things are happening in the picture?*

• Elicit what is happening in the picture.

Answer key
1 *Some ships are sailing from Mexico.*
2 *The divers are looking for treasure on the sea bed. They are worried about sharks.*
3 *The modern divers are looking for treasure on the sea bed. They have found some coins.*

• Ask for suggestions for the meaning of the title.

• Check students know where Florida is.

b • Ask students *So what do you think 'The Florida Galleons' is about?*

• Elicit suggestions.

2 • Say *These eight texts are in the wrong order. Read them and decide what the right order is.*

• Students read the texts. They order them 1–8.

• In pairs, students compare answers.

Answer key
The boxes should be numbered:
4   7   6   3   1   5   8   2

3 • Say *You're now going to hear the whole story on cassette. Listen carefully and check your order.*

• Play the cassette. Students listen and check.

• Rewind the cassette.

4 • Students read the instructions.

• Say *The extra pieces of information are very small. Add each one to one of the texts. You may also have to cross out one or more words in the texts.*

• ▣ Play the cassette.

• Students add the new information to their texts.

• In pairs, students compare answers.

• Check answers.

Answer key
(See items in brackets in tapescript.)

▣ **The Florida galleons**
In the summer of 1715, a fleet of Spanish galleons left Mexico. The (eleven) ships were carrying gold and silver worth more than £15 million.

As the ships were sailing past the coast of Florida, they were hit by a hurricane. The heavy ships were smashed against the rocks by the huge waves. All the ships were sunk by the storm and over a thousand sailors were drowned.

Immediately more ships were sent to find the treasure, but it was not easy. The sea around the Florida coast was very deep and dangerous. Many divers were drowned and others were eaten by sharks.

News of the disaster spread. Many pirate ships sailed to the Florida coast and attacked the divers. (About one third) of the treasure was found, but a lot of this was stolen by pirates. The rest of the treasure wasn't found and it stayed at the bottom of the sea.

Time passed and the wrecks were buried by the sand. The Florida galleons and their treasure were forgotten.

Then, over two hundred years later, a few coins were found on a beach in Florida. They were found by a treasure hunter called Buck Wagner.

Wagner and his friend, Doctor Kip Kelso, looked for the wrecks. They studied hundreds of old books (and maps). It took ten years. Finally, (in 1959) the galleons and their treasure were discovered.

Since then, nearly £3 million of gold and silver has been found. Among treasure hunters, the Florida Galleons' treasure is called 'the Big One'.

5 • Students read questions **a–e**.

• They read the whole story again and write answers to the questions.

• Check answers.

• Students explain their answers.

Answer key
a *They were going to Spain.*
b *No, because someone reported the disaster.*
c *The sea was deep and dangerous. There were dangerous sharks. The divers were attacked by pirates. So people gave up the search.*
d *Buck Wagner found the coins in 1959.*
e *Gold and silver worth £15 million was lost. About one third (i.e. £5 million) was recovered. £3 million has been found by the treasure hunters, so £7 million has not been found.*

WORD WORK

6 • Read the list of labels.

• Students label the picture.

• In pairs, students compare answers.

PROJECT

Your life

What forms of communication are there in your life? What do you know about them?

Choose an important form of communication in your life. Work out how it is done. Go to the library and find out more about it. If it is local, for example, local newspaper, radio or television, try to visit the office and interview someone.

Example
How is a record produced and distributed?
How is a TV news programme made and broadcast?
How is your favourite magazine produced and distributed?

Draw a flow chart for the process. Describe what happens at each stage.

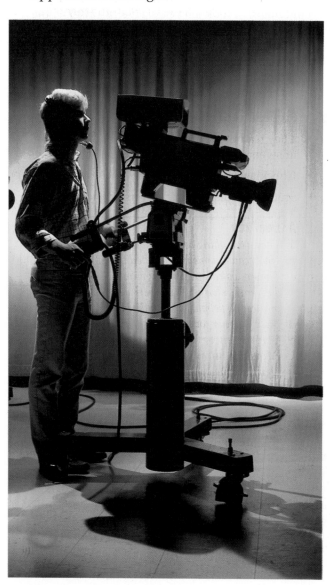

Learning diary

Look at the list on the first page of this unit.

11

A How well do you know each thing? Complete the circles to make faces.

B Try the self-check in the Workbook.

C Compare your self-check answers with a partner's. Do you understand everything? If you don't understand something, look in a grammar book or ask your teacher.

D What did you like best in this unit? Why?

▶ Pronunciation: page 113

12 revision

The Florida Galleons

1 **Look at these pictures.**

a What is happening in the picture?

b What do you think the story is about?

2 **Read the texts. Number them in the correct order.**

☐ News of the disaster spread. Many pirate ships sailed to the Florida coast and attacked the divers. Some of the treasure was found, but a lot of this was stolen by pirates. The rest of the treasure wasn't found and it stayed at the bottom of the sea.

☐ Wagner and his friend, Doctor Kip Kelso, looked for the wrecks. They studied hundreds of old books. It took ten years. Finally the galleons and their treasure were discovered.

☐ Then over two hundred years later a few coins were found on a beach in Florida. They were found by a treasure hunter called Buck Wagner.

☐ Immediately, more ships were sent to find the treasure, but it was not easy. The sea around the Florida coast was very deep and dangerous. Many divers were drowned and others were eaten by sharks.

☐ In the summer of 1715 a fleet of Spanish galleons left Mexico. The ships were carrying gold and silver worth more than £15 million.

☐ Time passed and the wrecks were buried by the sand. The Florida galleons and their treasure were forgotten.

☐ Since then nearly £3 million of gold and silver has been found. Among treasure hunters the Florida Galleons' treasure is called 'the Big One'.

☐ As the ships were sailing past the coast of Florida, they were hit by a hurricane. The heavy ships were smashed against the rocks by the huge waves. All the ships were sunk by the storm and over a thousand sailors were drowned.

- Students read the gapped interview.
- Divide the class into pairs.

a
- In pairs, students work out the interviewer's questions and fill in the gaps.
- They write the interviewer's words in the gaps.

b
- Ask one pair to read their interview for the class. Comment if necessary, e.g. if any of the interviewer's questions are clearly wrong, or if students use an incorrect tense.
- Repeat with a second pair.
- All pairs role play their interviews. Walk round and correct tenses as necessary.

> **Answer key**
> (possible answers)
> *What were they doing?*
> *What happened to the galleons?*
> *How many ships were there?*
> *When did the ships sink?*
> *Did the Spanish find any of the treasure?*
> *How did you discover the wrecks?*
> *Did anyone help you?* **or** *Who helped you?*
> *When did you discover the wrecks?*
> *How much treasure has been found?*
> *How much has not been found?*
> *Where are the wrecks?*

 (number 8)
- Read the questions in turn.
- Elicit suggestions.

FOLLOW UP

 (number 9)
- Number 1–8 round the class. Repeat until each student has a number.
- Say *All number ones, put up your hand.*
- Repeat with other numbers.
- Each student translates the paragraph of their number.

> **Important note!**
> Each student's number is also the number of the *correctly ordered text*. For example, students with the number 1 translate the paragraph starting *In the summer of 1715* because this is the first paragraph in the proper text.

- Students with the same number compare their translations.
- They amend their work as necessary.
- Each group chooses a spokesperson.
- Each spokesperson reads their text to complete the story from 1 to 8.
- Give feedback as necessary. Pay special attention to the passive voice and to tenses.

- Invite comments and questions.
- Respond to comments and questions.

EXTRA ACTIVITY

- One person from each group 1–8 copies out their translation.
- Display these as a continuous text, next to the story in English.

VICTORIA ROAD

 (number 1)
- Read the instructions.
- Divide the class into groups of five or six.
- Say that two minutes is a very short time, and in this time everyone must speak.
- Remind students to use at least five 'Useful expressions'.
- Each group chooses a 'secretary'.
- Groups write their plays.
- Students read through their play and time themselves.
- They cut parts out if the play is too long.

 (number 2)
- Each group acts out their play for the class.
- Give some positive feedback on each play.

(number 3)
- Say *Now I'll play the final episode of 'Victoria Road'. Listen carefully. Is it the same as your play at all?*
- ▄▄ Play the cassette.

▄▄ **Victoria Road – Goodbye Jackie**
Terry I'm going to say goodbye to Jackie, Mum. (dreamily) I know that you must leave, Jackie. I'll miss you. I hope you will remember me.
Jackie Oh, Terry. I don't want to leave you, Terry, but I must. I'll always love you, Terry. Promise me that you'll wait for me. I'll come back.
Terry It's all right, Jackie. I understand. I'll wait for you till the end of time. Don't cry. You must be strong.
(Later)
Jackie Oh hi, Terry … Yes, all right, Dad.
Terry I've come to say goodbye, Jackie. I know that you must leave. I'll …
Jackie Just a minute, Terry. Oh, yes. I'm really looking forward to it. I can't wait. I have to leave for the airport in a few minutes. Keep in touch. Bye, Grandma. Now, what were you saying, Terry?
Terry I know that you must leave. I'll miss you, but I hope that …

Delivery boy Flowers for Miss Jackie Wright.

Jackie For me? Oh how exciting! I'm sorry, Terry, what were you saying?

Terry Oh, er … I know that you must go, Jackie. I'll miss you and …

Mr Wright Come on, Jackie. It's time to go. You don't want to miss the plane.

Casey Bye, Jackie. Send us a postcard.

Kamala Have a good trip. Bye.

Vince See you next year.

Sue Goodbye.

Jackie Goodbye, everyone.

Sue There's a good film on at the cinema in town this evening. Do you fancy going?

Terry Yeah. Great idea. What time shall we meet?

Notes

I'll miss you. Terry means that he will think about Jackie a lot. He will be sad that she is not still living in Victoria Road.

You must be strong. This means 'Don't be upset. Try and bear it.'

Keep in touch. Jackie means 'Write to me' or 'Telephone me.'

People send flowers on important occasions. They can order the flowers from a shop, and the shop will then deliver the flowers.

- Ask *What happens in the final episode?*

Answer key
In this episode, Terry is imagining a very romantic goodbye, but the real goodbye is very different. Jackie has no time for Terry.
Terry decides he is better off with Sue.

- Read the instructions.
- Ask students what *tense* is best to describe the three things.
- Elicit answers.

Answer key
the journey: *past simple*
new home and friends: *present simple*
what you have done: *present perfect*

- Repeat for asking about people in Victoria Road.

Answer key
All of the above, plus present continuous

- Ask what other things Jackie might say.
- Elicit ideas.
- In class or for homework, students write Jackie's letter.
- Correct letters for paragraph organization, spelling and grammar. The grammar points you discussed *must* be correct.
- Students rewrite their letters.
- Display the letters. Students look at each other's work.

▶ **Pronunciation: page T113a**

LEARNING DIARY

- Students read the Learning diary.
- They look back at the other Learning diaries.
- They write down the twelve things.
- In pairs, students compare and discuss their lists. Rearrange the class into different pairs. They compare and discuss their lists again.
- Students write down three ways in which they think they learn best. Walk round and ask for an explanation if you do not understand. Do not correct unless you are asked.
- Students think about the question *What can you do to learn the things you are not sure about?*
- Students write down three ways to do this. Walk round, as before.
- If possible, give *general* advice about what students can do to learn the things they are not sure about. *Base this on their answers to the last question.*

3 ▶ Now listen. You will hear the whole story. Check your order.

4 Listen again. There are four extra pieces of information on the tape. Add them to your texts.

5 Read the whole story again and answer these questions.

   a Where do you think the galleons were going?

   b Were all the sailors on the galleons drowned?

   c Why couldn't the divers in 1715 find all the treasure?

   d When did Buck Wagner find the coins?

   e How much treasure has not been found?

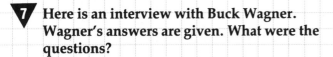

6 Label these things in the picture.

galleon	wreck	diver
treasure	coin	shark

7 Here is an interview with Buck Wagner. Wagner's answers are given. What were the questions?

   a Complete the interview.

Interviewer Mr Wagner, Can you tell me something about the treasure? Where did it come from?

Wagner From some Spanish galleons.

Interviewer ....?

Wagner They were taking the treasure from Mexico to Spain.

Interviewer ....?

Wagner They were hit by a hurricane near the coast of Florida.

Interviewer ....?

Wagner Eleven.

Interviewer ....?

Wagner In 1715.

Interviewer ....?

Wagner Divers found about a third of the treasure, but a lot of it was stolen by pirates.

Interviewer ....?

Wagner I found some gold coins on a beach in Florida. Then I read a lot of old books and maps. Finally we found the wrecks.

Interviewer You say 'we'. ....?

Wagner Yes, my friend, Kip Kelso.

Interviewer ....?

Wagner In 1959.

Interviewer ....?

Wagner About 5 million dollars' worth – that's nearly 3 million pounds.

Interviewer ....?

Wagner We don't know, but probably about seven million pounds' worth.

Interviewer ....?

Wagner I'm afraid I can't tell you that.

   b Role play your interview.

8 What do you think?

   a Who does the treasure belong to?

   b What would you do if you found some treasure?

FOLLOW UP

9 Translate part of the Florida galleons text into your own language. Compare your translation with that of other students. Do you agree?

VICTORIA ROAD

1 Jackie is going to America. What do you think will happen? Work in groups of five or six. Write a final episode, called: 'Goodbye, Jackie'.

Your episode must:

- have a part for every member of your group.
- be no more than two minutes long.
- contain at least five expressions from the Useful expressions sections.

2 Act your episode.

3 🔊 Listen to the final episode. Compare it to yours. Is it the same in any way?

FOLLOW UP

4 Jackie has been in America for three weeks. She writes a letter to her friends in Victoria Road. Imagine you are Jackie and write the letter. Describe:

- the journey
- your new home and friends
- what you have done

and ask about the people in Victoria Road.

Learning diary

12

You've come to the end of this book. But it's not the end of learning English.

How do you feel about the things that you have learnt? Look back at the Learning Diaries in the book. Write down:

- 3 things that you feel you know well now.
- 3 things that you are still not sure about.
- 3 things that you really enjoyed.
- 3 things that you didn't like much.

Discuss your lists with other members of your class. How do you learn best?

What can you do to learn the things you are not sure about?

Good luck with your next year of English!

► Pronunciation: page 113

PRONUNCIATION PRACTICE

Introduction
Phonetic alphabet revision

In this section students are revising only the vowels of English. The consonants are revised in Unit 4.

- Read the sounds and the words aloud. Students repeat.
- Divide the class into pairs.
- Demonstrate the activity with the first three sounds.
- In the second column students write a word with the same sound for each sound. They can check their ideas in a dictionary or in the worldlist on pages 114–19.
- Copy the table onto the board.
- Get students to come out and write words in the spaces.
- Other students say whether the word has the correct sound. They suggest other words.
- Students correct their own lists as necessary.

- Students draw lines to match the sounds to the words.
- Copy the list onto the board.
- Get students to come out and link the sounds and words on the board.
- Students read the words aloud.

> **Answer key**
> /ɜː/ bird
> /uː/ room
> /aɪ/ night
> /iː/ sleep
> /ʌ/ come
> /əʊ/ home
> /juː/ new
> /ɒ/ watch
> /ɔː/ walk
> /ɑː/ can't

- Students complete the words.
- Copy the list onto the board.
- Students come out and complete the words.
- Students check their own lists.
- Students read the words aloud.

> **Answer key**
> /meɪd/ made   /snəʊ/ snow
> /wɒz/ was   /sed/ said
> /brɔːt/ brought   /fɑːm/ farm
> /skuːl/ school   /jɪə/ year
> ? /faɪv/ five   /hɪm/ him

Unit 1 /z/ /ɪz/

- Students read the two pairs of sentences.
- You read them aloud.
- Ask *What do you notice about 'washes'?*
- Elicit an answer.

> **Answer key**
> *The ending is pronounced /ɪz/.*

- Students read the group of words.
- Read aloud the instruction below the words. Tell students they will hear the words on cassette. Point out that *watches* ends in /ɪz/, like *washes* – so the line has been drawn between them.
- Tell students to put their pens on *watches* – and to listen carefully for the next word.
- Say *So if the word you hear ends in /ɪz/, continue the line to that word. If it doesn't, leave your pen where it is, but listen for the next word.*
- Check understanding.
- Play the cassette.
- Students listen and draw the lines.
- Ask *What shape do you get?*
- Elicit answer.

> **Answer key**
> *a star*
>
>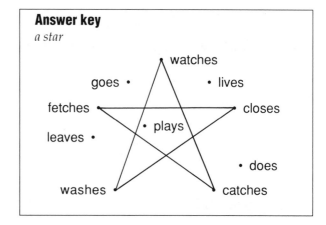

- Students complete the rule.
- Check answer.

> **Answer key**
> *After s, sh and tch, -es is pronounced /ɪz/.*

- Remind students that this is an important rule in the pronunciation of English. It applies to plural nouns as well as verbs.

Unit 2 -ed endings

- Tell students to listen carefully to the different pronunciation of the past tense forms in the two sentences they will hear on the cassette.
  - Play the cassette.
- Elicit differences.

Answer key
*Sometimes the past tense ending **-ed** is pronounced /d/ and sometimes it is pronounced /ɪd/.*

- Students draw two columns in their books, one with the heading *stopped* and the other with the heading *started*, as shown in the Student's Book.
- Students look at the words in the list and try to put each word in the correct column.

- Students listen to the cassette, and, as they hear each past tense verb, check that they have written it in the correct column.
- Check answers.

Answer key
stopped: *played   died   joined   stayed   received   lived   opened   saved*

started: *recorded   wanted   needed   painted   visited   collected   decided*

- Students work out the rule by looking at the characteristics of the words in each column.
- They write the rule in their books.

Answer key
*You pronounce the **-ed** when the letter before the **-ed** is a **d** or a **t**.*

Unit 3 /ɪ/ and /iː/

- Students look up in a dictionary any words they do not know.
- Check the understanding of words you think might be new to students.
- Say *Now, put your pen on 'hill'. I am going to play a cassette with these words on it. When you hear the next word, connect 'hill' to that word with a line. Continue in the same way and connect the words **in the order that you hear them.***
- Play the cassette.
- Students listen carefully and draw connecting lines.
- Ask *What have you drawn?*
- Elicit answer.

Answer key
a ship

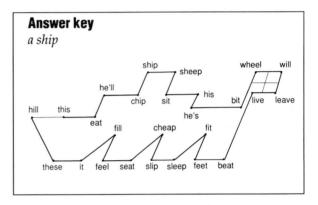

Unit 4 Phonetic alphabet revision

- Read the words aloud.

- Students write new words in the spaces.
- Students check their words in a dictionary or in the wordlist on pages 114–19.
- Copy the table onto the board.
- Students suggest words to put in the table.
- Check these answers with the phonetic transcription in the wordlist.

PRONUNCIATION PRACTICE

Introduction
Phonetic alphabet revision

Vowels: These are the vowel sounds of English.

/iː/	need	....
/i/	twenty	....
/ɪ/	did	....
/e/	ten	....
/æ/	cat	....
/ɑː/	car	....
/ʌ/	run	....
/ɒ/	not	....
/ɔː/	four	....
/ʊ/	book	....
/uː/	Sue	....
/juː/	computer	....
/ɜː/	work	....
/ə/	under	....
/eɪ/	day	....
/aɪ/	nine	....
/ɔɪ/	boy	....
/aʊ/	how	....
/əʊ/	go	....
/eə/	there	....
/ɪə/	here	....

1 In the second column write one more word with the same sound.

2 Match the sounds to the correct word.

/ɜː/	come
/uː/	watch
/aɪ/	bird
/iː/	can't
/ʌ/	room
/əʊ/	walk
/juː/	night
/ɒ/	sleep
/ɔː/	new
/ɑː/	don't

3 Complete these words with the correct symbol:

/m ....d/	made	/sn ..../	snow
/w ....z/	was	/s ....d/	said
/br ....t/	brought	/f........m/	farm
/sk ....l/	school	/j ..../	year
/f...........v/	five	/h ...... m/	him

Unit 1 /z/, /ɪz/

1 Read these pairs of sentences.

I live here.	I wash the car.
Sue lives here.	Casey washes the car.

What do you notice about 'washes'?

2 Look at these words.

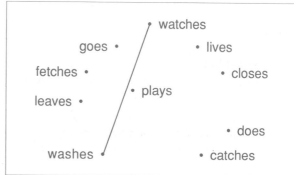

Now listen. If you hear the /ɪz/ ending, continue the line to connect the word. If you don't hear the /ɪz/ ending, don't draw the line. What shape do you get?

3 Complete this rule.

> After ...., ... and .... -es is pronounced /ɪz/.

Unit 2 -ed endings

1 Listen. What do you notice about the '-ed'?

The car started
The car stopped

110

2 Put these words in the correct column.

played   stayed   painted   decided
recorded   wanted   visited   opened
died   needed   collected   saved
joined   received   lived

stopped

started

3 Listen and check your answers.

4 When do you pronounce the '-ed'? Make a rule.

> You pronounce the -ed when the letter before the -ed is a .... or a ....

Unit 3 /ɪ/, /iː/

1 Look at the words. Use a dictionary. Find the meanings of any new words.

ship   • sheep   wheel   will

he'll   chip sit • his   bit live leave .

hill   this   eat   he's

fill   cheap   fit

these it feel seat slip sleep feet beat

2 Listen. You will hear the words. Draw a line to connect the words in the order that you hear them. If you connect the words correctly, you will find one of the things in the list.

Unit 4
Phonetic alphabet revision

Consonants. These are the consonant sounds of English.

/d/	**d**og	....
/t/	**t**o	....
/b/	**b**ig	....
/p/	**p**en	....
/g/	**g**ood	....
/k/	**c**ome	....
/ʃ/	**s**he	....
/tʃ/	ri**ch**	....
/ʒ/	lei**s**ure	....
/dʒ/	**j**acket	....
/f/	**f**rom	....
/v/	**v**ery	....
/ð/	**th**is	....
/θ/	four**th**	....
/s/	**s**ix	....
/ŋ/	si**ng**	....
/j/	**y**esterday	....
/z/	**z**oo	....
/h/	**h**ow	....
/m/	**m**an	....
/n/	**n**o	....
/l/	**l**eg	....
/r/	**r**ed	....
/w/	**w**et	....

1 In the second column write one more word with the same sound.

• Students complete the words.

> **Answer key**
>
> /tʃi:p/ cheap   /wʌn/ one
> /kæmrə/ camera   /ði:z/ these
> /tʃeɪndʒ/ change   /jes/ yes
> /ʃɔ:/ sure   /bɑ:θ/ bath
> /kæfeɪ/ cafe   /pli:z/ please

Unit 5 /r/

- Say *In spoken English, the letter 'r' is sometimes pronounced and sometimes not.*
- Students look at the sentence.
- Point out the four 'r's.
- Say *Listen carefully. I'm going to play the cassette. Which of the 'r' sounds can you hear?*
- Play the cassette.
- Students tick the words containing an audible 'r'.
- Elicit answers.

> **Answer key**
> *The 'r' in bRight and in Red.*

- Students repeat after you the four words containing /r/.
- Correct as necessary.

- Draw students' attention to the outlines of Africa and the Antarctic.
- Say *Look at the words and put them into 'Africa' if the 'r' is pronounced and 'the Antarctic' if the 'r' is silent.*
- Students write the words in the correct place.
- In pairs, students compare answers.

- Say *Now, you'll hear the words on the cassette. Listen carefully and check your answers. Correct any wrong answers.*
- Play the tape. Students check and correct their answers.
- Play the cassette again. Students repeat words.
- Do remedial pronunciation work as necessary.

> **Answer key**
>
> | Africa | Antarctic | |
> |---|---|---|
> | terrible | year | equator |
> | Africa | over | brother |
> | breakfast | sport | picture |
> | travel | dinner | north |
> | brother | bird | Arctic |

Unit 6 /h/

- Make the point that the letter '*h*' is usually pronounced in English.
- It is pronounced /h/. A word beginning with a vowel is *not* pronounced with /h/ at the beginning.
- Tell the students they are now going to practise the /h/ sound.
- Say *I'm going to play the cassette. Listen to the words. If you hear the /h/ sound, repeat the word.*
- Play the tape.
- Students listen and repeat, if necessary.
- Correct as you go along, if necessary.

 hear   at   hero   horrible   accident air   how   hat   ear   hair   old   hotel hold   easy

Unit 7 /tʃ/ and /ʃ/

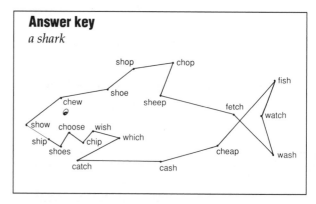
- Students read the words.
- Give students a few minutes to look up unfamiliar words in the dictionary.
- Check comprehension of words.

- Read the instructions aloud (from *Listen*).
- Check comprehension.
- Say *Start by putting your pen on the word **show**.*
- Play the cassette. Students listen and connect words.
- Ask *What have you drawn?*
- Elicit answer.

> **Answer key**
> *a shark*
>
>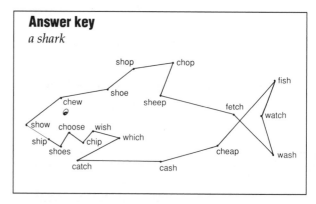

show   ship   shoes   choose   chip wish   which   catch   cash   cheap   fish watch   wash   fetch   sheep   chop   shop shoe   chew   show

Unit 8 A secret message

- Students look at the task.
- Explain the activity.
- Students write the sentences in words.
- Students compare their ideas in pairs.

Answer key
*You will escape at quarter to three
on Thursday the ninth of July.
Wait for a woman with long brown hair.
She will come in a yellow car.*

Answer key
/brɪŋ sʌm nju: kləʊðz fɔ:r ʌs/
/ðeə wɪl bi: wʌn ekstrə pɜ:sən/

Unit 9 Intonation

- Students look at the intonation curves and accompanying questions and statements. Explain as necessary and check understanding.

Note
Explaining may involve comparisons with the intonation of questions and statements in the mother tongue.

- Say *You are now going to hear a cassette of statements and questions. Each time you'll hear some sounds first of all, then real words. Listen carefully, and each time decide whether you're listening to a statement or a question.*
- Play the cassette. Students listen carefully.
- Rewind the cassette.
- Play the cassette again. Stop it after the first utterance. Ask whether it was a question or a statement.
- Repeat with remaining utterances.

Answer key
Q   Q   S   Q   S   S   Q   Q

- Rewind the cassette.

- Play the cassette again. Students listen and repeat.

Has your cousin arrived?
Did you go to the disco yesterday?
I've bought some new trousers.
Is Jackie from New York?
I'm from Australia.
I went to England last summer.
Have you ever seen a UFO?
Where have you been?

Unit 10 Plural endings /ɪz/

- Students read the list of words.
- Check understanding of the words.
- Say *On the cassette you will hear each of these words and then its plural form.*
- Read the two examples given. Say *You will hear these first.*
- Play the cassette.
- Students listen to the cassette. They write the plural next to each word.
- Play the cassette again.
- Students check their answers.
- Check answers (including spelling).

Answer key
*sandwiches   sausages   tomatoes   badges
potatoes   slices   bottles   tins   houses
lemons   oranges*

- Read the question. Say *Look at your list of singulars and plurals.*
- Students write down the rule.
- Students compare rules.
- Elicit answers.
- Write the rule correctly on the board.

Answer key
*If a word ends in **s**, **ch**, **ge**, **ce** or **se** in the singular, the plural ending will be pronounced /ɪz/.*

- Students copy the rule.
- Elicit examples.

Answer key
(possible examples)
gases   watches   pages   faces   suitcases

continued on T113a

2 Complete these words with the correct symbol.

/....... i:p/   cheap   /....... ʌn/   one

/....... æmrə/   camera   /....... i:z/   these

/tʃeɪn ..../ change   /....... es/   yes

/....... ɔ:/   sure   /bɑː ..../   bath

/....... æfeɪ/   cafe   /pliː ..../ please

Unit 5 /r/

1  Listen. Can you hear the /r/?

The aRctic teRn has bRight Red legs.

2 Put these words in Africa if we say the 'r' or the Antarctic if we don't say the 'r'.

year	breakfast	brother
terrible	dinner	picture
Africa	travel	north
over	bird	Arctic
sport	equator	

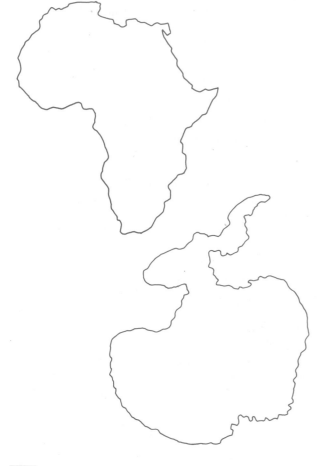

3  Listen and check your answers.

Unit 6 /h/

 Listen. If you hear the /h/ sound, repeat the word. If you don't hear /h/, stay silent.

Unit 7 /tʃ/, /ʃ/

1 Look at these words. Use a dictionary. Find the meaning of any new words.

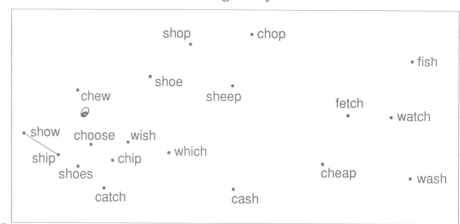

shop   • chop   • fish

• shoe   sheep   fetch   • watch

• chew

• show   choose   • wish   • which

ship   • chip

shoes   cheap   • wash

catch   cash

2  Listen. You will hear the words. Draw a line to connect the words in the order you hear them. If you connect the words correctly, you will find something that begins with /ʃ/.

Unit 8 A secret message

1 What is the message? Write it in words.

/juː wɪl əskeɪp ət kwɔːtə tə θriː/

....

/ɒn θɜːzdi ðə naɪnθ əv dʒuːlaɪ/

....

/weɪt fɔː rə wʊmən wɪð lɒŋ braʊn heə/

....

/ʃiː wɪl kʌm ɪn ə jeləʊ kɑː/

....

2 Write this reply in the phonetic alphabet.

Bring some new clothes for us.

There will be one extra person.

Unit 9 Intonation

1 Look.

Have you ever spoken to a tourist?

I've got an English penfriend.

2 📻 Listen. Is it a question or a statement?

3 Listen again and repeat.

Unit 10 /ɪz/ plural endings

1 📻 Listen and give the plural.

Example
glass   glasses
hamburger   hamburgers

sandwich ....   bottle ....

sausage ....   tin ....

tomato ....   house ....

badge ....   lemon ....

potato ....   orange ....

slice ....

2 When do you pronounce the plural ending /ɪz/? Make a rule. Give two more examples.

Unit 11 /n/ or /m/ + consonant

📻 Listen and repeat.

One hundred chimneys were blown down.

Band Aid's code number was one seven nine.

The numbers are sent to the central computer.

on Monday the twenty-ninth of June

We listened to an album on Sunday.

Who invented the greenhouse?

Unit 12 A secret message

1 What is the message? Write it in words.

/wi: həv dɪskʌvəd ðə treʒə frəm ðə gæliənz/

....

/ɪt ɪz əbaut θɜ:ti maɪlz sauθ i:st əv ðə kəust əv flɒridə/

....

/ðeərə fɔ: ʃɪps/

....

/ðeɪ ɑː berɪd ɪn ðə sænd ət ðə bɒtəm əv ðə si:/

....

2 Write this reply in the phonetic alphabet.

How much gold is there in the ships?

Will more divers be needed?

Jamaica Farewell

Chorus

But I'..... sad to say I'm on my ....

I .... be back for many a day.

.... heart is down. My .... is turning around.

I have ...... leave a little .... in Kingston Town.

1

Down the way where .... nights are gay

And the .... shines daily on the mountain ....

I .... a trip on a sailing ....

And when I .... Jamaica I made a stop.

2

Sounds .... laughter everywhere

.... the native girls .... to and fro.

I .... declare that my heart is ....,

Though I've .... to Maine and to ....

113

continued from T113

Unit 11 /n/ and /m/ + consonant

- Students read the sentences.
- Say *I'm going to play the cassette. Listen carefully, and repeat what you hear.*
- Play the cassette.
- Students repeat each sentence.
- Some students have no problems with this sound combination. If your students have no problems, congratulate them. Say *A lot of people have problems with this. You don't, and that's great.*
- Some students do have problems. These students often try to put a vowel between two adjacent consonants. They say *hun-ə-dred* and *chim-ə-ney.* If your students have problems, point out that there is often *no* vowel between adjacent consonants in English words. Repeat the exercise.

Unit 12 A secret message

▼ 1
- Students look at the task.
- Explain the activity.
- Students write the sentences in words.
- Students compare their ideas in pairs.

Answer key
We have discovered the treasure from the galleons.
It is about thirty miles south-east of the coast of Florida.
There are four ships.
They are buried in the sand at the bottom of the sea.

▼ 2
Answer key
/haʊ mʌtʃ gəʊld ɪz ðeər ɪn ðə ʃɪps/
/wɪl mɔ: daɪvəz bi: ni:dɪd/

SONG: JAMAICA FAREWELL

- Students look at the song.
- Students try to complete the gaps.
- Elicit ideas.
- Play the tape. Students listen.
- Students complete the gaps.
- Elicit answers.
- Play the tape again. Students check their songs.
- Play the tape again. Students sing along.

▣ Jamaica Farewell
Chorus
But I'm sad to say I'm on my way
I won't be back for many a day.
My heart is down. My head is turning around.
I have to leave a little girl in Kingston Town.

1

Down the way where the nights are gay
And the sun shines daily on the mountain top
I took a trip on a sailing ship
And when I reached Jamaica I made a stop.

2

Sounds of laughter everywhere
And the native girls dancing to and fro
I must declare that my heart is there
Though I've been to Maine and to Mexico.

WORDLIST

INTRODUCTION

surname /'sɜ:neɪm/
at the end /æt ðɪ 'end/
word processor /'wɜ:d
    prəʊsesə(r)/
grandma /'grænmɑ:/
grandpa /'grænpɑ:/
try /traɪ/
concentrate /'kɒnsntreɪt/
photo /'fəʊtəʊ/
mine /maɪn/
brain /breɪn/
mouth /maʊθ/
fool /fu:l/
worry /'wʌrɪ/
rude /ru:d/

postcode /'pəʊskəʊd/
barbecue /'bɑ:bɪkju:/
Australian /ɒ'streɪlɪən/
speak /spi:k/
understand /ˌʌndə'stænd/

UNIT 1 DAILY LIFE

bored /bɔ:d/
the same /ðə 'seɪm/
day /deɪ/
robot /'rəʊbɒt/
get undressed /get
    ˌʌn'drest/
again /ə'gen/, /ə'geɪn/
make the beds /meɪk ðə
    'bedz/
wash up /wɒʃ 'ʌp/
iron /'aɪən/
tidy /'taɪdɪ/
housework /'haʊswɜ:k/
phone /fəʊn/
around /ə'raʊnd/
stay /steɪ/
wash /wɒʃ/
except /ɪk'sept/
lazy /'leɪzɪ/
problem /'prɒbləm/

normal /'nɔ:ml/
person /'pɜ:sn/
simple /'sɪmpl/
baby /'beɪbɪ/
teenager /'ti:neɪdʒə(r)/
adult /'ædʌlt/, /ə'dʌlt/
kinds of /'kaɪndz əf/
deep /di:p/
temperature
    /'temprətʃə(r)/
active /'æktɪv/
rapid /'ræpɪd/
movement /'mu:vmənt/
dream /dri:m/
usually /'ju:ʒəlɪ/
remember /rɪ'membə(r)/
body /'bɒdɪ/
spend /spend/
sleepwalk /'sli:pwɔ:k/
amazing /ə'meɪzɪŋ/
pyjamas /pə'dʒɑ:məz/
shave /ʃeɪv/
dig /dɪg/

launderette /ˌlɔ:ndə'ret/,
    /lɔ:n'dret/
shopping bag /'ʃɒpɪŋ bæg/
asleep /ə'sli:p/
perhaps /pə'hæps/,
    /'præps/
rise /raɪz/
relax /rɪ'læks/
breathe /bri:ð/
hour /'aʊə(r)/

tourist /'tʊərɪst/
language school
    /'læŋgwɪdʒ sku:l/
weather /'weðə(r)/
too /tu:/
cold /kəʊld/
wrong /rɒŋ/
hungry /'hʌŋgrɪ/
tired /'taɪəd/

musical instrument
    /ˌmju:zɪkl 'ɪnstrʊmənt/
pet /pet/
average /'ævərɪdʒ/
stranger /'streɪndʒə(r)/

intelligent /ɪn'telɪdʒənt/
play cards /pleɪ 'kɑ:dz/
lose /lu:z/
all the time /ɔ:l ðə taɪm/

UNIT 2 THE PAST

weekend /ˌwi:k'end/
paint /peɪnt/
laugh /lɑ:f/
busy /'bɪzɪ/
ill /ɪl/
tease /ti:z/
listen to /'lɪsn tu:/
She's only kidding. /ʃi:z
    əʊnlɪ' kɪdɪŋ/
fed up with /fed ʌp wɪð/
stupid /'stju:pɪd/
to fancy /'fænsɪ/

king /kɪŋ/
rock and roll /ˌrɒk ən 'rəʊl/
choir /'kwaɪə(r)/
recording studio /rɪ'kɔ:dɪŋ
    ˌstju:dɪəʊ/
secretary /'sekrətrɪ/
manager /'mænɪdʒə(r)/
single /'sɪŋgl/
radio station /'reɪdɪəʊ
    ˌsteɪʃn/
wild /waɪld/
sexy /'seksɪ/
the following year /ðə
    fɒləʊɪŋ jɪə(r)/, /-jɜ:(r)/
a hit (record) /hɪt/
army /'ɑ:mɪ/
lonely /'ləʊnlɪ/
fat /fæt/
depressed /dɪ'prest/
mansion /'mænʃn/
album /'ælbəm/
electronic /ˌɪlek'trɒnɪk/
machine /mə'ʃi:n/

plate /pleɪt/
poster /'pəʊstə(r)/

statue /'stætʃu:/
mirror /'mɪrə(r)/
teddy bear /'tedɪ beə(r)/
club /klʌb/
autograph /'ɔ:təgrɑ:f/
never /'nevə(r)/
anyone /'enɪwʌn/
show /ʃəʊ/
wipe /waɪp/
sweat /swet/
chest /tʃest/
audience /'ɔ:dɪəns/
fantastic /fæn'tæstɪk/
special /'speʃl/

UNIT 3 PLACES

mend /mend/
hurt /hɜ:t/
knee /ni:/
place /pleɪs/
cross the road /krɒs ðə
    'rəʊd/
move in /mu:v ɪn/
gorgeous /'gɔ:dʒəs/
round the corner /ˌraʊnd
    ðə 'kɔ:nə(r)/
show around /ʃəʊ
    ə'raʊnd/
accent /'æksent/,/ 'æksənt/

spanner /'spænə(r)/
a moment /ə'məʊmənt/

field /fi:ld/
bridge /brɪdʒ/
tunnel /'tʌnl/
lie /laɪ/
valley /'vælɪ/
station /'steɪʃn/
factory /'fæktərɪ/
modern /'mɒdn/
shopping centre /'ʃɒpɪŋ
    sentə(r)/
centre /'sentə(r)/
opposite /'ɒpəzɪt/
bus stop /'bʌs stɒp/
secondary school
    /'sekəndrɪ sku:l/
in front of /ɪn 'frʌnt əv/
library /'laɪbrərɪ/
behind /bɪ'haɪnd/
entrance /'entrəns/
newsagent /'nju:zeɪdʒənt/ ·
petrol station /'petrəl
    steɪʃn/
hairdresser /'heə(r)
    dresə(r)/
parade /pə'reɪd/
above /ə'bʌv/

ladder /'lædə(r)/
children /'tʃɪldrən/
cat /kæt/
dog /dɒg/
settee /se'ti:/

down /daʊn/
turning /'tɜ:nɪŋ/
on the right /ɒn ðə 'raɪt/ ·
on the left /ɒn ðə 'left/
get to /get tə/, /tʌ/, /tu:/
end /end/
turn /tɜ:n/

sheep /ʃi:p/
bit /bɪt/
beat /bi:t/
fit /fɪt/
ship /ʃɪp/
seat /si:t/

UNIT 4 REVISION

kiss /kɪs/
optician /ɒpˈtɪʃn/
writer /ˈraɪtə(r)/
boxer /ˈbɒksə(r)/
sold /səʊld/
bend /bend/
shopper /ˈʃɒpə(r)/
unusual /ʌnˈju:ʒl/
customer /ˈkʌstəmə(r)/
organize /ˈɔ:gənaɪz/
everything /ˈevrɪθɪŋ/
idea /aɪˈdɪə/
simple /ˈsɪmpl/
per cent /pəˈsent/
charity /ˈtʃærətɪ/
sign /saɪn/
rang /ræŋ/
trouble /ˈtrʌbl/

———

sandwich /ˈsænwɪdʒ/
tennis racquet /ˈtenɪs
   rækɪt/
knife /naɪf/

———

fabulous /ˈfæbjʊləs/

UNIT 5 TRAVEL

hot /hɒt/
in the country /ɪn ðə
   ˈkʌntrɪ/
coast /kəʊst/
forever /fəˈrevə(r)/
wonderful /ˈwʌndəfl/
sunbathe /ˈsʌnbeɪð/
excited /ɪkˈsaɪtɪd/
seaside /ˈsi:saɪd/
passport /ˈpɑ:spɔ:t/
ticket /ˈtɪkɪt/
panic /ˈpænɪk/
aunt /ɑ:nt/
airport /ˈeə(r)pɔ:t/
luggage /ˈlʌgɪdʒ/
on my own /ɒn maɪ ˈəʊn/

———

feel homesick /fi:l
   ˈhəʊmsɪk/
How long . . . ? /haʊ lɒŋ/

———

a long way /ə lɒŋ ˈweɪ/
tern /tɜ:n/
inch /ɪntʃ/
bright /braɪt/
beak /bi:k/
tail /teɪl/
begin /bɪˈgɪn/
incredible /ɪnˈkredəbl/
journey /ˈdʒɜ:nɪ/
the Earth /ðɪ ɜ:θ/
the Arctic /ðɪ ˈɑ:ktɪk/
the Antarctic /ðɪ
   ænˈtɑ:ktɪk/
the Equator /ðɪ ɪˈkweɪtə(r)/
the North Pole /ðə ˌnɔ:θ
   ˈpəʊl/

the South Pole /ðə ˌsaʊθ
   ˈpəʊl/
northern /ˈnɔ:ðən/
southern /ˈsʌðən/
hemisphere /ˈhemɪsfɪə(r)/
north /nɔ:θ/
south /saʊθ/
east /i:st/
west /west/
spring /sprɪŋ/
summer /ˈsʌmə(r)/
autumn /ˈɔ:təm/
winter /ˈwɪntə(r)/
Asia /ˈeɪʃə/
Europe /ˈjʊərəp/
Africa /ˈæfrɪkə/
Australasia /ˌɒstrəˈleɪʃə/
the Atlantic Ocean /ðɪ
   ətˈlæntɪk əʊʃn/
the Pacific Ocean /ðɪ
   pəˈsɪfɪk əʊʃn/
Ireland /ˈaɪələnd/
sun /sʌn/
star /stɑ:/
foggy /ˈfɒgɪ/
cloudy /ˈklaʊdɪ/

———

hard luck /hɑ:d ˈlʌk/
just /dʒʌst/
cost /kɒst/
fare /feə(r)/
return (ticket) /rɪˈtɜ:n/
fun fair /ˈfʌnfeə(r)/
hire /ˈhaɪə(r)/
boat /bəʊt/
boating lake /ˈbəʊtɪŋ leɪk/
sunburnt /ˈsʌnbɜ:nt/
nose /nəʊz/
back /bæk/
Octopus /ˈɒktəpəs/
feel sick /fi:l ˈsɪk/
pirate /ˈpaɪrət/

———

single (ticket) /ˈsɪŋgl/

UNIT 6 PROBLEMS

put /pʊt/
shelf /ʃelf/
for a long time /fə(r), fɔ:(r)
   ə lɒŋ taɪm/
magazine /mægəˈzi:n/
cigarette /ˌsɪgəˈret/
to smoke /sməʊk/
pocket /ˈpɒkɪt/
steal /sti:l/
shoplift /ˈʃɒplɪft/
It serves him right /ɪt sɜ:vz
   hɪm ˈraɪt/
idiot /ˈɪdɪət/

———

bone /bəʊn/

———

tailor /ˈteɪlə(r)/
village /ˈvɪlɪdʒ/
receive /rɪˈsi:v/
parcel /ˈpɑ:sl/
cloth /klɒθ/
damp /dæmp/
hang /hæŋ/
fire /ˈfaɪə(r)/
a few /əˈfju:/

purple /ˈpɜ:pl/
ring /rɪŋ/
plague /pleɪg/
cure /kjʊə(r)/
city /ˈsɪtɪ/
disease /dɪˈzi:z/
safe /seɪf/
everybody /ˈevrɪbɒdɪ/
local /ˈləʊkl/
vicar /ˈvɪkə(r)/
spread /spred/
hole /həʊl/
full of /ˈfʊl əf/
vinegar /ˈvɪnɪgə(r)/
sweetheart /ˈswi:thɑ:t/
each other /i:tʃ ˈʌðə(r)/
relative /ˈrelətɪv/
smell /smel/
sweet /swi:t/
sign /saɪn/

———

somewhere /ˈsʌmweə(r)/
everywhere /ˈevrɪweə(r)/
anywhere /ˈenɪweə(r)/
nowhere /ˈnəʊweə(r)/

———

gran /græn/
Up you go /ʌp ju:gəʊ/
blooming /ˈblu:mɪŋ/
scratch /skrætʃ/
arm /ɑ:m/
frightened /ˈfraɪtnd/

———

tractor /ˈtræktə(r)
plough /plaʊ/
forehead /ˈfɔ:hed/, /ˈfɒrɪd/
ambulance /ˈæmbjʊləns/
stitch /stɪtʃ/
lucky /ˈlʌkɪ/

UNIT 7 COMPARISONS

slim /slɪm/
better /ˈbetə(r)/
best /best/
smile /smaɪl/
lovely /ˈlʌvlɪ/
article /ˈɑ:tɪkl/
borrow /ˈbɒrəʊ/
attractive /əˈtræktɪv/
figure /ˈfɪgə(r)/
look after /lʊk ɑ:ftə(r)/

———

make up /ˈmeɪk ʌp/
less /les/
perfume /ˈpɜ:fju:m/
handbag /ˈhændbæg/
maybe /ˈmeɪbi/
worst /wɜ:st/
worse /wɜ:s/
lend /lend/
a couple of /ə ˈkʌpl əv/
quid /kwɪd/
to pay back /peɪ ˈbæk/

———

deaf /def/
pardon /ˈpɑ:dn/

fashion /'fæʃn/
moustache /mə'sta:ʃ/
stiff /stɪf/
corset /'kɔ:sɪt/
narrow /'nærəʊ/
waist /weɪst/
uncomfortable /ʌn'kʌmftəbl/
the first time /ðə 'fɜ:st taɪm/
straight /streɪt/
bust /bʌst/
fashionable /'fæʃnəbl/
hat /hæt/
wide /waɪd/
leg /leg/
popular /'pɒpjʊlə(r)/
the age of /ði: (j)'eɪdʒ əv/
pink /pɪŋk/
tight /taɪt/
jumper /dʒʌmpə(r)/
blouse /blaʊz/
pointed /'pɔɪntɪd/
toe /təʊ/
high /haɪ/
stiletto /stɪ'letəʊ/
heel /hɪəl/
revolution /revə'lu:ʃn/
miniskirt /mini'skɜ:t/
boot /bu:t/
century /'sentʃərɪ/
haircut /'heəkʌt/
hippy /'hɪpɪ/
style /staɪl/
colourful /'kʌləfl/
beard /bɪəd/
common /'kɒmən/

bra /bra:/
knickers /'nɪkəz/
vest /vest/
shorts /ʃɔ:ts/
underpants /'ʌndəpænts/

floor /flɔ:(r)/
escalator /'eskəleɪtə(r)/
size /saɪz/
try on /traɪ ɒn/
first class /'fɜ:st kla:s/
second class /'sekənd kla:s/
feet /fi:t/
department store /də'pa:tmənt stɔ:(r)/

trainers /'treɪnəz/
comfortable /'kʌmftəbl/

chew /tʃu:/

UNIT 8 REVISION

prisoner /'prɪznə(r)/
prison /'prɪzn/
escape /ɪ'skeɪp/
reporter /rɪ'pɔ:tə(r)/
take off /teɪk ɒf/
towards /tə'wɔ:dz/
police inspector /pə'li:s ɪnspektə(r)/
describe /dɪ'skraɪb/
glasses /'gla:sɪz/

UNIT 9 VISITORS

seen /si:n/
gone /gɒn/
the States /ðə 'steɪts/
cousin /'kʌzn/
paper round /'peɪpə raʊnd/
been /bi:n/
cowboy /'kaʊbɔɪ/
met /met/
introduce /ˌɪntrə'dju:s/
heard /hɜ:d/
Good Lord /gʊd 'lɔ:d/
dustbin /'dʌstbɪn/
thrown /θrəʊn/
had /hæd/
got /gɒt/
brought /brɔ:t/
done /dʌn/

Prime Minister /ˌpraɪm 'mɪnɪstə(r)/
British /'brɪtɪʃ/
since /sɪns/
Houses of Parliament /ˌhaʊzɪz əv 'pa:ləmənt/
official /ə'fɪʃl/
palace /'pælɪs/
built /bɪlt/
most of /məʊst əv/
destroy /dɪ'strɔɪ/
clock tower /klɒk taʊə(r)/
bell /bel/
brontosaurus /ˌbrɒntə'sɔ:rəs/
royal /rɔɪəl/
hunting forest /'hʌntɪŋ fɒrɪst/
waxworks /'wækswɜ:ks/
model /'mɒdl/
display /dɪ'spleɪ/
battle /'bætl/
Chamber of Horrors /ˌtʃeɪmbər əv 'hɒrəz/
gift /gɪft/
huge /hju:dʒ/
collection /kə'lekʃn/
plant /pla:nt/
including /ɪŋ'klu:dɪŋ/
butterfly /'bʌtəflaɪ/
whale /weɪl/
dinosaur /'daɪnəsɔ:(r)/
skeleton /'skelɪtn/
cafeteria /ˌkæfə'tɪərɪə/
contain /kən'teɪn/
telescope /'telɪskəʊp/
astronomy /ə'strɒnəmɪ/
international /ˌɪntə'næʃnəl/
meridian line /mə'rɪdɪən laɪn/
observatory /əb'zɜ:vətrɪ/
execution /ˌeksɪ'kju:ʃn/
zoo /zu:/
jewel /dʒu:əl/
crown /kraʊn/

constable /'kʌnstəbl/
on patrol /ɒn pə'trəʊl/
mountain /'maʊntɪn/
thief /θi:f/
look for /'lʊk fɔ:(r)/
base /beɪs/

UNIT 10 FOOD

broke /brəʊk/
present /'preznt/
glass /gla:s/
milk /mɪlk/
ham /hæm/
chicken /'tʃɪkɪn/
chips /tʃɪps/
packet /'pækɪt/
crisps /krɪsps/
steak /steɪk/
onion /'ʌnɪən/
salad /'sæləd/
slice /slaɪs/
cheese /tʃi:z/
tomato /tə'ma:təʊ/
lettuce /'letɪs/
cucumber /'kju:kʌmbə(r)/
childish /'tʃaɪldɪʃ/
see for yourself /si: fə:(r) jɔ:'self/

automobile /'ɔ:təməbi:l/
gas /gæs/
drug store /'drʌg stɔ:(r)/
pants /pænts/
truck /trʌk/
lift /lɪft/
motorway /'məʊtəweɪ/

coffee /'kɒfi:/
paper /'peɪpə(r)/
plastic /'plæstɪk/
iron /'aɪən/
leather /'leðə(r)/
information /ˌɪnfə'meɪʃn/
bread /bred/
wood /wʊd/
meat /mi:t/
shampoo /ʃæm'pu:/
soap powder /'səʊp paʊdə(r)/
carrot /'kærət/
potato /pə'teɪtəʊ/
sausage /'sɒsɪdʒ/

soup /su:p/
mineral water /'mɪnərəl wɔ:tə(r)/
cake /keɪk/
fruit /fru:t/
pancake /'pæŋkeɪk/
garlic /'ga:lɪk/
starter /'sta:tə(r)/
home-made /ˌhəʊmmeɪd/
jacket potato /ˌdʒækɪt pə'teɪtəʊ/
salad bar /'sæləd ba:(r)/
peppers /'pepəz/
sweetcorn /'swi:tkɔ:n/

search /sɜ:tʃ/
police station /pə'li:s steɪʃn/
light /laɪt/
mine /maɪn/
close /kləʊs/
go dead /gəʊ 'ded/
a UFO /ə ju: ef 'əʊ/
calendar /'kælɪndə(r)/
county /'kaʊntɪ/

English-speaking /'ɪŋglɪʃ spi:kɪŋ/

bean /bi:n/
traditional /trədɪʃənl/
pizza /'pi:tsə/
salami /sə'lɑ:mɪ/
olive /'ɒlɪv/
mushroom /'mʌʃrʊm,
    -ru:m/
tuna /'tju:nə/
mussels /'mʌslz/
anchovy /'æntʃəvɪ/
sardine /sɑ:'di:n/
chillies /'tʃɪlɪz/
healthy /'helθɪ/
alternative /ɔ:l'tɜ:nətɪv/
exotic /ɪg'zɒtɪk/
pineapple /'paɪnæpl/
wholemeal /'həʊlmi:l/
delicious /dɪ'lɪʃəs/
extra /'ekstrə/
topping /'tɒpɪŋ/
dessert /dɪ'zɜ:t/
lemon /'lemən/
cheesecake /'tʃi:zkeɪk/
pie /paɪ/
cream /kri:m/
sauce /sɔ:s/
diet /'daɪət/
lemonade /ˌlemə'neɪd/
pure /pjʊə(r)/
beverage /'bevərɪdʒ/
alcoholic /ˌælkə'hɒlɪk/
beer /bɪə(r)/
bottle /'bɒtl/
wine /waɪn/
serve /sɜ:v/

recipe /'resəpɪ/
ingredients /ɪŋgri:dɪənts/
minced /mɪnst/
beef /bi:f/
clove /kləʊv/
breadcrumbs
    /'bredkrʌmz/
nut /nʌt/
salt /sɔ:lt/
pepper /'pepə(r)/
bun /bʌn/
peel /pi:l/
chop /tʃɒp/
grill /grɪl/
bowl /bəʊl/
appetite /'æpɪtaɪt/
fork /fɔ:k/
refrigerator
    /rɪ'frɪdʒəreɪtə(r)/
fridge /frɪdʒ/
fry /fraɪ/
toast /təʊst/
tin /tɪn/
finally /'faɪnəlɪ/
loaf /ləʊf/

UNIT 11
COMMUNICATION

written /'rɪtn/
discover /dɪs'kʌvə(r)/
test /test/
exam /ɪg'zæm/
found /faʊnd/
to copy /'kɒpɪ/
stolen /'stəʊlən/
warn /wɔ:n/
sent /sent/
invite /ɪn'vaɪt/
party /'pɑ:tɪ/
to ground /graʊnd/
done /dʌn/
properly /'prɒpəlɪ/
pocket money /'pɒkɪt
    mʌnɪ/
laziness /'leɪzɪnəs/
trip /trɪp/
stuck /stʌk/
main /meɪn/
to check /tʃek/
to process /'prəʊses/
result /rɪ'zʌlt/

remove /rɪ'mu:v/
develop /dɪ'veləp/
print /prɪnt/
laboratory /lə'bɒrətrɪ/
printer /prɪntə(r)/

south-east /ˌsaʊθ'i:st/
storm /stɔ:m/
hurricane /'hʌrɪkən/
fireman /'faɪəmən/
fire engine /'faɪər ˌendʒɪn/
injure /'ɪndʒə(r)/
wreck /rek/
wind /wɪnd/
roof /ru:f/
chimney /'tʃɪmnɪ/
rip off /rɪp 'ɒf/
smash /smæʃ/
hotel /həʊ'tel/
blow down /bləʊ 'daʊn/
rare /reə(r)/
without /wɪ'ðaʊt/
electricity /ɪˌlek'trɪsətɪ/
power line /'paʊə(r) laɪn/
repair /rɪ'peə(r)/
block /blɒk/
crush /krʌʃ/
harbour /'hɑ:bə(r)/
wave /weɪv/
ferry /'ferɪ/
MP /ˌem'pi:/
warning /'wɔ:nɪŋ/
given /'gɪvn/
Meteorological Office
    /ˌmi:tɪərə'lɒdʒɪkl ɒfɪs/
weather forecast /'weðə(r)
    fɔ:kɑ:st/
midnight /'mɪdnaɪt/
direction /dɪ'rekʃn/, /daɪ-/
follow /'fɒləʊ/
flood /flʌd/
damage /'dæmɪdʒ/
extinct /ɪk'stɪŋkt/

chart /tʃɑ:t/
release /rɪ'li:s/
switch on /swɪtʃ ɒn/
broadcast /'brɔ:dkɑ:st/
produce /prə'dju:s/
sample /'sɑ:mpl/
code number /'kəʊd
    nʌmbə(r)/
all over /ɔ:l'əʊvə(r)/
central /'sentrəl/
sort (out) /sɔ:t (aʊt)/
producer /prə'dju:sə(r)/
present /prɪ'zent/
compact disc /ˌkɒmpækt
    'dɪsk/
sales /seɪlz/
copy /'kɒpɪ/

UNIT 12
REVISION

worth /wɜ:θ/
past /pɑ:st/

against /ə'genst/, /ə'geɪnst/
rock /rɒk/
sunk /sʌŋk/
sailor /'seɪlə(r)/
drown /draʊn/
treasure /'treʒə(r)/
diver /'daɪvə(r)/
eaten /'i:tn/
disaster /dɪ'zɑ:stər/
attack /ə'tæk/
bury /'berɪ/
sand /sænd/
galleon /'gælɪən/
forgotten /fə'gɒtn/
coin /kɔɪn/
hunter /'hʌntə(r)/
study /'stʌdɪ/

promise /'prɒmɪs/

USEFUL SETS

Days of the week

Monday /'mʌndɪ/
Tuesday /'tjuːzdɪ/
Wednesday /'wenzdɪ/
Thursday /'θɜːzdɪ/
Friday /'fraɪdɪ/
Saturday /'sætədɪ/
Sunday /'sʌndɪ/

Months of the year

January /'dʒænjʊərɪ/
February /'februərɪ/
March /mɑːtʃ/
April /'eɪprəl/
May /meɪ/
June /dʒuːn/
July /dʒuː'laɪ/
August /'ɔːgəst/
September /sep'tembə(r)/
October /ɒk'təʊbə(r)/
November /nəʊ'vembə(r)/
December /dɪ'sembə(r)/

The seasons

spring /sprɪŋ/
summer /'sʌmə(r)/
autumn /'ɔːtəm/
winter /'wɪntə(r)/

Geographical names

the Earth /ðɪ ɜːθ/
the Arctic /ðɪ ɑːktɪk/
the Antarctic /ðɪ æn'tɑːktɪk/
the Equator /ðɪ ɪ'kweɪtə(r)
the North Pole /ðə nɔːθ'pəʊl/
the South Pole /ðə ˌsaʊθ 'pəʊl/
northern hemisphere /ˌnɔːðən 'hemɪsfɪə(r)/
southern hemisphere /ˌsʌðən 'hemɪsfɪə(r)/
Asia /'eɪʃə/
Europe /'jʊərəp/
Africa /'æfrɪkə/
Australasia /ˌɒstrə'leɪʃə/
the Atlantic Ocean /ðɪ ət'læntɪk əʊʃn/
the Pacific Ocean /ðə pə'sɪfɪk əʊʃn/

Points of the compass

north /nɔːθ/
south /saʊθ/
east /iːst/
west /west/

Cardinal numbers

one /wʌn/
two /tuː/
three /θriː/
four /fɔː(r)/
five /faɪv/
six /sɪks/
seven /'sevn/
eight /eɪt/
nine /naɪn/
ten /ten/
eleven /ɪ'levn/
twelve /twelv/
thirteen /ˌθɜː'tiːn/
fourteen /ˌfɔː'tiːn/
fifteen /ˌfɪf'tiːn/
sixteen /ˌsɪk'stiːn/
seventeen /ˌsevn'tiːn/
eighteen /ˌeɪti:n/
nineteen /ˌnaɪnti:n/
twenty /'twentɪ/
twenty-one /ˌtwentɪ'wʌn/
twenty-two /ˌtwentɪ'tuː/
twenty-three /ˌtwentɪ'θriː/
twenty-four /ˌtwentɪ'fɔː(r)/
twenty-five /ˌtwentɪ'faɪv/
twenty-six /ˌtwentɪ'sɪks/
twenty-seven /ˌtwentɪ'sevn/
twenty-eight /ˌtwentɪ'eɪt/
twenty-nine /ˌtwentɪ'naɪn/
thirty /'θɜːtɪ/
forty /'fɔːtɪ/
fifty /'fɪftɪ/
one hundred /wʌn 'hʌndrəd/
two hundred /ˌtuː 'hʌndrəd/
one thousand /wʌn 'θaʊznd/
two thousand /ˌtuː 'θaʊznd/
ten thousand /ˌten 'θaʊznd/
one hundred thousand /wʌn ˌhʌndrəd 'θaʊznd/
one million /wʌn 'mɪlɪən/

Ordinal numbers

first /fɜːst/
second /'sekənd/
third /θɜːd/
fourth /fɔːθ/
fifth /fɪfθ/
sixth /sɪksθ/
seventh /'sevnθ/
eighth /eɪtθ/
ninth /naɪnθ/
tenth /tenθ/
eleventh /ɪ'levnθ/
twelfth /twelfθ/
thirteenth /ˌθɜː'tiːnθ/
fourteenth /ˌfɔː'tiːnθ/
fifteenth /ˌfɪf'tiːnθ/
sixteenth /ˌsɪk'stiːnθ/
seventeenth /ˌsevn'tiːnθ/
eighteenth /ˌeɪ'tiːnθ/
ninteenth /ˌnaɪn'tiːnθ/
twentieth /'twentɪəθ/
twenty-first /ˌtwentɪ'fɜːst/
twenty-second /ˌtwentɪ'sekənd/
twenty-third /ˌtwentɪ'θɜːd/
twenty-fourth /ˌtwentɪ'fɔːθ/
twenty-fifth /ˌtwentɪ'fɪfθ/
twenty-sixth /ˌtwentɪ'sɪksθ/
twenty-seventh /ˌtwentɪ'sevnθ/
twenty-eighth /ˌtwentɪ'eɪtθ/
twenty-ninth /ˌtwentɪ'naɪnθ/
thirtieth /'θɜːtɪəθ/
thirty-first /ˌθɜːtɪ'fɜːst/

Irregular verbs

Infinitive	Past tense	Past participle
be /bɪ, bi:/	was /wɒz/	been /bi:n/
become /bɪ'kʌm/	became /bɪ'keɪm/	become /bɪ'kʌm/
blow /bləʊ/	blew /blu:/	blown /bləʊn/
break /breɪk/	broke /brəʊk/	broken /'brəʊkən/
bring /brɪŋ/	brought /brɔ:t/	brought /brɔ:t/
buy /baɪ/	bought /bɔ:t/	bought /bɔ:t/
catch /kætʃ/	caught /kɔ:t/	caught /kɔ:t/
come /kʌm/	came /keɪm/	come /kʌm/
do /du:/	did /dɪd/	done /dʌn/
drive /draɪv/	drove /drəʊv/	driven /'drɪvn/
eat /i:t/	ate /et/	eaten /'i:tn/
fall /fɔ:l/	fell /fel/	fallen /'fɔ:lən/
feed /fi:d/	fed /fed/	fed /fed/
fight /faɪt/	fought /fɔ:t/	fought /fɔ:t/
find /faɪnd/	found /faʊnd/	found /faʊnd/
fly /flaɪ/	flew /flu:/	flown /fləʊn/
forget /fə'get/	forgot /fə'gɒt/	forgotten /fə'gɒtn/
get /get/	got /gɒt/	got /gɒt/
give /gɪv/	gave /geɪv/	given /'gɪvn/
go /gəʊ/	went /went/	gone /gɒn/
have /hæv/	had /hæd/	had /hæd/
hear /hɪə(r)/	heard /hɜ:d/	heard /hɜ:d/
hit /hɪt/	hit /hɪt/	hit /hɪt/
hold /həʊld/	held /held/	held /held/
leave /li:v/	left /left/	left /left/
make /meɪk/	made /meɪd/	made /meɪd/
meet /mi:t/	met /met/	met /met/
pay /peɪ/	paid /peɪd/	paid /peɪd/
put /pʊt/	put /pʊt/	put /pʊt/
read /ri:d/	read /red/	read /red/
ride /raɪd/	rode /rəʊd/	ridden /'rɪdn/
ring /rɪŋ/	rang /ræŋ/	rung /rʌŋ/
run /rʌn/	ran /ræn/	run /rʌn/
say /seɪ/	said /sed/	said /sed/
see /si:/	saw /sɔ:(r)/	seen /si:n/
sell /sel/	sold /səʊld/	sold /səʊld/
send /send/	sent /sent/	sent /sent/
sink /sɪŋk/	sank /sæŋk/	sunk /sʌŋk/
steal /sti:l/	stole /stəʊl/	stolen /'stəʊlən/
take /teɪk/	took /tʊk/	taken /'teɪkən/
think /θɪŋk/	thought /θɔ:t/	thought /θɔ:t/
throw /θrəʊ/	threw /θru:/	thrown /θrəʊn/
wake up /weɪk ʌp/	woke up /wəʊk ʌp/	woken up /wəʊkən ʌp/
write /raɪt/	wrote /rəʊt/	written /'rɪtn/

WORKBOOK KEY

Introductory unit

INTRODUCTION

1 Come in.
2 Come on, Ann's here.
3 See you,
4 Hang on a minute. Don't worry about it,
5 hurry up.
6 just now.
7 The bus is coming.
8 I'm sorry,
9 Don't be rude,

your
his   our
her   their

b
1 is 's   5 'm 're
2 are   6 's 's
3 're   7 are 're
4 's 's 're   8 'm

c
1 I'm not from London.
2 My sister isn't seventeen.
3 You aren't in these photos.
4 We aren't from Italy.
5 Your camera isn't in the living room.
6 Terry isn't at home.
7 Vince and Sue aren't at the bus stop.
8 I'm not late for my appointment.
9 Casey and I aren't very good at Maths.
10 Geography isn't my favourite subject.

b
1 have   6 have
2 has   7 has
3 have   8 have
4 have   9 has
5 has   10 have

c
1 We haven't got a dog.
2 Our school hasn't got a good football team.
3 She hasn't got green eyes.
4 I haven't got a penfriend.
5 You haven't got the right answer.
6 I haven't got the new Madonna record.
7 We haven't got a lot of homework today.
8 Our flat hasn't got a garden.
9 My grandparents haven't got a video recorder.
10 This camera hasn't got an automatic focus.

two

five

seven

eleven
twelve
thirteen

sixteen
seventeen

twenty-one

twenty-three
twenty-four

twenty-seven
twenty-eight
twenty-nine
thirty

first

third
fourth

sixth

eighth
ninth
tenth

fourteenth
fifteenth

eighteenth
nineteenth
twentieth

twenty-second

twenty-fifth
twenty-sixth

thirty-first

a
's your   's your
are you   's your
's   have you got
are you   Is
Have you got have you got
Have you got Are you

b
Student's own answers

a

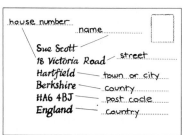

house number
name
Sue Scott
18 Victoria Road — street
Hartfield — town or city
Berkshire — county
HA6 4BJ — post code
England — country

b
Mrs P. Wright
165 Windermere Road
Preston
Lancashire
P23 8KJ
Great Britain

Tony Clarence
29 Biscay Street
Birmingham
B7 9YT
United Kingdom

c
Student's own answers

Unit 1

VICTORIA ROAD

1 I've got nothing to do.
2 There's nothing to do around here.
3 You're in my way.
4 That's funny.
5 It's time you were up.
6 What's the matter with you?

Why don't you do your homework?
Why don't you tidy your room?
Why don't you go to the shops?
Why don't you clean the car?
Why don't you make your bed?
Why don't you iron your trousers?
Why don't you cook the dinner?
Why don't you wash up?

LANGUAGE WORK

a

quarter past seven

half past ten

twenty to five

twenty past eleven

five past two

ten to six

twenty-five to three

ten past four

five to nine

quarter to twelve

eight o'clock

twenty-five past one

b

twenty-three minutes past twelve
eleven minutes past eight
twenty past nine
twelve minutes to twelve
half past six
twenty-nine minutes past seven
nineteen minutes to three
four minutes to five

 b

1 live   2 go   3 works
4 travels   5 works   6 watch
7 go   8 drives   9 live
10 works   11 studies   12 sings

c

Student's own answers

READING

 a second; a minute; an hour
a day; a week; a month; a year

 b and c

 1 this   2 These   3 This   4 this
5 these   6 this   7 this   8 these

 women   watches
men   a baby
teeth   a person
children   families

LISTENING

 b

She tidies her room.
She doesn't cook dinner.
She doesn't wash her clothes.
She doesn't iron her clothes.
She doesn't clean the car.
She doesn't wash up.
She goes shopping.
She doesn't set the table.
She makes her bed.
She babysits.
She doesn't sweep the floor.
She makes drinks.

c

Student's own answers

 on   at   on
at   in   on
in   on   at … in
in   at   at … on
on

 Student's own answers

INTERACTION

 a

1 goes   2 washes   3 plays
4 does   5 watches   6 cleans
7 catches   8 closes   9 goes
10 misses   11 starts
12 finishes   13 practises

 b

Where do you live?
Do you live in a house or a flat?
Why do you live in England?
Do you play tennis every day?
Where do you practise?
What time do you get up?
What do you have for breakfast?
What do you do in your free time?
When do you go to bed?

PROJECT

 This is John's day. He gets up at half
past seven. He gets dressed and he
has his breakfast. Then he catches
the bus to school. He comes home at
four o'clock, and then he watches
television and does his homework.
On Thursday evenings he goes
swimming.

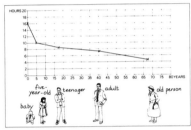

LEARNING DIARY

 five past eight
twenty to eleven
six o'clock
half past three
twenty-five past twelve
ten to seven

 on   at
in   on
in   in
at   at
on   at
on

 spend   sleep   needs   go
get up   says   does   reads
watches   don't   close   sleeps
goes   gets up

 When do you get up?
What do you do with all that extra
time?

Do you go out?
does your wife sleep?
When does she go to bed?
When does she get up?

 1 doesn't need   4 doesn't go
2 don't go   out
3 doesn't watch   5 don't get up

Unit 2

VICTORIA ROAD

 Did you have a good weekend?
Yes, we had a good laugh.
I didn't want to.
Oh, very funny.
I'm only kidding.
I'm fed up with your silly jokes.
She fancies him.

LANGUAGE WORK

 b
Were
was
Was
was … weren't
wasn't … Was
was
was
wasn't … was

 b

1 played   6 cleaned
2 worked   7 helped
3 stayed   8 watched
4 practised   9 washed
5 painted   10 telephoned

c

1 didn't play … Casey did.
2 didn't work… Sue did.
3 didn't stay … Terry did.
4 didn't practise … Vince did.
5 didn't paint … Sue and Kamala
   did.
6 didn't clean … Casey did.
7 didn't help … Vince did.
8 didn't watch … Terry did.
9 didn't wash … Kamala did.
10 didn't telephone … Sue did.

READING

 1 in   6 in … in
2 at   7 in
3 to   8 to
4 at   9 in
5 to   10 at

 loved   went   sang   bought
his   wanted   didn't   made
was   birthday

special   dream   voice   heard
told   That's   played   went
could

b
1 a railway station
2 a police station
3 a space station
4 a radio station

c
Student's own answers

LISTENING

 a

January	February
March	April
May	June
July	August
September	October
November	December

b
Student's own answers

 went got made left took arrived said looked wasn't took couldn't found drove stopped gave missed caught had did saw bought wasn't

INTERACTION

 b
1 did she go
2 Did he play
3 did he sing
4 did you buy
5 did you get up
6 did she paint
7 Did you have
8 did you do
9 Did you see
10 did he (or Elvis) live

 was he born (or did he come from)
When was he born
When did he make his first hit record
did he die
hit singles did he have
was … about him
How many songs did he write
did he play with
Did they visit
When did they go to Australia
did he marry
did he give his last
When did he die

PROJECT

 b

robbed	worried
needed	played
loved	used
hurried	pulled
stayed	knitted
wanted	picked
moved	arrived

 a
(Possible answer)
He was born on 7 September 1936.
He played with the Crickets.
He wrote 33 songs.
His first hit was 'That'll be the Day'.
He went to Australia.
He married Maria Elena Santiago.
He died in a plane crash.

b
Student's own answers

LEARNING DIARY

1	sang	7	met
2	were	8	worked
3	played	9	married
4	made	10	died
5	rode	11	was
6	left	12	had

1 did she go
2 did you find
3 did she buy them
4 did she get it
5 were they there
6 did you watch
7 did he do it
8 did he break it
9 was he there
10 did he stop you

1 Vince wasn't ill yesterday.
2 Terry didn't forget his homework.
3 Kamala didn't see Vince with a girl.
4 Sue didn't play badminton last night.
5 Casey and Terry didn't go to the cinema.
6 I didn't have a salad for my lunch.
7 We weren't late for the train.
8 I couldn't do the homework easily.
9 Mr Moore didn't drive too fast.
10 He didn't put his passport in his pocket.

Unit 3

VICTORIA ROAD

 over there … I'm in love.
She's gorgeous.
Is there anything to do around here?
It's a great place.
Are you doing anything at the moment?
Would you like to show me around?
I've hurt my foot.
I don't believe it.
round the corner.

LANGUAGE WORK

 b
The men aren't playing basketball. They're playing American football.
The boy isn't eating a hamburger. He's eating an ice cream.
The girl isn't buying a pair of jeans. She's buying a T-shirt.
The people aren't waiting for a bus. They're waiting for a train.
The girl isn't playing a guitar. She's playing a piano.
The two men aren't carrying a piano. They're carrying a table.
The astronauts aren't mending a bicycle. They're mending a satellite.
The man and woman aren't watching a football match. They're watching TV.
The woman isn't reading a book. She's reading a magazine.
The boy isn't painting a picture. He's painting a chair.

 b
1 's getting up
2 works
3 have
4 're going
5 'm having
6 'm looking
7 's raining … rains
8 'm doing
9 travels …'s travelling
10 's doing … does

READING

 1 above   2 over   3 on top of
4 through   5 behind
6 in front of   7 at the top of
8 at the bottom of   9 on the left
10 on the right   11 in
12 in the middle of   13 between
14 under   15 opposite   16 next to

 b
The treasure is just between the bridge and the railway bridge, opposite the castle.

c
Student's own answers

 is one tunnel   are two lakes
are six bridges   are three rivers   is one castle   is one town
is one station   are three villages

LISTENING

 b
2 Who are you waiting for?
We're waiting for Tony.
3 What are you listening to?
I'm listening to Jason Donovan.
4 Are you going to the disco?
No, I'm going to the cinema.

T122

5 Is Terry doing his homework?
  No, he's writing a letter.
6 What's he making?
  He's making a table.
7 What are you watching?
  I'm watching the news.
8 Are you doing anything at the moment?
  Yes, I'm having lunch.

 a

1	desk	10	dressing table
2	lamp	11	fridge
3	bed	12	cooker
4	wardrobe	13	stereo
5	bath	14	armchair
6	mirror	15	settee
7	toilet	16	television
8	sink	17	table
9	cupboard	18	chair

b
Upstairs, left to right:
study, bedroom, bathroom.
Downstairs, left to right:
dining room, living room, kitchen.

INTERACTION

Excuse me. Can you tell me how to get to the station, please?
Yes. Go down here. Take the third turning on the left. The station is on the left.

Excuse me. Can you tell me how to get to the library, please?
Yes. Go down here. Turn left. Take the second turning on the right. The library is on the right.

Excuse me. Can you tell me how to get to the post office, please?
Yes. Go down here. Turn right. The post office is on the corner of the next street.

 wardrobe valley factory kitchen toilet settee castle lake island bedroom church armchair

PROJECT

 b

going	**shopping**
seeing	hitting
carrying	stopping
going	clapping
walking	
feeling	
cleaning	**arriving**
following	living
	coming
	taking
	having
	making

a
(Possible order)
Warwick is near Birmingham.
It is quite an old town.

It has got a modern shopping centre.
It has got a lot of interesting buildings.
A lot of tourists come to see them.
I live in Stratford Road.
My house is number 42.

b
(Possible answer)
Warwick is near Birmingham. It is quite an old town, but it has got a modern shopping centre. It has got a lot of interesting buildings and a lot of tourists come to see them. I live in Stratford Road and my house is number 42.

c
Student's own answer

LEARNING DIARY

 1 Where's Casey going?
  He's going to a football match.
2 Why are they taking the television?
  It's making a funny noise.
3 Why are you sitting here?
  We're waiting for our friends.
4 Are you getting up?
  No, I'm staying in bed.
5 Is Kamala working in the shop today?
  No, she's helping Sue.
6 What are Vince and Terry doing?
  They're talking to Jackie.

1	does	6	's putting
2	'm not going	7	watch
3	's wearing	8	's mending
4	likes	9	isn't having
5	are/is moving	10	gets

1	behind	5	next to
2	opposite	6	on
3	on	7	in the middle of
4	between	8	under

Unit 4

Unit 5

VICTORIA ROAD

(Left hand column)
Oh, I'm all right.
That's all right.
you'll be all right.
It's all right now.

(Right hand column)
It's all right,
All right.
Yes, all right.
She's all right.

LANGUAGE WORK

 b

1	'll spend	6	won't take
2	'll stay	7	will be
3	won't help	8	'll need
4	will be	9	'll bring
5	won't go	10	will be

a

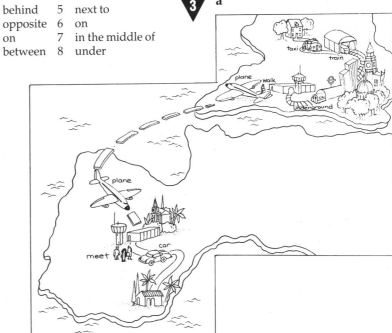

b

('travel' can be used instead of 'go'.)

2 She'll go ... by train
3 She'll go ... by underground
4 She'll walk
5 She'll go ... by plane
6 will meet
7 'll go ... by car

 b

1 When will we leave London?
2 When will we arrive?
3 How long will the flight take?
4 Will someone meet us at the airport?
5 How long will we stay in Athens?
6 Will we visit the Parthenon?
7 Where will we stay?
8 Will we need a visa?
9 When will we get back?
10 How much will it cost?

READING

 1 The North Pole
2 The Equator
3 The Pacific Ocean
4 North America
5 South America
6 The Atlantic Ocean
7 Europe
8 Africa
9 Asia
10 The Indian Ocean
11 Antarctica
12 Australasia
13 The South Pole

 b

If you go on the Octopus, you'll feel sick.
If you eat too much, you'll get fat.
If you eat sweets, you'll get bad teeth.
If you get up late, you'll miss the train.
If you sunbathe too long, you'll get sunburnt.
If you leave your handbag open, you'll lose your money.
If you stand up in a boat, you'll fall in the water.
If you drive too fast, you'll have an accident.

LISTENING

b

1	mustn't	6	must
2	must	7	mustn't
3	needn't	8	mustn't
4	needn't	9	needn't
5	mustn't	10	must

c

Student's own answers

 8

ship	port
aeroplane	airport
train	station
boat	boating lake
car	garage
bus	bus stop

INTERACTION

 9

1	train	5	timetable
2	ticket office	6	passenger
3	ticket clerk	7	ticket
4	platform		

 10 **a**

please	time ... train
return	from
will	Thank

b

London, please.
Single or return?
Return, please.
That will be £25.
What time is the next train?
Eleven fifteen from platform nine.
Thank you.

PROJECT

 11 **b**

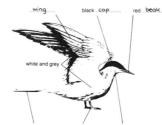

wing ..... black ..cap..... red ..beak....
white and grey
...tail..... ...red.... ...legs..... ....head......

c

It has a ...   It has ... and a ...   It is not a very large bird.   It has a ... of ...   It eats ...   It spends the ... and then ... the ... the ...

d

(Possible answer)

The Foreign Tourist is red and white. It has got a red face and legs. It has a hat on its head and it wears shorts. It carries at least two cameras. It is fat. It eats fish and chips, hamburgers and chips, and pizza and chips. It spends fifty weeks of the year in northern Europe and America and then it migrates to southern coasts in summer.

 12

you're	she'll
he doesn't	I'm not
I'm	they haven't
he isn't	he's
they don't	I'll
you've	we aren't
I won't	she didn't
I've	it hasn't
it's	

LEARNING DIARY

 1

When will you leave London?
How will you travel?
Will you fly?
How long will the journey take?
How many continents will you visit?

 2

Single or return?
That will be ... please

 3

're ...'ll telephone
's ...'ll stay
want ...'ll show
're ...'ll stop
's ...'ll go
comes ...'ll take

 4

1	must	5	needn't
2	mustn't	6	must
3	must	7	needn't
4	needn't	8	mustn't

Unit 6

VICTORIA ROAD

 1

into; to; at; up; back
for; in; out; for

LANGUAGE WORK

 2 **b**

1 was walking
2 was robbing
3 were coming
4 were playing
5 wasn't washing
6 weren't having

3 **a**

1 was taking the dog for a walk
2 was looking in a shop window
3 were talking to a boy
4 was crossing the street
5 was painting
6 were carrying a large box
7 were waiting for a bus
8 was buying a newspaper
9 was telephoning
10 were eating hamburgers

b

2 No, she wasn't waiting for a bus. She was looking in a shop window.
3 No, they weren't crossing the street. They were talking to a boy.
4 No, he wasn't buying a newspaper. He was crossing the street.
5 No, he wasn't cleaning the windows. He was painting.
6 No, they weren't carrying a table. They were carrying a large box.

7 No, they weren't shopping. They were waiting for a bus.
8 No, he wasn't eating a hamburger. He was buying a newspaper
9 No, she wasn't looking in a shop window. She was telephoning.
10 No, they weren't reading magazines. They were eating hamburgers.

READING

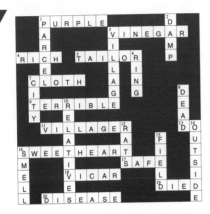

b
1 from ... of   7 of
2 of ... of   8 from
3 from   9 from
4 of   10 of
5 of   11 of
6 of ... of   12 from ... of

LISTENING

b
1 was flying ... talked
2 were driving ... stopped
3 met ... was sunbathing
4 was staying ... learnt (or learned)
5 was staying ... took
6 was coming ... lost
7 saw ... was coming

b
1 was watching ... rang
2 rang ... switched
3 was going ... saw
4 saw ... said
5 was standing ... ran
6 saw ... shouted
7 started ... was waiting
8 started ... put
9 was carrying ... scratched
10 scratched ... fell

INTERACTION

Labels should read down:

Left	Right
forehead	eyes
hair	nose
face	mouth
arm	chest
hand	thumb
leg	knee
	foot

b
Where were you standing?
What were you doing?
Were you carrying anything?
Why were you carrying a bag?
What was the man carrying?
Was he running?
Was he carrying a gun?
Where was he going?
Was anyone waiting for the man?
What were the shop assistants doing?

PROJECT

b
Let's go to Matthew's party. It's at his house.
What's Matthew's address? I don't know it.
I haven't got his address, but he lives opposite Jane's friend.

John's late again. He's always late.
Well, if he isn't here by nine o'clock, we'll go on our own.
We can't do that, John's got the tickets.
Look. He's coming now. That's his parents' car.

write   wrote
buy   bought
break   broke
go   went
can   could
eat   ate
do   did
ride   rode
have   had
run   ran
get   got
make   made
see   saw (or be/was)
take   took
come   came
drive   drove
leave   left (or feel/felt)
find   found
put   put
say   said
lose   lost

LEARNING DIARY

was coming ... saw
was carrying
saw ... stopped
was standing ... ran
saw ... turned
was running ... fell
were talking ... happened
fell ... arrested

1 The thief wasn't carrying a gun.
2 Rebecca wasn't coming home from school.
3 The two policemen weren't talking to a shop assistant.

4 Rebecca wasn't looking at a ring.
5 The two policemen weren't driving a car.

What were you doing?
Were you buying anything?
Where was the man standing?
What was he doing?
Was he carrying anything?
What were the shop assistants doing?

Unit 7

VICTORIA ROAD

Can you lend me some money?
I'll pay you back next week.
Who are you kidding?
a couple of quid.
That's not true.
what do you want more money for?
I don't know what you see in him.
Doesn't it make you sick?

1 lent   borrowed
2 borrowed   lent
3 lent   borrowed

LANGUAGE WORK

richer   wider
dirtier   wetter
cheaper   easier
funnier   bigger
nearer   more boring
thinner   drier
more interesting   greater

1 cheaper
2 hotter
3 more expensive
4 wetter
5 further
6 more difficult to reach
7 noisier
8 more boring
9 easier to reach
10 nearer

1 Club Islandia is the nearest.
2 Barracuda Village is the wettest.
3 Club Islandia is the most difficult to reach.
4 Club Islandia is the driest.
5 Barracuda Village is the hottest.
6 Club Islandia is the most expensive.
7 Akibo Island is the furthest.
8 Club Islandia is the easiest to reach.
9 Akibo Island is the most interesting.
10 Club Islandia is the quietest.
11 Akibo Island is the noisiest.
12 Barracuda Village is the cheapest.

READING

 6 The picture should be labelled down in this order:
hat; shoes; jacket; tie; coat; trousers; dress; boots.

 7 **a**

wide	narrow
loose	tight
low	high
light	dark
dull	bright
far	near
hot	cold
dry	wet
cheap	expensive
easy	difficult

b

uncomfortable   unfashionable
uninteresting   unpopular
unexciting

 8 **b**

3 I like this dress, but it's too small.
4 I like this sweatshirt, but it's too big.
5 I like these shorts, but they're too bright.
6 I like these trousers, but they're too short.
7 I like these knickers, but they're too small.
8 I like this jacket, but it's too tight.
9 I like these shoes, but they're too wide.
10 I like this skirt, but it's too long.

LISTENING

 9 Fares, please.
Two to the town centre, please.

That's 80p, please.

20p change.
Thank you.

Any more fares, please?

Town Centre.
Come on. This is our stop.

 10 Furniture is on the third floor.
They're on the first floor.
They're on the third floor.
Ladies' fashions are on the ground floor.
They're on the second floor.

 11 **a**
2 pairs of shorts
4 pairs of knickers
2 pairs of socks
2 pairs of shoes
1 dress
3 bras
1 pair of trainers
2 skirts

b
Student's own answers

INTERACTION

 12 **a**

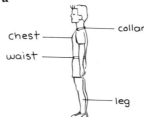

 13 **a**
1 help ... like ... and ... in
2 you ... to ... with ... heels
3 size ... take
4 Here ... you ... try ... on
5 right ... they're ... Have ... in ... bigger
6 a ... and ... look
7 do ... comfortable ... better ... fit ... much
8 They're ... take
9 That's ... very ... change ... Goodbye

PROJECT

 14 a man with a moustache
a car with three wheels
a blouse with large buttons
a man with pointed ears
boots with high heels
trousers with wide legs
a woman with long hair
a bird with a forked tail
a dress with long sleeves
a spider with long legs

 15

LEARNING DIARY

 1
1 taller than   slimmer than
2 better than   worse than
3 cleaner than   dirtier than
4 more modern than
   more expensive than
5 further than   closer than

 2
1 the largest
2 the most difficult
3 the heaviest
4 the fattest
5 the most expensive

 3 two shirts, two pairs of shorts, three pairs of socks, a sweatshirt and a pair of boots.

Unit 8

Unit 9

VICTORIA ROAD

 1 Is that the time?
Hurry up, ... you know.
we've only just got back the States.
You must introduce me.
Pleased to meet you.
We must go,
See you around.

LANGUAGE WORK

 2 **b**
He has cleaned the windows.
He has painted the door.
He has bought a record.
She has taken a photograph.
He has had a shower.
They have seen a ghost.
He has written a letter.
They have played football.
She has broken her leg.
They have gone to the Moon.

3 **a**
He has written to the local newspaper.
He has taken some photographs.
He hasn't visited the museum yet.
He has talked to the Geography teacher.
He has got some books from the library.
He hasn't found a map yet.
He hasn't collected any leaflets from the town hall yet.
He hasn't interviewed people yet.
He hasn't made a plan yet.
He hasn't written the project yet.

b

I've written to the local newspaper.
I've taken some photographs.
I haven't visited the museum yet.
I've talked to the Geography teacher.
I've got some books from the library.
I haven't found a map yet.
I haven't collected any leaflets from the town hall yet.
I haven't interviewed people yet.
I haven't made a plan yet.
I haven't written the project yet.

READING

1 The Tower of London
2 Big Ben
3 Madame Tussaud's
4 10 Downing Street
5 Buckingham Palace
6 The Houses of Parliament

Student's own answers

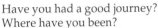 **b**

1 's gone   4 's gone
2 've been   5 've been
3 've been   6 've gone

1 a bookshop   2 a toy shop
3 a clothes shop   4 a shoe shop
5 a sports shop   6 a record shop
7 a souvenir shop   8 a flower shop

LISTENING

 b

1 has made   6 talked
2 made   7 He's gone
3 has written   8 went
4 wrote   9 started ... hasn't
5 took   finished

 a

She has made a hit single.
She has appeared on TV.
She has moved into a new flat in London.
She has bought a sports car.
She has recorded an album.
She has met the Queen at Buckingham Palace.
She has had a holiday in the West Indies.
She has taken part in a charity concert.
She has done a concert tour of the States.
She has starred in a video.
She has won an award for the best record of the year.
She has got married.

b

She made a hit single in January.
She appeared on TV in February.

She moved into her new flat in March.
She bought a sports car in April.
She recorded her album in May.
She met the Queen in June.
She had a holiday in July.
She took part in a charity concert in August.
She did her concert tour in September.
She starred in a video in October.
She won the award in November.
She got married in December.

INTERACTION

 b

1 Has Sue painted her room?
2 Has Carmen been to England?
3 Where have Jackie and Greg gone?
4 What has Terry done with his cowboy hat?
5 How long have McLintock and Owen been away?
6 Have you seen my money?
7 What have you bought?
8 Has it stopped raining?

Have you had a good journey?
Where have you been?
Have we visited the planet before?
Have you brought anything back?
How many people have you brought?
Have you talked to them?
Has the computer examined them?
What has it found?
Has the computer finished its examination?
Have the people woken up yet?
How long have they been away from Earth?

PROJECT

 b

Our homework for Friday is about the countries of South America.

Jackie Wright has moved from Manchester to Victoria Road in Hartfield.

I can speak Spanish, Greek, Italian and English.

My birthday is in July and my sister Jane's is in December.

Sue Scott has got a Spanish penfriend.

Our teacher is Mr Clarke.

We have French on Monday.

The British Prime Minister lives at 10 Downing Street.

be		been
	broke	broken
	brought	brought
buy		bought
come	came	
	ate	eaten
	got	got
	went	gone
have		had
	made	made
	said	said
	saw	seen
speak	spoke	
	took	taken
tell	told	
	wrote	written

LEARNING DIARY

Sue has booked the hall.
Casey hasn't bought the drinks.
Sue and Vince have written the invitations.
Terry and Jackie haven't made a poster.
Jackie has hired a disco.

2

1 Has Casey bought the drinks?
2 Have Sue and Vince written the invitations?
3 Have Terry and Jackie made a poster?
4 Has Jackie hired a disco?

3

1 's gone   4 has ... lived
2 Have ... done   's lived
  did   did ... live
3 've seen   lived
  did ... see   5 Have ...
  saw   been
                was

Unit 10

VICTORIA ROAD

1

Are you coming to the cafe?
I've got to
I'm broke.
I'll pay.
Come on, you lot.
Can I help you?
Could we have
five of us.
I wish I wasn't here.

2 a

He's got to mend the TV.
She's got to do the washing up.
She's got to do the ironing.
She's got to make her bed.
He/She's got to get up.

b

I've got to mend the TV.
I've got to do the washing up.
I've got to do the ironing.
I've got to make my bed.
I've got to get up.

LANGUAGE WORK

b

any   some   any   some
any   some   any
some   any   some   some   some
any
some   any   some

b

countable	uncountable
onions	milk
hamburgers	ice cream
apples	orange juice
newspapers	ham
sausages	pop music
postcards	cheese
carrots	water
stamps	soap
bananas	coffee
eggs	whisky
potatoes	salt
tomatoes	cloth
	cola
	fish
	fruit

3   How many do you want?
4   How much do you want?
5   How much do you want?
6   How many do you want?
7   How much do you want?
8   How much do you want?
9   How much do you want?
10   How many do you want?

READING

a

honey   tea   coffee   toast
jam   butter   cereal
CORN FLAKES
HONEY
JAM
milk   fried egg   mushroom   sugar
orange juice   sausage   tomato   bacon

b

Student's own answers

meat	fish	fruit
chicken	tuna	pineapple
ham	sardines	bananas
beef	mussels	oranges
	anchovies	apples

vegetables

peppers   mushrooms
olives   cucumber
lettuce   carrots
onions

---

dairy products	drinks
cream	beer
ice cream	apple juice
cheese	wine
milk	milk
chocolate	mineral water

loaves	potatoes	women
bottles	children	teeth
glasses	men	feet
sandwiches	classes	knives
tomatoes		

LISTENING

1   peel ... chop
2   Put ... bowl
3   Add ... mix ... fork
4   mixture ... Put ... refrigerator
5   take ... out of ... grill ... fry
6   cut ... toast
7   Wash ... Slice ... open
8   bit ... few ... top ... salad ... slice ...
      ring ... bun
9   pick

INTERACTION

4 bottles of beer; 3 packets of crisps;
2 cups of tea; 2 glasses of milk; 3 tins
of tuna; 3 slices of tomato; 2 loaves
of bread

chicken	apple
sweetcorn	cream
pineapple	potatoes
mushrooms	hamburger
pizza	cheese

Yes, please.
Could I have a cheese and tomato
pizza and a glass of orange juice,
please?

And for you?
Could I have a tuna and sweetcorn
pizza, please?
Would you like anything to drink?
Yes, I'll have an orange juice, too,
please.
Anything else?
No, thank you.

So that's one cheese and tomato
pizza and one tuna and sweetcorn
pizza and two glasses of orange
juice. Do you want a large or a
standard orange juice?
Standard, please.

Cheese and tomato?
That's for me.

That will be £9.60, please.

PROJECT

garlic bread
a cheese sandwich
orange juice
tomato soup
fruit salad
a meat and potato pie
a ham sandwich
mushroom soup
a tuna and anchovy pizza
pineapple juice

LEARNING DIARY

1   any   4   any   7   any
2   any   5   any   8   some
3   some   6   some   9   any

... a few ... a little ... a little ...
a few ... a few ... a little ... a little

2 loaves of bread
3 glasses of milk
2 cheese sandwiches
4 bottles of lemonade
4 tins of beans
5 potatoes

help
like ... please
drink
Yes ... have ... glass
Anything
thank
That's
you

Unit 11

VICTORIA ROAD

I've been invited to a party
You're grounded.
this is terrible.
it serves you right.
the week before last.
that's that.
Can you give me a hand
Is that clear?
What's wrong?
I'm stuck.
This is no laughing matter.
I'm off.

LANGUAGE WORK

b

1   Flour and water are mixed.
2   The pizza base is made.
3   Tomatoes and cheese are put on
      the base.
4   Toppings are added.
5   The pizza is cooked in the oven.
6   The pizza is taken out of the
      oven.
7   The pizza is served.

3

are dug up	are taken
are stored	are added
are washed	are put
are peeled	are put
are sliced	are stored
are cooked	are sent

READING

4 **b**

were recorded
have been recorded
are recorded
will be recorded

5 **b**

The telephone was invented by Alexander Graham Bell.
The space rocket was invented by Werner von Braun.
Gravity was discovered by Isaac Newton.
'She Loves You' was recorded (written) by the Beatles.
The Mona Lisa was painted by Leonardo da Vinci.
America was discovered by Christopher Columbus.
Australia was discovered by Jan van Diemen.
Macbeth and *Othello* were written by William Shakespeare.
Penicillin was discovered by Alexander Fleming.
The car was invented by Gottfried Daimler.
The telescope was invented by Galileo.
'Blue Suede Shoes' was recorded by Elvis Presley.
Don Quixote was written by Cervantes.
The electric guitar was invented by Adolf Rickenbacker.

6 **a**

1	tree	5	wave
2	railway line	6	boat
3	roof	7	beach
4	chimney		

b

(Possible answers)
Some trees have been blown down.
The telephone lines have been brought down.
A car has been crushed by a tree.
The railway line has been blocked by a tree.
Boats have been smashed by the waves.
Roads have been flooded by the sea.
A lot of houses have been damaged.
Roofs have been ripped off.
A chimney has been broken.
A lot of windows have been smashed.
The school has been closed.

LISTENING

7

blown	made
eaten	given
blocked	broadcast
broken	injured
thrown	terrified
crushed	said
taken	sent
warned	sold
brought	

8

1 will be arranged
2 will be prepared
3 will be sent
4 will be interviewed
5 will be recorded
6 will be taken
7 will be written
8 will be checked
9 will be developed
10 will be printed

INTERACTION

9

Can I help you?
Have you got 'Love Boogie'?
Who's it by?
It's by the Mind Machine.

Have you looked on the shelves over there?
Yes, but I can't see it.

Do you know what label it's on?
Virgin, I think.

Just a minute. I'll see if we've got it.

No, I'm sorry. We haven't got it.
But I can order it for you.
How long will that take?

A week.
OK.
Can I have your name, please?

PROJECT

10

to ... by ... their ... Where
They're
there
wear
too
two
buy

11

1 Greg is from America
2 He has come to visit Jackie's family.
3 He is Jackie's cousin.
4 Jackie has got a lot of relatives in the States.
5 Who has got my pen?
6 It is on Vince's desk.
7 Vince's guitar is in his dad's car.
8 Sue's penfriend is from Spain.
9 Terry's bag has been stolen.
10 Jackie has gone to the airport.

LEARNING DIARY

1

1	is collected	5	is sorted
2	are taken	6	is drawn
3	is sent	7	is written
4	are received	8	is broadcast

2

1 Four windows were broken by the wind.
2 The power lines will be repaired by the Electricity Board tomorrow.
3 Twenty boats have been destroyed by the waves.
4 Floods will be brought by the heavy rain.
5 'Thriller' was recorded by Michael Jackson.
6 Our new single will be released by the record company next week.
7 Casey's bike has been stolen by some boys.
8 *Romeo and Juliet* was written by Shakespeare.
9 Most crisps are eaten by children.

Unit 12

1 Put the verbs in brackets into the correct tense.

1 I ___ at seven o'clock every day. (get up)
2 Vince ___ his guitar at the moment. (play)
3 Mr Moore ___ a shower now. (have)
4 He ___ a shower every morning. (have)
5 Where's Sue? She ___ a letter. (write)
6 Kamala ___ in her parents' shop on Saturdays. (help)
7 Terry ___ television on Saturday afternoons. (watch)
8 Excuse me. You ___ in my seat. (sit)
9 I ___ an English test at the moment. (do)
10 Mr Scott ___ to work by train. (go)

| **2 marks for each verb** |
| 1 for correct tense |
| 1 for correct spelling |

2 Make these sentences negative.

1 I'm going to school.
2 Kamala lives in Victoria Road.
3 Elvis wanted a guitar.
4 I've got dark hair.
5 Vince was at the football match.
6 We're having a party.
7 Elvis's parents were rich.
8 You like hamburgers.
9 Jackie's moving in today.
10 Terry went to London.
11 Jackie's got a brother.
12 Sue and Jackie are good friends.

| **2 marks for each answer** |
| 1 for correct form |
| 1 for correct spelling |

3 This is Sue's day. Put the sentences into the past tense to say what happened yesterday.

1 She gets up at seven o'clock.
2 She has a shower.
3 She catches the bus to school.
4 She arrives at ten to nine.
5 School starts at nine o'clock.
6 She goes home at 3.30.
7 She watches television for an hour.
8 She does her homework.

| **2 marks for each answer** |
| 1 for correct form |
| 1 for correct spelling |

4 Turn these statements into questions.

1 Casey lives in Victoria Road.
2 You're going to the shops.
3 Kamala was at school yesterday.
4 Elvis died in 1977.
5 Jane's got a new coat.
6 Terry's doing his homework.
7 You were a John Lennon fan.
8 John Lennon sang with the Beatles.
9 They've got a big car.
10 Casey's parents work in Hartfield.

| **2 marks for each answer** |
| 1 for correct form |
| 1 for correct spelling |

5 Look at these answers. Write the questions to complete the dialogue.

_____?
Vince Scott.

_____?
Sixteen.

_____?
12th September.

_____?
In Hartfield.

_____?
18 Victoria Road, Hartfield.

_____?
754921.

| **2 marks for each question** |
| 1 for correct question construction |
| 1 for correct spelling |

6 Write these times in words.

Example
6.15 *Quarter past six*

3.10 _____   10.20 _____
8.30 _____   4.45 _____
11.00 _____   5.55 _____
4.30 _____   2.50 _____

| **1 mark for each correct time** |

| **TOTAL   100** |

1 Put these into the future tense to talk and ask about tomorrow.

1 Terry goes to school at 8.15.
2 He doesn't travel by car.
3 He catches the bus with his friends.
4 Does he come home at three o'clock?
5 I don't have lunch at school.
6 When do you do your homework?

2 marks for each answer
1 for correct tense construction
1 for correct spelling

2 Make these sentences negative.

1 Kamala was eating a hamburger.
2 Terry and Jackie were looking at the magazines.
3 I was watching Jackie.
4 Terry was stealing sweets.
5 Mr Wijeratne was cleaning the shelves.

1 mark for each answer

3 Turn these statements into questions.

1 You were lying on the beach.
2 Carmen was buying an ice cream.
3 The boys were playing football.
4 Carmen's aunt was making a sandwich.
5 Carmen's uncle was swimming in the sea.

1 mark for each answer

4 Put the verbs in brackets into the correct tense.

My earliest memory
1 I ___ with my friends, when I ___ an accident. (play / have)
2 While I ___ my bike, I ___ off. (ride / fall)
3 When I ___ off, I ___. (fall / cry)
4 When my friends ___ me, they ___ to get my mother. (see / run)
5 My mother ___ the garden, when they ___ her. (dig / tell)
6 She ___ to find me and she ___ me up. (run / pick)
7 She ___ me indoors and ___ my hands. (take / wash)
8 While she ___ my hands, my father ___ home. (wash / come)

2 marks for each verb
1 for correct tense construction
1 for correct spelling

5 Complete these with the comparative or the superlative of the adjectives in brackets.

1 Jackie is ___ than Sue. (tall)
2 I think Sue is ___ than Jackie. (attractive)
3 Casey is the ___ footballer in the team. (good)
4 I'd like to be ___ than I am. (slim)
5 This must be the ___ suit in the shop. (expensive)
6 The blue whale is the ___ animal in the world. (big)
7 He has got a ___ computer than I have got. (good)
8 I think Kamala is the ___ girl in the class. (pretty)
9 I washed my hair, but now it's ___ than before. (bad)
10 These jeans are much ___ than those. (nice)
11 Tuesday was the ___ day for ten years. (hot)
12 Rome is ___ away from London than Paris. (far)

2 marks for each answer
1 for correct form
1 for correct spelling

6 Complete these with 'this' or 'these'.

1 Do you like ___ trousers?
2 I'd like ___ shirt, please.
3 How much are ___ scissors?
4 ___ shorts are too tight.
5 Do you like ___ dress?
6 I'll take ___ jeans, please.

1 mark for each

7 Look at the packing list. Complete the sentence below.

3 x shirts   5 x knickers   2 x belts   2 x shorts
3 x skirts   1 x jumper   1 x trousers
For my holiday I'll need three shirts, five...

1 mark for each

8 Complete the dialogue.

Can I ___ you?
Yes. ___ you got these in a ___ 32, please?
Yes. ___ you are. Do you ___ to try ___ on?
Yes, please.
There's a ___ room over there.
Are ___ all right?
Yes, they're fine. How ___ are they?
They're £21.80.
I'll ___ them.

1 mark for each word

TOTAL   100

1 Put the verbs in brackets into the present perfect tense.

1 Vince and Kamala ___ to London. (go)
2 The storm ___ thousands of trees. (destroy)
3 I ___ my project. (do)
4 Someone ___ my bag. (steal)
5 Terry ___ two hamburgers. (eat)

> **2 marks for each answer**
> 1 for correct form
> 1 for correct spelling

2 Make these sentences negative.

1 We've been to London.
2 Sue has met Greg.
3 Greg has written to his parents.
4 I've had my lunch.
5 He's bought a record.

> **2 marks for each answer**
> 1 for correct form
> 1 for correct spelling

3 Turn these statements into questions.

1 You've been to New York.
2 Greg's taken a lot of photographs.
3 They've finished their project.
4 Kamala's borrowed my pen.
5 You've bought a new car.

> **2 marks for each answer**
> 1 for correct form
> 1 for correct spelling

4 Put the verbs in brackets into the correct tense.

1 We ___ to France for our holidays last year. (go)
2 I ___ to France yet. (not be)
3 I don't want to go to the movies. I ___ that film. (see)
4 I ___ that film last year. (see)
5 Sue ___ a new dress on Saturday. (buy)
6 I ___ it yet. (not see)
7 We ___ down half an hour ago. (sit)
8 But the waitress ___ our order yet. (not take)
9 Kamala ___ her hair and it's still wet. (wash)
10 Greg ___ yesterday. (leave)

> **2 marks for each answer**
> 1 for correct tense construction
> 1 for correct spelling

5 Complete these sentences with 'some' or 'any'.

1 Do you need ___ new clothes for your holiday?
2 Well, I haven't got ___ beach shoes.
3 And I need ___ new shorts.
4 But I don't need ___ T-shirts.
5 Have you got ___ money for the new things?
6 I've got ___ money in the bank.

> **1 mark for each correct answer**

6 Complete this list with 'a bit of' or 'a few'.

To make this you need ___ paper, ___ old bottles, ___ plastic, ___ tins, ___ boxes and ___ soap.

> **1 mark for each correct answer**

7 Complete these with 'How many' or 'How much'.

1 ___ bottles of water do we need?
2 We need some tomatoes for the soup.
   ___ do you need?
3 ___ wood have you got?
4 ___ bread is there in the cupboard?
5 Have you got any oranges?
   Yes. ___ do you want?
6 ___ milk do you have in your tea?

> **1 mark for each correct answer**

8 Turn these sentences into the passive.

1 The main computer checks the information.
2 Workmen will repair the electricity lines.
3 Thieves have stolen five cars.
4 Carl Lewis has broken the world record.
5 An ambulance took the people to hospital.
6 The river destroyed the bridge.
7 The police have closed the road.
8 The teacher warned Terry.
9 Bruno Brookes presents the Top 40.
10 Millions of people hear the programme.
11 A new DJ will present the show next week.
12 Huge waves threw the ferry onto the beach.

> **2 marks for each answer**
> 1 for correct tense construction
> 1 for correct spelling

9 Make these sentences negative.

1 Terry's bag was stolen.
2 Sue and Vince have been grounded.
3 Mr Moore was invited to the party.
4 The road will be repaired by the end of the week.
5 Our houses were damaged.
6 Sonia's new record has been released.
7 Tigers are found in Africa.
8 The information is sorted by the shop's computer.

> **1 mark for each answer**

> **TOTAL 100**

TEST ANSWERS Unit 4

1
1 get up
2 's playing
3 's having
4 has
5 's writing
6 helps
7 watches
8 're sitting
9 'm doing
10 goes

2
1 I'm not going to school.
2 Kamala doesn't live in Victoria Road.
3 Elvis didn't want a guitar.
4 I haven't got dark hair.
5 Vince wasn't at the football match.
6 We aren't having a party.
7 Elvis's parents weren't rich.
8 You don't like hamburgers.
9 Jackie isn't moving in today.
10 Terry didn't go to London.
11 Jackie hasn't got a brother.
12 Sue and Jackie aren't good friends.

3
1 She got up at seven o'clock.
2 She had a shower.
3 She caught the bus to school.
4 She arrived at ten to nine.
5 School started at nine o'clock.
6 She went home at 3.30.
7 She watched television for an hour.
8 She did her homework.

4
1 Does Casey live in Victoria Road?
2 Are you going to the shops?
3 Was Kamala at school yesterday?
4 Did Elvis die in 1977?
5 Has Jane got a new coat?
6 Is Terry doing his homework?
7 Were you a John Lennon fan?
8 Did John Lennon sing with the Beatles?
9 Have they got a big car?
10 Do Casey's parents work in Hartfield?

5
What's your name?
How old are you?
When is your birthday?
Where do you live?
What's your address?
What's your telephone number?

6
ten past three
twenty-five to nine
eleven o'clock
half past four
twenty past ten
quarter to five
five to six
ten to three

TEST ANSWERS Unit 8

1
1 Terry will go to school at 8.15.
2 He won't travel by car.
3 He'll catch the bus with his friends.
4 Will he come home at three o'clock?
5 I won't have lunch at school.
6 When will you do your homework?

2
1 Kamala wasn't eating a hamburger.
2 Terry and Jackie weren't looking at the magazines.
3 I wasn't watching Jackie.
4 Terry wasn't stealing sweets.
5 Mr Wijeratne wasn't cleaning the shelves.

3
1 Were you lying on the beach?
2 Was Carmen buying an ice cream?
3 Were the boys playing football?
4 Was Carmen's aunt making a sandwich?
5 Was Carmen's uncle swimming in the sea?

4
1 was playing / had
2 was riding / fell
3 fell / cried
4 saw / ran
5 was digging / told
6 ran / picked
7 took / washed
8 was washing / came

5
1 taller
2 more attractive
3 best
4 slimmer
5 most expensive
6 biggest
7 better
8 prettiest
9 worse
10 nicer
11 hottest
12 further

6
1 these
2 this
3 these
4 These
5 this
6 these

7 For my holiday I'll need three shirts, five pairs of knickers, two belts, two pairs of shorts, three skirts, one jumper and one pair of trousers.

8 help Have size Here want them changing they much take

TEST ANSWERS   Unit 12

1
1 have gone
2 has destroyed
3 've done
4 has stolen
5 has eaten

2
1 We haven't been to London.
2 Sue hasn't met Greg.
3 Greg hasn't written to his parents.
4 I haven't had my lunch.
5 He hasn't bought a record.

3
1 Have you been to New York?
2 Has Greg taken a lot of photographs?
3 Have they finished their project?
4 Has Kamala borrowed my pen?
5 Have you bought a new car?

4
1 went
2 haven't been
3 've seen
4 saw
5 bought
6 haven't seen
7 sat
8 hasn't taken
9 has washed
10 left

5
1 any
2 any
3 some
4 any
5 any
6 some

6
a bit of   a few   a bit of a few   a few
a bit of

7
1 How many
2 How many
3 How much
4 How much
5 How many
6 How much

8
1 The information is checked by the main computer.
2 The electricity lines will be repaired by workmen.
3 Five cars have been stolen by thieves.
4 The world record has been broken by Carl Lewis.
5 The people were taken to hospital by an ambulance.
6 The bridge was destroyed by the river.
7 The road has been closed by the police.
8 Terry was warned by the teacher.
9 The Top 40 is presented by Bruno Brookes.
10 The programme is heard by millions of people.
11 The show will be presented by a new DJ next week.
12 The ferry was thrown onto the beach by huge waves.

9
1 Terry's bag wasn't stolen.
2 Sue and Vince haven't been grounded.
3 Mr Moore wasn't invited to the party.
4 The road won't be repaired by the end of the week.
5 Our houses weren't damaged.
6 Sonia's new record hasn't been released.
7 Tigers aren't found in Africa.
8 The information isn't sorted by the shop's computer.